IRISH TOURISM
1880–1980

Tourism Ireland is the body responsible for promoting the island of
Ireland overseas as a tourist destination. The author and publisher would
like to gratefully acknowledge the support of Tourism Ireland
in the production of this book.

Tourism **Ireland**

Marketing the island of Ireland overseas

For my family

IRISH TOURISM 1880–1980

IRENE FURLONG

IRISH ACADEMIC PRESS

DUBLIN • PORTLAND, OR

First published in 2009 by Irish Academic Press

44 Northumberland Road,
Ballsbridge,
Dublin 4, Ireland

920 NE 58th Avenue, Suite 300
Portland, Oregon,
97213-3786, USA

www.iap.ie

British Library Cataloguing-in-Publication Data
An entry can be found on request

978 0 7165 2945 3 (cloth)

Library of Congress Cataloging-in-Publication Data
An entry can be found on request

Printed by Biddles Ltd, King's Lynn, Norfolk

Contents

céao míle fáilce

(A HUNDRED THOUSAND WELCOMES)

Fly TWA to Ireland for An Cóstal

In April, Ireland will be "at home" to her friends. What better way to visit this country than by flying TWA? You will enjoy the service, comfort and dependability of TWA's world-proved Constellations. TWA operates frequent services through Shannon from:—

New York, Boston, Paris, Rome, Geneva/Zurich

Consult your travel agent or call TWA. TWA offices in all the major cities of the world.

FLY TWA

TRANS WORLD AIRLINES

USA · EUROPE · AFRICA · ASIA

Issued by Trans World Airlines, 44 Upr. O'Connell Street, Dublin. Phone 45651.

An advertisement by Trans World Airlines urging Americans to visit Ireland for An Tóstal in 1953. Courtesy of Harmonia Publications.

Black and white illustrations

Colour plates

1. Painting of Bray, Co. Wicklow, in 1862, by Erskine Nichol, showing wide variety of leisure activities. *Courtesy of National Gallery of Ireland.*

2. Poster of Bray for the Lancashire and Yorkshire Railway Company, Courtesy of Wordwell Ltd.

3. 'Come to Ulster' poster c. 1930, Ulster Tourist Development Association. *Courtesy of National Museum of Ireland.*

4. 'Angling in Ireland' brochure distributed at the 1939 New York World's Fair, probably by the Irish Tourist Association.

5. Advertisement for Coca-Cola in *Life* magazine in 1943, showing American troops based in Ulster using stereotypical Irish images such as the jaunting car, thatched cottage and winsome colleen along with Nissen huts used to house the troops. The use of the Irish Tourist Board's slogan – Céad Míle Fáilte – with translation for American readers, is interesting. *Courtesy of Coca Cola Company.*

6. Selection of postcards from Bray, Co. Wicklow, up to the 1950s. *Courtesy of Henry Cairns.*

7. Cover of *Northern Ireland gives a great welcome*, published by the Northern Ireland Tourist Board in 1951 and featuring Finn MacCoul, the iconic builder of the Giant's Causeway. *Courtesy of Northern Ireland Tourist Board.*

8. Poster for the aerial chairlift built in 1950 to take visitors to the Eagle's Nest on Bray Head by Eamon Quinn, who also ran the Red Island holiday camp in Skerries, Co. Dublin.

9. Fógra Fáilte poster for An Tóstal, the cultural festival launched in 1953 to attract visitors in the off season.

10. Cover for *Ireland – an illustrated guide to the counties of Ireland*, published by Fógra Fáilte in 1953 and illustrating the multitude of activities available to visitors.

11. Irish farmers meet a creamery lorry – one of the first six postcards produced by John Hinde in 1957. *Courtesy of John Hinde Limited.*

12. A well-known image by John Hinde, of which he said that Bord Fáilte discouraged the use of donkeys in postcards because the government regarded them as symbols of a backward country and wanted portrayals of skyscrapers. *Courtesy of John Hinde Limited.*

13. Poster for the 1992 International James Joyce Symposium. Bord Fáilte was most instrumental in fostering the use of Irish literary figures such as Joyce in developing cultural tourism, especially as the number of Irish Nobel literary prize-winners was disproportionately large. *Courtesy of Robert Ballagh.*

14. Poster for the 'Today' radio programme in Australia featuring an Irish week, with co-operation from Cathay Pacific airlines, the Northern Ireland Tourist Board, the Traveland group and Tourism Ireland.

15. With 'black taxi' tours heralding a return to tourism in Belfast, loyalist and nationalist iconic images were popular attractions. These commemorate the building of the *Titanic* in Belfast in 1911 and Bobby Sands, the republican hunger-striker who died in 1981. *Courtesy of Irina Raffo.*

16. Poster issued by Irish Airlines in 1959 featuring Shannon airport, with emphasis on the duty-free facilities available there. *Courtesy of National Museum of Ireland.*

17. Bord Fáilte 1970s poster of a Paul Henry painting which was made available to overseas travel companies for promotion purposes. *Courtesy of National Museum of Ireland.*

18. Brochure illustrating charms of Northern Ireland's 'coast of beauty.'

19. Aer Lingus advertisement, 1960s.

20. Illustration by Rowel Friers, a well-known Northern Ireland cartoonist, for a map of the province.

21. A brochure for Dublin.

22. John Hinde postcard for Dublin airport with glamorous Aer Lingus stewardess. *Courtesy of John Hinde Limited.*

Acknowledgements

I would like to acknowledge gratefully the assistance and support I received from so many people during the writing of this book. They include staff in the National Archives of Ireland, especially Brian Donnelly, and the National Library of Ireland; Aidan O'Hanlon, Michael Gorman, Kevin O'Doherty, Seaghan Ó Briain and Thomas O'Gorman, formerly of Bord Fáilte, the last three now sadly deceased; Donal Guilfoyle and Derek Cullen in Fáilte Ireland; Desmond McGimpsey, Ken Powles and Robert Blair, formerly of the Northern Ireland Tourist Board; Major Jock Affleck, formerly of Bangor Borough Council; Lucia King and Gary McCracken in the Northern Ireland Tourist Board; Margaret O'Shaughnessy in the Foynes Flying Boat Museum; Mary Davies; John Kennedy of John Hinde Ltd; Allie Pigott; Alastair Durie, Frank Miller and Maeve Collins. A special 'thank-you' to Professor Vincent Comerford for his unceasing encouragement, and to the staff of the Department of History in NUI Maynooth for help over the years. I must acknowledge the debt I owe to the Irish Research Council for the Humanities and Social Sciences for funding the research for this work. I would also like to convey my deepest gratitude to Mark Henry of Tourism Ireland for his significant material and moral support. My sincere thanks to Lisa Hyde of Irish Academic Press for her patience. And last, but not least, I must express my appreciation of my long-suffering family, who have endured neglect and preoccupation while I devoted myself to this work.

CIE

for comfortable holiday travel

The Lakes of Killarney . . . Tropical Parknasilla, the Irish Riviera . . . lovely Galway Bay . . . visit these and many other lovely and historical parts of Ireland in complete comfort and yet at little cost.

Conducted, 6, 9, 11, and 13-day, luxury motor coach tours leave Dublin during the Summer and Autumn. Day tours from Dublin, Cork, Limerick, Waterford, Galway, Tralee, Sligo, Youghal, etc.

Go-as-you-please tours are available for those who prefer to travel their own leisurely, unconducted way, and the world-famous Radio Train takes you on all-in day excursions from Dublin to Killarney and Galway.

ASK YOUR TRAVEL AGENT ABOUT THESE DELIGHTFUL WAYS OF DISCOVERING IRELAND

CÓRAS IOMPAIR ÉIREANN

(IRELAND'S TRANSPORT COMPANY)

An advertisement for Coras Iompair Éireann for rail and coach tours in 1953. Courtesy of Harmonia Publications.

Notes on references in the text and in endnotes

Tourist organisation	Established
Irish Tourist Association	1925
An Bord Cuartaíochta (The Irish Tourist Board)	1939
An Bord Fáilte (The Irish Tourist Board)	1952
Fógra Fáilte (Tourist Publicity Board)	1952
Bord Fáilte Éireann (The Irish Tourist Board)	1955

TEXT

In the text, use has been made of acronyms to denote the following organisations:

BEA	British European Airways
BOAC	British Overseas Airways Corporation
BTA	British Tourist Association
BTHA	British Travel and Holidays Association
CIE	Coras Iompair Éireann
ETC	European Travel Commission
IDA	Industrial Development Authority
IHF	Irish Hotels Federation
ITA	Irish Tourist Association
ITB	Irish Tourist Board
IUOTO	International Union of Official Tourism Organisations
NITB	Northern Ireland Tourist Board
OECD	Organisation for Economic Co-operation and Development
OPW	Office of Public Works
RTO	Regional Tourism Organisation
UK	United Kingdom
USA	United States of America
UTDA	Ulster Tourist Development Association

In endnotes, the use of a file number preceded by the letter 'S' denotes that it is located among the Department of the Taoiseach files in the National Archives of Ireland. For other material, 'NA' denotes the National Archives of Ireland.

Throughout the text the terms 'Ireland' and 'Irish' refer to independent Ireland post-1922. 'Northern Ireland' and 'Ulster' refer to Northern Ireland. The terms 'South' and 'North' also denote the respective states.

Introduction

> When I come here in the evenings to meditate on my madness; to watch the shadow of the Round Tower lengthening in the sunset; to break my heart uselessly in the curtained gloaming over the dead heart and blinded soul of the island of the saints, you will comfort me with the bustle of a great hotel and the sight of the little children carrying the golf clubs of your tourists as a preparation for the life to come.[1]

It reads just like an Irish tourist marketing ploy in the year 2008, appealing to foreign visitors to leave behind their humdrum existence and transport themselves to an Ireland replete with medieval heritage, spiritual refreshment, scenic beauty and the consolation of a luxury hotel, complete with facilities for the fastest growing sport in Ireland today. However, this was written by George Bernard Shaw over a hundred years ago, at a time when the first bout of promotion of the island as a tourist destination was well under way. Even then, there were fears expressed about the effects of tourist development on the heritage and scenic beauty of the country, and Shaw, in *John Bull's Other Island*, mocked the pretensions of his English anti-hero, Broadbent, who wished to transform people, landscape and antiquities into attractions and who saw tourism as the ideal vehicle for their exploitation. Shaw was not the only Irish writer to focus on tourism in twentieth-century Ireland, as many writers embraced the notion of the country as a suitable locus for rest and recreation. But commentators also posed the question of what we would become when subjected to the 'tourist gaze' as specified by Urry: 'Part of that experience is to gaze upon or view a set of different scenes, of landscapes or townscapes which are out of the ordinary.'[2]

Ireland at the beginning of the twentieth century was certainly a place with a difference for those intrepid travellers who came to visit, replete with that picturesque wilderness so beloved of Victorians, and with the added frisson of possible danger due to its political situation. Over the decades tourism has played an increasingly significant role in culture, society and the economy and its possibilities and consequences have been explored by a wide spectrum of Irish writers, who seek to place it within a literary or political discourse in modern Ireland. The Irish language writers from the Blasket Islands, who experienced what may have been the first wave of cultural tourists in Ireland, those scholars and students who flocked there in order to study Irish language and culture, were ambivalent about their visitors. Tomás Ó Criomhthain was the author of *An tOileánach* (*The Islandman*), an autobiographical work published in 1929, and also of *Allagar na hInise* (*Island Cross-Talk*), a series of dramatised sketches based on his observations of the Great Blasket island in the years 1919–22. Máirín Nic Eoin argues that his work, and that of his contemporaries Peig Sayers and Muiris Ó Súilleabháin, was as much the outcome of cultural tourist encounters as it was of native genius, as Ó Criomhthain's home became a destination for renowned Celtic scholars Robin Flower and Kenneth Jackson. She sees the consequent descent of younger generations of scholars upon the region, and the translation and marketing of these works, as proof that the books have become 'part and parcel of the tourist experience'.[3] Be that as it may, they offer an interesting perspective on the response of the islanders to the scholarly invasion. In *Allagar na hInise*, Ó Criomhthain presents the reaction of the natives, whose main preoccupation appears to be the cost of the hospitality they mete out free of charge:

> It's a holiday. There's nothing to be seen but naomhógs making for the island from every direction. They move like sea monsters, each of them carrying six or eight people. They don't leave either without their dinner. Someone said that you'd think the islanders were paid by the government to prepare tea for them every Sunday and holiday.[4]

Indeed, there is a paradox between the islanders' ingrained tradition of hospitality and their increasing resentment of the visitors, whom they see as people of a higher social order, privileged by class and wealth, but whom they criticise for their tight-fistedness and for their consumption of the scarce resources on the islands. Nevertheless, Ó Criomhthain gives credit to the visitors for keeping him from starvation: 'I hear many an idle fellow saying that there's no use in our native tongue; but that hasn't been my experience. Only for it I should have been begging my bread!'[5]

Many Irish writers did not confine themselves to presenting the tourist phenomenon as an experienced event. Some of them utilised the genre of the tourist guide to offer a political polemic on the conditions in the country. Liam O'Flaherty, a native of the Aran Islands, penned *A Tourist's Guide to Ireland* in 1929 while he was living in London, but anyone expecting a paean of praise for his homeland was to be severely disappointed. His work consisted of a vicious denunciation of clergy, politicians, publicans and peasants, written for the benefit of visitors to Ireland. He accused the Jesuits of robbing the tourist of pleasure by setting the tone of Irish education and thus the development of culture: 'The heavy, hairy garment of Puritanism has fallen and enshrouded the whole of society.'[6] He foresaw the tourist's 'sense of dignity being offended by the sight of penniless scholars and of all culture being held in suspicion and treated with contumely'.[7] He also pointed to the accumulation of property by religious orders as turning the country into a religious kingdom, and concluded that the tourist would get an impression of Ireland as 'a beautiful, sad-faced country that is being rapidly covered by a black rash'. Pointing out that the tourist would want to know why taxation is so high, why Dublin is the most expensive city in Europe, why Irish whiskey is dearer in Ireland than in England and 'why Irish roads are bad for motorists compared with English roads'.[8] O'Flaherty's analysis of the tourist situation in 1929 sounds all too similar to that which prevails in 2008. A ruthless indictment of the condition of the nation, this tourist guide to Ireland in the late 1920s offered a fascinating insight into the miserable existence afforded to many by the infant state, and it was echoed in the 1940s by Peadar O'Donnell, editor of *The Bell* from 1946 to 1954. He applied the form when he wrote a 'Tourist guide to Irish politics' for that publication in 1947.[9] Berating the Fianna Fáil party for its failure to carry through its 1932 promises of full employment and self-sufficiency, he declared that it was no longer in a position to make new gestures towards national sentiment and was therefore unprotected against social unrest. However, it is the utilisation by O'Flaherty and O'Donnell of the tourist guide format that is intriguing. Jonathan Raban has described travel writing as 'literature's red-light district',[10] and it is arguable that in publications intended for native consumption, but ostensibly addressed to the tourist, that genre is so devalued as 'serious' writing that it can accommodate subversive messages in an easier manner than other publications. Other Irish writers to engage with tourism in a dramatic format were Brian Friel, who in 1971 wrote *The Mundy Scheme*, a satire in which it was proposed to send dead Americans to spend their eternity in Ireland, and Hugh Leonard, whose *The Patrick Pearse Motel*, written in the same year, lampooned the notion of a motel with rooms named after the heroes of Ireland's struggle for independence. Their literary engagement with the tourist industry demonstrates the extent to which it had entered the national consciousness by then as both a benefit and a menace, and mirrors contemporary concerns in Ireland today.

Now, in the first decade of the new millennium, tourism has become a crucial component in the Irish economy and an integral part of Irish life, but it may come as a surprise to many people to discover how long the promotion of Ireland as a tourist destination has been going on. The history of tourism in Ireland has not been found interesting in the context of academic studies, although the topic of tourism *per se* is now considered a rich source for critical theory and literary analysis. A survey of the existing secondary material does not divulge much on the topic, with Irish historians having little to say on the subject of the Irish tourism industry until the 1960s, possibly because statistical data exists only from the late 1940s. For this reason, this book will look at developments in Ireland up to that period in considerable detail, concentrating on some of the personalities involved, whether as entrepreneurs, politicians or public servants, in an effort to rescue them from the neglect, in historical terms, in which they have languished. It is worth bearing in mind that Ireland is not unique in this neglect of an important aspect of its history, which in the mid-twentieth century was expected to overtake agriculture as its biggest industry, as the history of tourism on a worldwide basis is only beginning to be written. Indeed, Alastair Durie, in *Scotland for the Holidays: A History of Tourism in Scotland*, suggests that the academic community takes a low view of tourism for three reasons. The first is that the service sector has until recently been under-researched and written up; the second is that the nature of the subject hinders analysis, as tourism is an umbrella term covering a very wide range of experiences; and the third relates to the sources, for which there are both too few and too many.[11] In addition, before undertaking an account of the industry in any country, it is necessary to define the terms *tourism* and *tourist*, especially as the latter term is often used in a pejorative sense when unfavourably compared with that of *traveller*.

What is tourism? The word *tour* is said to emanate from a Greek word that describes a tool used to make a circle, the parallel in human terms being the return to the point of origin that identifies the temporary nature of the tourist trip.[12] In an international context, tourism is possibly the fastest-growing industry in the world; it represents the only economic hope for some areas of the planet unsuited to industrial development, but it can also be the golden goose which finds itself rendered barren by the production of too many eggs in a short space of time. In other words, it is a Janus-faced phenomenon, an inescapable element of the human experience, whether it is as user or provider, but one that has the capacity to create as many problems as it solves. Nevertheless, at the beginning of the third millennium, it is an integral component of life for the inhabitants of the developed world, as leisure and recreation are regarded as human rights on a scale never before experienced. Travel is seen as the reward for hard work carried out on a sustained basis, and getting away from it all has become the light at the end of the tunnel replacing the promise of a heavenly reward for a post-religious society. At any one time there may be millions of tourists up in the air surrounding the earth, a possibility that summons up an apocalyptic vision of airborne ants desperate to leave their grounded reality for the possibility of possessing the exotic dream elsewhere.

What is a tourist? Ireland's official tourism bodies use the definition of the World Tourism Organisation to categorise and quantify the visitors who travel to their country: 'A tourist is a person travelling to and staying at least one night in a country other than his or her country of usual residence for a period not exceeding twelve months, for leisure, business or other purposes.'[13] While this might appear to constitute an extremely broad definition, it does not include day-trippers or excursionists who swell the coffers of heritage sites, interpretive centres or many other attractions. Dubliners who travel to Bray for an afternoon on the promenade, although remaining substantially in their own domestic environment, may also be classified as tourists in that they contribute financially to the local economy by leaving behind some of their disposable income. In any reckoning of the economic benefits of the industry, spending by these categories must be included in the final figures. Such are the difficulties inherent in calculating what exactly tourism is, and who precisely is the tourist, but these problems are not peculiar to the Irish situation, and an internationally accepted quantitative base is a necessity in order to allow forward planning by tourism organisations, in both the public and private sectors.

The calculation of statistics is a problem that has bedevilled every national tourist organisation since the birth of the industry.

For many years, it was impossible to plan ahead due to a lack of concrete information on tourist movements and expenditure, and various systems have been put in place over the decades to quantify the figures. In the Republic of Ireland, the Central Statistics Office carries out two sample surveys of passengers, and these are used in conjunction with passenger movement figures supplied by transport companies to provide estimates for overseas tourism and travel.[14] The Country of Residence Survey is a continuous sample survey of inward and outward passengers at all major sea and air ports, and is used to provide estimates of the numbersof Irish visits abroad and visits to Ireland by non-residents, with visits to Ireland being further categorised into areas of residence. In 2006 the sample size was just over 665,500 passengers. The Passenger Card Inquiry is also a continuous sample survey of incoming and departing passengers at major points of entrance and exit, and provides information on the reason for journey, area of residence, length of stay, expenditure and fare cost. The results are combined with the overall visitor estimates from the previous survey to provide overseas tourism and travel estimates. The sample size in this survey in 2006 was just over 383,000 passengers, of which 213,000 were inward and 170,000 outward.[15] Cross-border visits on rail and scheduled bus services are estimated from this document and from passenger movement statistics. These results are used to estimate the country of residence distribution as well as the reason for journey, average length of stay, expenditure and fare costs. However, the estimates of expenditure by cross-border visitors using private cars or unscheduled bus services are based on very limited information and are regarded as subject to error. In addition, Fáilte Ireland, the national tourism development authority, carries out its own surveys of overseas travellers, occupancy and visitor attractions, which also contribute to overall figures.

Arising from this methodology, it has been estimated that in the year 2007, overseas visits to the Republic of Ireland totalled over 7.7 million, continuing an upward trend from 2005 of over ten per cent.[16] This was more than twice the World Tourism Organisation's preliminary estimates of 4.5 per cent in world arrivals, and well over the 3.9 per cent growth in European arrivals. Expenditure by out-of-state tourists amounted to €4.1 billion, with a further €726 million by overseas visitors on fares to Irish carriers and almost €29 million spent by overseas resident same-day visitors. Domestic tourism added over €1.5 billion, making a total of almost €6.5 billion earnings from tourism in 2007.[17] There was substantial growth in visitor numbers from mainland Europe, with German visitors at

436,000 continuing to outstrip all other European markets. The North American figure increased by 4 per cent, almost back to the record level of 2000 before the events of 9 September 2001 had such a harmful effect on that market. This means that the Republic has increased its share of United States travellers to Europe, which grew by 4 per cent in 2007. However, as usual, the bulk of tourists came from Britain, with 3,776,000, followed by mainland Europe at 2,577,000. What is interesting in this context is that 14 per cent of visitors from mainland Europe came to Ireland for business purposes, and that 24 per cent of visitors of them stated that they were visiting friends and relatives, which was traditionally one of the main reasons for visits from Britain and the United States. As Irish people spread their wings in other countries and nationals of those countries come to work in Ireland, the resulting tourist figures take on a new complexion. In financial terms, for every Euro spent by out-of-state tourists, fifty-two cents eventually accrue directly to the exchequer, through Value-Added Tax, excise duties and PAYE, with a resulting €2.77 billion being contributed in 2006, of which €2.27 billion came from foreign tourism. As the value of exported goods and services for that year was estimated at €140.15 billion, the tourism industry's input of €4.69 billion accounted for 3.3 per cent of exports. According to the Central Statistics Office Quarterly Survey, this would amount to 3.8 per cent of Gross National Product. Fáilte Ireland's Tourism Business and Employment Survey for the year estimated that the Irish tourism and hospitality industry employed almost 250,000 people in 2006, an increase of 1.4 per cent on the numbers employed in 2005, with the largest increases occurring in the hotel and restaurant sectors. Of that number, 203,000 were year-round employees, of which 62 per cent were Irish nationals, while the remainder were of international origin.

In Northern Ireland, the Northern Ireland Tourist Board (NITB) carries out its own Passenger Survey (NIPS), which closely follows the methodology of the UK Office for National Statistics International Passenger Survey, in which passengers are sampled on all major routes in and out of the UK, but with some differences. A systematically chosen sample of travellers is interviewed on country of residence, reason for visit and details of expenditure and fares. No interviews are carried out with Northern Ireland or Republic of Ireland residents, and NIPS deals only with visitors who have stayed overnight in the Province. Information on Republic of Ireland residents staying overnight is derived from the Central Statistics Office's Household Travel Survey, and information on

other overseas visitors who stay overnight but enter or exit the
island from the Republic is derived from Fáilte Ireland's Survey of
Overseas Travellers. For 2007, there were 6,905 interviews completed in the NIPS. Tourism revenue accruing to Northern Ireland in
2007 amounted to £535 million, consisting of £376 million from out
of state visitors, an increase of 1 per cent in real terms, and £159 million from the domestic market. While there was an increase of 6 per
cent in out of state visitors, excluding Great Britain and the Republic
of Ireland, there were some ups and downs. Visitor numbers from
North America as a whole were up, with traffic from the United
States increasing by 12 per cent, while that from Canada was up 50
per cent. The number of British visitors was static, while those from
the Republic of Ireland were up by 3 per cent. The most dramatic
increase was in visitors from Australia and New Zealand, up 36 per
cent to 57,000, and outnumbering those from Canada at 45,000.18
Visits to friends and relatives were down by one per cent, which
was attributed to the competition from short break destinations and
low cost travel for British travellers. Business travel was down 4 per
cent, and the number of nights spent in that sector declined due to
a reduction in the average length of stay of a business visitor.
However, business trips were evenly spread throughout the year,
while over half of holidaymakers arrived during the July to
September period. It can be seen that in both jurisdictions, tourism
is a significant contributor to the economy, with the difference that
in Northern Ireland there is no question of its having to act as a
factor in the balance of payments sphere, as its promotion there is
financed from the United Kingdom.

However, it is acknowledged on both sides of the border that
Ireland will never be in the top echelon of global tourist destinations and that it faces constant competition from emerging markets
around the world. Furthermore, with low-cost air fares and more
disposable income than ever before, many Irish people can now
consider a weekend in Dubai a reasonable suggestion, a far cry
from the early days of travel that eventually evolved into what we
know as 'tourism'. In the second half of the sixteenth century,
members of the English nobility began to cross the English
Channel in search of the latest and best in European culture, in
what became known as the 'Grand Tour'. These travellers journeyed with
the intention of completing their education by acquiring a gloss of
Renaissance culture and were concerned with developments in art,
science and politics. By the eighteenth century, the Grand Tour had
evolved into a prolonged visit to continental countries for the purpose of pleasure as much as learning, and although some successful

merchants and professional men did partake of shorter, less expensive trips to Europe, it still remained the province of a tiny elite. Popular tourism was a British invention, inextricably linked with technological advances in transport and communications. By the late 1830s, as railways extended their networks across Britain and industrialisation created a new class of urban workers searching for an escape from their everyday environment, the material and social conditions to enable the ordinary man to 'get away from it all' were in place. The time was ripe for an entrepreneur who would build a business on this foundation by offering special outings at reduced fares for instruction and pleasure. An unlikely candidate emerged from the Harborough Temperance Society, a man convinced that he had been chosen by Providence to become the pioneer of modern travel. Thomas Cook was firmly committed to the cause of temperance, and in 1841 he organised a trip between Leicester and Loughborough to facilitate the attendance of a group of teetotallers at a temperance rally.[19] He arranged for 570 people to be carried eleven miles, entertained by a band, harangued for three hours about the 'monster intemperance' and returned home for the price of one shilling, and thus the 'excursion' was born.[20] By the 1850s he was taking this work seriously as a social crusade to bring the educational advantages of travel to ordinary people, and in a treatise on the subject entitled *Physical, Moral and Social Aspects of Excursions or Tours*, he firmly averred that the chief value of tourism was to 'unite man to man, and man to God'.[21] While he did not invent it, he developed the concept of the package tour, and by the end of the nineteenth century British tourists could travel in groups to the furthest parts of the British Empire. As inhabitants of that empire, Irish men and women of means were not slow to avail themselves of the facilities offered by Cook and his imitators, and having seen what tourists could contribute by way of financial reward to regions which had been by-passed by the Industrial Revolution, by 1900 there was a small but vociferous body of Irish entrepreneurs anxious to promote the charms of the 'Emerald Isle' as a tourist destination. This description of Ireland was coined by Dr William Drennan, chairman of the United Irishmen, in a poem entitled 'When Erin first rose' written in the late eighteenth century, and has since entered into the tourism discourse as the accepted shorthand for the island of Ireland.

In the last decade of the nineteenth century and the first of the twentieth, there were determined efforts made to elevate Ireland's profile as a tourist destination. As domestic tourism was restricted by the relatively small size of Ireland's urban and professional classes, so significant to tourism in mainland Britain, Irish tourism had to depend more than was true elsewhere in the United Kingdom on visitors from abroad. With no mass resorts such as Blackpool, or Douglas in the Isle of Man, nor any select resorts of international reputation such as the spas of the Continent, Ireland's attractiveness to visitors consisted of its portfolio of natural attractions, which included the Giant's Causeway and the lakes of Killarney, along with its antiquities and sporting possibilities, but it was never more than a small-scale phenomenon. However, many seaside resorts made strenuous attempts to cater for foreign visitors, and the goodwill of the British administration in Dublin was obtained, with significant results. The willingness of the government to take an active interest in promotion was an exceptional circumstance in the United Kingdom, where nothing comparable was done for Scotland or England, and can be attributed to the determination and perseverance of one man, Frederick Crossley, who succeeded in uniting members of the peerage, commercial interests and transport companies in an association which campaigned vociferously for state aid. However, with the outbreak of war in Europe in 1914, the Easter Rising in Dublin in 1916, and the subsequent War of Independence and the Civil War that followed the signing of the Anglo-Irish Treaty in 1922, tourism was abandoned and the brave new pre-war ventures crumbled away to nothing. However, it was ever thus in Irish tourism. Just as it appeared that the tourist industry was on the right track, some external event such as recession, terrorism, animal diseases or human epidemics demonstrated the vulnerability of that ephemeral trade to factors outside Irish control.

The Cumann na nGaedheal administration which took office in the Irish Free State in December 1922 was preoccupied with matters of economy, politics and international prestige, and the devastation wreaked on the infrastructure in many parts of the country during the various conflicts, along with damage to what hotel stock still existed, made any serious moves to promote the country as a tourist destination an impossibility. Nevertheless, once again some resolute individuals succeeded in having the industry placed on the political agenda, and a start was made through the formation of a centralised tourist association. There was an awareness of the economic potential of tourism from the early days of both the Irish Free State and Northern Ireland, and certain politicians and civil servants, along with dedicated and inspired individuals, set out to exploit that potential to the full. That their efforts met with limited success was sometimes the result of the unfortunate collision of international events, such as the Second World War, with Irish initiatives which were groundbreaking in their time, and the opposition of the Department of Finance in the Republic of Ireland to early development proposals was an obstacle to be faced by politicians and entrepreneurs alike. In Northern Ireland, the success of traditional industries such as shipbuilding, linen, rope-making and heavy industry relegated tourism to a situation of low priority, and it was only when these industries began to fail that it was regarded as having serious potential. It is revealing to see the evolution of state support for the tourist industry in Ireland across the different administrations which handled it, and its transition from its perception by C.S. (Todd) Andrews, one of the first employees of the Irish Tourist Association, as 'a shoddy business'[22] to its present status as First Cause of the restoration and commodification of our cultural heritage. However, the ideological conflict between preservation, presentation and packaging of Irish culture and civilisation for foreign consumption is the subject of intense debate, as opposing interests seek to impose their criteria on those things Irish that are most attractive to overseas visitors, who may well become the architects of our cultural demise. The sweet smell of success underpinning the economic miracle of the Celtic Tiger could be regarded as being undermined by tourism promotion of Ireland as the misty, green isle of red-haired colleens, elderly men leaning over country gates and cheerful children ushering the cattle home. It is worth bearing in mind that this opposition in thematic terms is nothing new; the debate has been ongoing since the earliest days of tourism promotion and development.

One of the most valuable sources for establishing the workings of the tourist bodies from the 1940s onwards has been the co-operation of people who were involved in tourism at that time. I was fortunate in that I had maintained contact with former colleagues in Bord Fáilte, which facilitated my access to information and enabled me to interview many of the protagonists of the events I wished to research. I was also lucky enough to be put in contact with former employees of the Northern Ireland Tourist Board, and found them equally prepared to share their experiences with me. The willingness of these witnesses to be interviewed was motivated by their feeling that this was an unwritten chapter in Irish history. They were imbued with a strong sense of the patriotism of most of the protagonists in the early days, at a time when the two states were attempting to forge new and separate identities. As independent Ireland emerged from its dependence upon Britain as the principal market for its manufactured and agricultural goods during the second half of the twentieth century, so tourist interests in the country determined to cast the tourism promotion net over a wider area. In Northern Ireland, the state's financial dependence on the United Kingdom has perhaps proven a stumbling block in developing a competitive attitude in the tourism sphere. As the world shrinks in time and space thanks to technological advances, the fight for a place in the tourism marketplace in the third millennium presents as many challenges now as it did to those who were attempting to pioneer its development over a hundred years ago.

Turn of the century tourism in Ireland

> There is nothing in these isles more beautiful and picturesque than the South and West of Ireland. They who know the fairest portions of Europe still find in Ireland that which they have seen nowhere else, and which has charms all its own.[1]

Quoted by Mr and Mrs Hall in their 1865 opus *A Week at Killarney*, this tribute to the Emerald Isle in the *Times* that year set the scene for a renewed interest in the sister island by British visitors, but it would be some decades before organised travel would become possible. In that time advances in transport would combine with the efforts of entrepreneurs to emulate the success of the Victorian holiday experience across the Irish Sea. Ironically, it was an Englishman who became the driving force of the industry at the turn of the century, and his efforts were responsible for the active interest of the British government in Irish tourist promotion. In a manner unparalleled elsewhere in the UK, it offered material support for the two main avenues of achieving this, the extension of the Irish light railway system by the Railways (Ireland) Act of 1896 and the passing of the Health Resorts and Watering-Places (Ireland) Act in 1909.

Despite widely held perceptions to the contrary, tourism was not a new phenomenon in nineteenth-century Ireland. Visitors had travelled and written of their experiences in the country for many centuries, with guidebooks to Ireland appearing as early as 1800. Certainly, early travel was a hit-and-miss affair because of the poorly developed road network. However, major changes resulted from the dramatic impact of the industrial revolution in Great Britain between 1750 and 1850, and these were to have an effect also in Ireland, because of its proximity to Britain. There, a rise in population from 5.5 million to 25 million was accompanied by a drift from rural areas to the newly emerging industrial towns. In their turn, urban households with increased purchasing power became the principal markets for the newly emerging modes of transport.

In Ireland, it was the building of canals in the second half of the eighteenth century that provided the first transport network and also led to the establishment of the first hotel chain. The first trunk canal, the Grand, opened its inaugural section from Dublin in 1780 and eventually crossed the midlands to reach the River Shannon.[2] Four years later the first hotel opened at Sallins, and hotels were also built at Robertstown, Tullamore, Portobello (Dublin) and Shannon harbour, the last being completed in 1806. They cost £30,000 to build and maintain up to 1812, but they were not a financial success.[3] The horse-drawn boats were comfortable but too slow; sailings from Dublin to Athy, a distance of 42 miles, took thirteen hours. The Methodist preacher, John Wesley was one of the first overseas visitors to use the canal on a trip to Kildare in 1785.[4] Unfortunately, the standard of onboard catering was not an inducement to use this mode of travel: the novelist Anthony Trollope wrote of 'the eternal half-boiled leg of mutton floating in a bloody sea of grease and gravy'. The fly-boats (*bateaux-mouches*), introduced in 1834, were lighter and faster, though still horse-drawn.

For those wishing to travel by road, the towns of Ireland were linked with Dublin by Royal Mail coaches at the beginning of the nineteenth century. These carried mail and passengers, but were expensive and slow. Popular transport was changed by an Italian immigrant, Charles Bianconi, who recognised the need for a reasonably cheap and speedy passenger service.[5] He began operations in 1815 on the Clonmel to Cahir route and was soon carrying mail and passengers between towns not served by the post office coaches. Bianconi invented the famous long cars which could carry sixteen to twenty passengers and within twenty-five years his network extended over most of Munster, Leinster and Connacht. By 1845 he had bought out many of his rivals, owned 1,400 horses and covered 3,800 miles daily through twenty-three counties, carrying all classes of society. Coaching inns and hotels were built to cater for his customers, and many of today's established hotels such as Hunters hotel in Rathnew, Co. Wicklow, began as such, while Dublin's Royal Hibernian hotel was the metropolitan terminus. The service was gradually eclipsed in the 1850s and 1860s, however, by the railway network, which had begun to spread across the country.

As in other countries, the railways had a tremendous impact on Irish life. Travel on the roads and canals had remained relatively slow and was always subject to the vagaries of the weather. Trains were faster, cheaper and more reliable, and they transformed ordinary people's ideas about travel. Up to this time, travel had been viewed as a burden, a task to be undertaken only when absolutely necessary for business, employment or official purposes. By providing a more comfortable and inexpensive means of transport, trains encouraged ordinary people to travel for both business and pleasure. In addition, an important feature was the development of excursions and the emergence of the day-tripper, whose numbers soon superseded those of the elite, first class traveller, and provided the clientele for the burgeoning seaside resorts throughout the British Isles. In Ireland, the first railway in 1834 linked the mail-boat port of Kingstown (now Dun Laoghaire) with the capital, and by 1852 the Irish railway network extended from Dublin to Galway, Bandon, Clonmel, Limerick and Kilkenny. Its expansion helped the development of holiday resorts enormously, and the growth of Killarney as a tourist resort was closely connected with the completion of the railway line from Dublin in 1853. The Great Southern hotel, which opened in 1854, was the first railway hotel in Ireland, and it marked the extension of the railway companies' activities into construction. It was built on land given by Lord Kenmare, who owned most of the lakes and picturesque areas around Killarney. Keen to promote tourism to cover the ever-increasing costs of maintaining his estate, he began a system of issuing tickets that allowed visitors to tour the lakes, the Torc waterfall and other scenic parts of his demesne.[6] Other hotels built by railway companies included those at Galway, Kenmare, Parknasilla, Bundoran, Warrenpoint and Rostrevor. Becoming an hotelier was also a method of survival for some of the landed families in Ireland who were the object of the activities of the Land League. Caroline Blake, widow of the owner of the Renvyle estate in Co. Galway, faced ruin in 1883 as a result of her defiance of that organisation, and turned her home into a hotel in order to survive, a move made possible by the Blake Fund Committee, which numbered the British prime minister, Arthur Balfour, among its subscribers.[7] However, the railways were also responsible for the demise of some early efforts in tourism. Jonathan Binns, an Englishman travelling in Clare in 1835, stayed in 'an immense inn' at Miltown Malbay, which was 'a partnership concern, built about thirty years ago by four gentlemen, including ninety beds, cold and warm baths and stabling for eighty horses, at a cost of £7,000'.[8] Harriet Martineau, arriving in the village in 1852

and expecting to stay at the hotel, found it transformed into an auxiliary workhouse for Ennistymon.[9] Coinciding with the growth of
the railway system, the advances made in steamship technology
enabled the relatively rapid crossing of the Irish Sea by this method
from 1843 onwards. In 1861 Irish tourism was given a boost when
Queen Victoria, the prince consort and three of their children, with
a retinue of over a hundred, visited Killarney. This trip received
extensive coverage in newspapers all over the world,[10] but it is difficult to gauge how many British visitors came to Ireland as a result,
as political unrest engendered by the spread of Fenianism contributed to an image of the country as being unsettled and therefore unsafe.

Many holiday resorts and watering-places had come into being
in Ireland during the seventeenth and eighteenth centuries.
Killarney had become the best known among foreign visitors, and
Richard Pococke, visiting there in 1758, described it as having 'good
inns, lodgings and accommodations for strangers who come …
mostly in the months of July and August'. As the railways opened
up formerly inaccessible areas, other small resorts began developing
facilities and amenities to attract tourists. Most of these were located beside the sea and catered for the Victorian passion for bathing
as a healthy and restorative practice, enabling British visitors to
escape from increasingly polluted industrial cities. The status of sea
bathing and seaside resorts acquired a new aura of respectability
and popularity inspired by the royal residence at Brighton, which
altered the image of the seaside as a resort for invalids and presented it instead as a fashionable place in which to be seen. Tramore, a
small fishing hamlet on the Waterford coast, and Bray, a Wicklow
market town, experienced phenomenal growth as local entrepreneurs sought to maximise the potential of this new industry. The
first hotel in Tramore was built by Bartholomew Rivers, a Catholic
ship-owner, merchant and banker, who also provided many new
houses for letting, a thatched chapel, assembly rooms and numerous bathing lodges. Although his ambitious ventures eventually led
to bankruptcy, Rivers undoubtedly laid down the groundwork for
the development of Tramore as a resort, and the opening of the
Waterford–Tramore railway line in 1853 gave a tremendous boost
to the town. Bray, on the other hand, was established as a small
market town by the mid-1700s, and its population consisted of small
traders, fisherman, sub-tenant farmers and a number of labourers,
together with the military personnel at the garrison. The location of
the town just ten miles south of Dublin on the main road to
Wicklow and Wexford was of major importance in its development

as a tourist destination, and by the time the first mail-coach service was inaugurated in 1814 the presence of a good hotel – Quin's – made Bray an obvious staging post on the route.[11] Bray became the starting point for tours to adjacent beauty spots such as the Dargle Valley, Powerscourt waterfall, the Glen of the Downs and the Wicklow mountains, which pandered to an increasing interest in the natural landscape and rugged mountain scenery. With improved communication and transport systems facilitating excursions by foreigners and day-trippers from Dublin, Bray acquired the title of 'the gateway to the Garden of Ireland' and featured prominently in many of the popular travel guides of the day. However, the town's popularity was not confined to seasonal visitors, as the rise in fashion of permanent seaside residency prompted the construction and remodelling of large, fashionable residences on the outskirts of the town.[12] As with Tramore, the coming of the railway to Bray in July 1854 offered developers the opportunity to transform the town, and this was done on the lines of Brighton, which, while it was an elegant seaside resort, also functioned as a fashionable residential town within easy reach of London. William Dargan, the country's most distinguished railway entrepreneur and organiser of the Dublin Industrial Exhibition of 1853, brought the railway to Bray, and he set about developing the town as an elegant resort and residence.

The emergence of that other vital ingredient in tourism traffic, the travel agent, also coincided with these developments. In 1818 a Mr Emery of Charing Cross in London began organising fourteen-day coach tours of Switzerland at a cost of 20 guineas.[13] He was followed in 1841 by Thomas Cook, who also organised excursions and who began operations in Ireland in 1849, taking a group of travellers from the Potteries to Dublin. In 1852 Cook introduced his short excursions and longer tours to Ireland, writing enthusiastically: 'From Derby to Dublin and back for 13s.! is an astounding announcement; and the artizan [sic] and mechanic classes may now regale their spirits with the pleasurable libations of travel.'[14] The following year he took thousands to the Dublin Exhibition, part of an effort to stimulate industry and to revive the Irish economy after the Famine. The importance of this initiative by Cook was that it proved that large numbers of the less moneyed British could be drawn to Ireland if the terms were right. Cook conducted a number of parties to Ireland, filling two special trains with about 1,500 people in 1856. Unfortunately, the rivalry of the railway companies frustrated his efforts, as they felt that they could provide excursion services themselves. Nevertheless, his son, John Mason

Cook, opened the first Cook office in Dublin in 1874, just two years after the Irish railways began accepting Cook's tickets for the first time in seventeen years.[15] By 1888 Cook was advertising tours in Ireland by rail, steamer and coach and in 1895 his first package tour from the United States arrived in Killarney and Glengarriff. Offices were opened in Belfast, Cork and Queenstown and in 1900 the company's brochure, *Cooks' Tours in the Emerald Isle*, was a hundred pages long, providing an extensive range of holidays of varying duration in all parts of the country and using lake steamers to take visitors on cruises on the River Shannon, Lough Corrib and Lough Erne. Queen Victoria's visit to Dublin in that year contributed largely to 'the most extraordinary season' ever in transatlantic travel, with new hotels being built in the capital as England's 'Sister Isle … roused from her Rip Van Winkle sleep'.[16]

The growth of interest in Ireland as a destination for travellers may have been facilitated by the huge technological advances in transport systems which took place during the late eighteenth and early nineteenth centuries, but these events were paralleled by the appearance of a spate of books about travel in Ireland. Arthur Young's *Tour of Ireland*, published in 1780, was one of the first guidebooks for travellers who were fit enough to cover large distances on horseback. His comments on Killarney describe a town not catering adequately for tourists.[17] Young advocated the construction of a 'large, well-built inn' on the lake shore, with numerous good apartments, '… and as great a variety of amusements as could be collected, especially within doors; for the climate being very rainy, travellers wait with great impatience in a dirty common inn'. Recommending the accommodations of the English 'spaw' as a model, he suggested that reasonable prices, prominently displayed, would help to retain visitors.[18] Young also wrote of Wicklow's 'most magnificent scenery', describing Powerscourt House as being 'in the most beautiful situation in the world' and publishing a glowing description of the Glen of the Downs, the Dargle Glen and Powerscourt waterfall.[19]

During the nineteenth century over seven hundred books were written about the country, with the Famine years of 1840–1850 producing up to fifty books, and early in the century the term 'Emerald Isle' came into common usage. Prominent among the writers were the intrepid Frenchman Alexis de Tocqueville and the English writer William Makepeace Thackeray. However, the most assiduous and enthusiastic writers about Ireland in the nineteenth century were undoubtedly Samuel Carter Hall and his wife, who wrote about their travelling experiences from 1829 onwards, when their *Sketches of Irish Character* was published. Describing the country and its inhabitants with a sympathetic and constructive eye, the Halls produced numerous works and *Hall's Ireland: Mr. and Mrs. Hall's Tour of 1840* is an earnest effort to inform the British reader about economic conditions in Ireland. In 1864 Murray's *Guide on Ireland* was published, and this was the first instance of Ireland being incorporated into an international series of guides.

Irish tourism development faced a number of disadvantages, in addition to its isolated situation on the periphery of Europe. Along with its almost total dependence on visitors from abroad and the relative absence of well-known attractions, Ireland also suffered from deficiencies of accommodation, amenities and transport facilities, along with an image of lawlessness and political unrest. The lack of a literary figure to romanticise the Irish landscape, as Scott and Wordsworth had done respectively for Scotland and the Lake District, was another drawback. The image of Ireland portrayed in the novels of Maria Edgeworth, a figure of comparative stature whose works had served as an inspiration to Scott, was not an alluring one, as it evoked impressions of clamouring and unruly masses, and hordes of beggars.[20] The presence of clamouring and unruly beggars was a constant theme in travel literature on Ireland well into the twentieth century, and along with fears of disturbance on political grounds, it constituted a major public relations problem for tourism promoters. The development of the tourist industry in the late nineteenth century was clearly a Herculean task, requiring inexhaustible optimism and untiring energy on the part of anyone prepared to take it on. Ironically, the person who became the engine of Irish tourism at this time was not an Irishman at all, but a native of Lancashire who came to Ireland to work in Thomas Cook's Dublin office.[21]

Frederick W. Crossley was born in Birmingham in 1862 and worked with Thomas Cook & Son there before moving to Dublin. He became convinced of the economic potential of Irish tourism but failed to interest his employers in a plan for investment and promotion. In 1891 he resigned from his post and founded the Irish Tourist Development Association with the object of bringing together all those in the country who stood to benefit from its tourism potential.[22] Crossley was an indefatigable worker. He threw himself into the cause of Irish tourism development, and quickly established himself as the main mover and shaker of that movement. Most crucially, he forged contacts with the influential peers and businessmen who made up the Royal Dublin Society, and also with the proprietors and managers of hotels and transport companies. His success in this

direction can be gauged by the fact that by August 1893 he had
established himself as their spokesman and had obtained a meeting with the Lord Lieutenant, Lord Houghton, at the vice-regal
lodge, at which he explained his interest in developing Ireland as a
tourist resort.[23]

Realising the importance of propaganda, Crossley established a
publishing company and in June 1894 he began publication of a
monthly journal, the *Irish Tourist*, with two specific aims: 'to make
better known to the world Ireland's charm and beauty, and to
attract multitudinous visitors'.[24] The first edition of the journal contained articles on 'Ireland's beauty spots', 'Notes on Irish history',
'In and around Dublin' and other helpful information on the country, while in a column entitled 'Opinions on Ireland' Crossley quoted William Makepeace Thackeray, who had visited Ireland in 1842:

> What sends picturesque tourists to the Rhine and Saxon
> Switzerland? Within five miles round the pretty inn of
> Glengarriff, there is a country of the magnificence of which no
> pen can give an idea. Were such a bay lying upon English
> shores, it would be a world's wonder. Perhaps, if it were on
> the Mediterranean or the Baltic, English visitors would flock
> to it by hundreds. Why not come and see it in Ireland?[25]

At the same time, he was instrumental in the establishment of the
Hotel and Restaurant Proprietors' Association of Ireland, the earliest organisation for the trade in the country.[26] At its first conference
in April 1894, Crossley was elected to the executive committee, and
it was agreed that a fund be established to advertise the scenic and
sporting attractions of Ireland by posters in the principal towns
and railway stations of Great Britain.[27] Public awareness of the economic potential of tourism was growing and the *Standard*, a
London newspaper, voiced a popular opinion when it said of
Ireland:

> With proper encouragement and enterprise the island might
> become the dairy farm and pleasure-ground of Great Britain,
> and the districts into which the money of the tourist could so
> easily be diverted are precisely those that are least hopeful
> from an agricultural point of view.[28]

Crossley agreed that the areas in Ireland where scenic attractions
were to be found were also those of the most marked poverty, but
he also used his influence to drum up support in urban areas. In
August 1894, the lord mayor of Dublin agreed to convene a meeting
of businessmen to devise means of making Ireland better known as

a tourist destination.[29] Crossley worked hard to garner support among the influential 'committee men' who ran so many Irish undertakings, and his efforts were successful. In April 1895, a meeting was held in Leinster House, Dublin, under the auspices of the Royal Dublin Society.[30] Presided over by Lord Houghton, it was held during the annual Spring Show, to maximise the attendance of prominent gentry and politicians,[31] and in this respect it could be said that tourism, in bringing together men from all classes of society with the same aim, was unusual in that it transcended the social divisions so prevalent in Victorian society. This meeting brought about the formation of the Irish Tourist Association, and Lord Houghton agreed to become the first president of the organisation. The issue of security in a colony with a history of rebellion was of concern to potential British visitors, and the association was sensitive to the problem and wished to dispel the impression of Ireland as a wild and uncivilised region through effective advertising.[32] The meeting attracted favourable publicity, with the *Irish Times* devoting an entire page to an account of the proceedings, and a large amount of correspondence regarding the movement was published in the following weeks. The newspaper unequivocally supported the efforts being made:

> The presence of these sympathisers with the particular effort, and the trouble to which all of them put themselves for the purpose, are a proof that 1895 has been properly described as the Tourist Year amongst us, in the sense of being that period in which we become again in a practical way alive to this source of industry and profit.[33]

The change of government in Britain in June 1895 brought about the removal of Lord Houghton from the viceroyalty, but he wrote to the lord mayor of Dublin confirming that he would remain as a member of the ITA and pledging his continued support for the movement.[34] In July 1895 the *National Review* published an article by him giving his impressions of the various parts of Ireland he had visited during his sojourn in the country.[35] Unfortunately, this positive opinion was countered by an article in the *Field* magazine which comprehensively denigrated Irish hotel accommodation, the lack of cleanliness in railway carriages and the inability of the inhabitants of the remoter districts to provide hospitality for visitors: 'The Irish as a race do not understand catering for the traveller, or indeed, for anyone with different tastes of their own.'[36] 'Rusticans Expectans', a correspondent to the *Times*, was also highly critical of an Irish hotel: 'The plates and dishes are filthy, the lamps are still

1.1
F.W. Crossley, from
an article in the
Irish Tourist in 1895.
*Courtesy of the
National Library of
Ireland.*

dirtier. I have to keep my bedroom shutters closed with my dressing-table and the door with my portmanteau.'[37] Crossley, styling himself 'the founder of the Irish Tourist Development movement', rushed to defend Irish hotels and railways, alleging that Anglo-Irishmen and American-Irishmen were 'most hypercritical' and pleading for consideration and forbearance for the infant tourism industry: 'No good purpose can be served by chronic grumblers recording their singular experience; let them bear in mind that Rome was not built in a day.'[38]

During the summer of 1895 Crossley led a deputation to the new lord lieutenant, Earl Cadogan, who was accompanied at the meeting by the chief secretary for Ireland, Gerald Balfour. Earl Cadogan agreed to succeed Lord Houghton as president of the association, and to support plans to hold a meeting in London to publicise their existence and aims. The chief secretary also agreed to become a member and to promote its aims in every way.[39] Meanwhile, the association was spreading its wings around the country. An Ulster committee was formed at a public meeting on 13 April 1896 in Belfast, of which the lord mayor, W.J. Pirrie, became chairman. On 30 May 1896 a public meeting convened by the Earl of Bandon, lord lieutenant of Cork county, was held in Municipal Buildings, Cork, for the purpose of establishing a branch there.

During the spring of 1896 Crossley announced that the lord lieutenant would preside at a public meeting in the Imperial Institute, London, on 24 June in connection with the association. The lord mayor of London and a large number of the Irish gentry who were taking an active interest in tourist development attended, as did the lord mayors of Dublin, Belfast and the mayor of Cork.[40] The meeting was pronounced an outstanding success, with over 500 people present, and among those who spoke were Irish members of parliament John Redmond and Horace Plunkett. The meeting received a large amount of publicity from the British media, both national and regional, and Crossley's aim of bringing Irish tourist development to the notice of a wider public was certainly achieved.[41]

This event marked the beginning of Crossley's successful career as a tourism entrepreneur, which would bring him huge financial rewards in the era before the outbreak of war in Europe in 1914. He moved swiftly to take advantage of the concessions that had been won from the British government and established a number of enterprises which would ensure him the most prominent position in Irish tourism for almost twenty years. Following the meeting in London, Crossley interviewed Gerald Balfour and received his promise of support for an undertaking which came into being as the Development Syndicate (Ireland) Ltd. Crossley boasted that 'over a million of money will be expended on public works through the influence of the Syndicate, which proposes to first direct its attention to the proper 'hotelling' of Ireland.[42] In fact, the syndicate was formed with a view to taking advantage of the Railways (Ireland) Act of 1896, which offered government subsidies for coach and steamer services in places not served by the railways.[43] The company began by investing in various public works in Ireland, acquiring a tourist car and posting service, and also a valuable posting establishment at Bantry. Crossley set about buying and constructing hotels and improving tourist services in scenic areas, building the Golfer's hotel at Sutton Cross in Dublin and the Lakeside hotel in Killaloe, and later acquiring the Claremont hotel in Howth, the Royal Mail hotel (now the Royal Marine) in Kingstown and the Laharna hotel on the Co. Antrim coast.[44] These hotels were sold when the company went into liquidation in 1915. In December 1896, he established another enterprise, the Shannon Development Company, which was funded with £20,000 capital and subsidised by the government with an annual grant of £9,500, as well as receiving grants from local authorities in the counties bordering the Shannon.[45] Crossley's networking skills are demonstrated by the Shannon Development Company's list of directors, which included Lord Iveagh, head of the Guinness firm, and an eclectic mix consisting of a merchant, stockbroker, printer, jeweller, solicitor, publisher and landed proprietor.[46]

Steamer services had operated on the River Shannon from 1825, but regular services had ceased in 1865. Crossley's company began a steamboat service in 1897 with the inaugural sailing of the SS *Fairy Queen* on 18 June, and had among its first customers the Duke of York (later King George V), who travelled from Killaloe to Banagher in September of that year. Naturally, Crossley was quick to take advantage of this event by naming that stretch the 'Duke of York route', as the practice of using endorsement by members of the royal family was an important marketing ploy in tourism ventures at that time. While the intention was to build hotels along the river at the various stopping-points, Crossley also hoped to extend the route from Killaloe to Dromod, Co. Leitrim, a distance of one hundred miles, in order to establish a connecting link between the kingdom of Kerry and the Donegal highlands.[47] By 1900 the company had acquired six steamers at a cost of £5,000, with the three new boats being named *The Countess Cadogan*, *The Countess of Mayo* and *The Lady Betty Balfour*, as Crossley kept an eye to the importance of influential patronage. Extensive schedules included stops at Athlone, Rooskey, Killaloe, Carrick-on-Shannon, Banagher, Portumna, Meelick and Shannonbridge, and necessitated a minimum of five vessels, with one free for emergencies, as there was one sailing in each direction on weekdays on all routes. Services were organised to coincide with railway termini, which gave connections as far north as Belfast and Derry, and publicised circular tours which extended all over the country, the most ambitious of which was probably the Belfast–Killarney–Bantry excursion. Unfortunately, the steamer service was not a profitable proposition, and the withdrawal of subsidies necessitated the curtailment, first of winter services, and eventually of the entire service. After 1904 the steamers were no longer seen north of Athlone, and the dispersal of the fleet began soon after. By 1914, the final steamer was disposed of and, although Crossley's son, Lieutenant Frederick Crossley, had become a director of the company by 1918, the Great War effectively destroyed the Irish tourist industry and the company was wound up in 1923.[48]

1.2
Advertisement for Crossley's Tourist Development publications in the *Irish Tourist* of 1901 showing hapless British tourist, complete with bag of money (£.s.d.) being hooked. *Courtesy of the National Library of Ireland.*

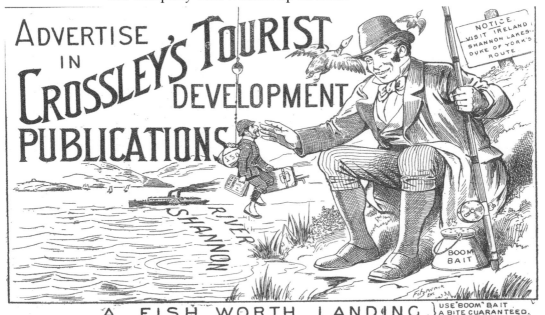

A FISH WORTH LANDING.

Crossley's publishing company also acquired the Irish Tourist Development Publishing Company, a firm engaged in publishing and advertising guidebooks, pamphlets, maps and photographs connected with tourist traffic and travelling in Ireland, while also operating as tourist and excursion agents and hotel and restaurant proprietors. Several of the directors were the same as those in the Shannon Development Company, with the exception of the Earl of Mayo, who replaced Lord Iveagh as the token peer, but a number of hotel proprietors and managers were also included. This company survived for thirty years, being dissolved in 1926.[49] In addition to his commercial activities, Crossley was to the fore in opposing measures detrimental to the development of the industry. On 2 July 1896 the Belfast Committee of the ITA held a public meeting in the town hall to fight proposals by a syndicate to enclose access to the Giant's Causeway and charge for admission. Crossley was incensed:

> If the Syndicate succeeded in placing barbed wire around the Causeway, the probability was that soon every cross, round tower, and ruin in the country, and ultimately the country itself, would be enclosed by barriers, and so the tourist invasion of Ireland would be prevented.[50]

He suggested the establishment of a shilling fund to defend the right of way at the causeway and obtained the support of Lord Antrim to oppose the syndicate.[51] Unfortunately, the battle was not so easily won, and the controversy continued for some time. The syndicate took the case to the courts, and despite the efforts of the defence committee, was victorious.[52] However, the syndicate made many improvements at the site, including a path around the bays, and the Causeway electric railway, built in 1883 and the first of its kind in the United Kingdom, took tourists there from Portrush every half-hour during the summer.[53] At the same time, Crossley threw himself with enthusiasm into another campaign. The Irish Road Improvement Association was formed in the spring of 1897 with the Earl of Mayo as its president, and Crossley and R.J. Macredy, editor of the *Irish Cyclist*, as its honorary secretaries, and had as its aim to make Irish roads, which had a well-deserved bad reputation, an attraction for native and visiting cyclists.[54] However, little progress was made, and four years later Macredy was imploring the readers of the *Irish Times* to rally around the association: 'It is like flogging a dead horse to try and induce cyclists or motorists to tour in this country when the roads … are in such a shocking condition.'[55] A leading article in the newspaper concurred: 'It is the

1.3
Drawing of the
Strand Hotel
(formerly the
Golfer's hotel and
now the Marine) in
Sutton, Co. Dublin,
in 1905. *Courtesy of
the National Library
of Ireland.*

worst economy to neglect the roads, and especially at the present day in Ireland when such laudable efforts are being made in various directions to induce tourists to our shores.'[56]

However, there were those in Ireland who did not see the incursion of tourists in such a positive light. R.A.S. Macalister, professor of Celtic archaeology at University College, Dublin, questioned the assumption that the tourist movement would provide a remedy for the lack of money in Ireland and the existence of misunderstandings between the English and Irish races. He dreaded the arrival of an army of trippers, who would encourage pauperism in the Irish peasant by tipping the mobs of young children who would follow them. He feared the desecration of Ireland's national monuments, citing the example of the disfiguration by graffiti of Westminster Abbey and Stonehenge as examples of the English tripper's lack of respect for such ancient edifices.[57] While Macalister's concern for Ireland's antiquities was genuine enough, it is difficult to escape the impression that there was also an element of snobbery in his views. The hordes of trippers that he anticipated would mainly consist of the lower orders, and he saw that phenomenon as being culturally corrosive. In any case, an anonymous writer to the *Irish Tourist* was quick to refute his allegations, laying blame for the despoliation of Irish beauty spots squarely at the door of the natives. The writer described conditions in the Glen of the Downs on a bank holiday evening, replete with evidence of vandalism in which the much-maligned cockney tourist had no share: 'I'm afraid that the Celt with all his poetry, all his mysticism, all his artistic pos-

sibilities, is scarcely in a sufficiently perfect state of civilisation himself to justify him in indulging in any very severe criticism of his
neighbours.' Not all criticism came from those outside the industry;
it was also encountered from within, as there was some carping
about the formation of Crossley's development syndicate at the
annual convention of the Hotel and Restaurant Proprietors'
Association in 1897. Some hoteliers protested that it was making
tourist development a mercantile and commercial matter, but
Walter Holder, president of the association, sprang to his defence,
citing Crossley's success in developing tourist traffic on the
Shannon as an example of what could be done in areas formerly
bereft of tourist facilities.[58]

The issue of the establishment of a royal residence in Ireland was
one which surfaced continuously in the late nineteenth century, in
political as well as tourism circles, as it was felt that such a presence
would increase the loyalty of Irish people to the British monarchy,
while also attracting the wealthy tourists who followed in the wake
of royalty wherever they went. Crossley constantly alluded to this
possibility, and in a special Horse Show issue of the *Irish Tourist* in
1894 he claimed that a permanent royal establishment would also
give an impetus to business houses and manufacturers.[59] There was
a general belief that the royals attracted tourism business, and
Scotland's growth in popularity as a holiday destination was often
attributed to the queen's purchase of the Balmoral estate. The possibility of a royal residence in Ireland was raised by Daniel
O'Connell in 1821 during the visit of King George IV, and William
Dargan had informed the queen during her 1853 visit to the Dublin
Exhibition that the greatest honour she could confer on him would
be to order him to build her a palace in Ireland.[60] The British press
concurred in this view of tourism as a cure for Ireland, with the
Times commenting on the queen's 1849 visit in most positive terms,
'She will draw in her train an imitative host of tourists and travellers',[61] and the *London Review* perceiving her Scottish sojourns as
improving the relationship between England and Scotland: 'It is a
singular and cheering sight in these modern days to see Queen
Victoria treading the heather and wandering among the mountains
and streams where the people once rose *en masse* to resist the
dynasty of which she is so illustrious an ornament.'[62]

Successive British prime ministers also saw the establishment of
a royal residence in Ireland in those terms, but following the death
of Prince Albert in 1861, the queen seems to have developed a
strong antipathy to the 'sister' island. The growth of political unrest
and dissident factions, some of whose members had proposed the

kidnapping of the monarch during her 1849 visit,[63] diminished the attractiveness of the country, and a suggestion in the House of Commons in February 1865 that the lord lieutenant be replaced by the Prince of Wales residing there for three months annually was greeted with laughter.[64] Nevertheless, the prime minister, William Gladstone, was in favour of the idea, and in May 1867 the *Court Circular* suggested that such an arrangement was indeed likely. The queen was adamant on the subject, however, and, writing to Benjamin Disraeli in 1868, she insisted: 'For health and relaxation, no one would go to Ireland, and people only go there who have their estates to attend to. But for health and relaxation thousands go to Scotland.'[65] Having trenchantly disposed of the nascent Irish tourism industry, she further stressed that visits by her children to Ireland were for duty, not amusement, and as such would have to be paid for by the government. This issue was one cause of a running battle between the queen and William Gladstone during most of the first five years of his administration, and she articulated her opposition strongly in 1871, on the grounds that it would oblige the royal family to visit Ireland more regularly 'when Scotland and England deserved it much more'.[66] The strength of her hostility to the idea did not augur well for those involved in the Irish tourism industry in the late nineteenth century, and it proved a vain aspiration. However, Crossley was nothing if not determined in his efforts to woo the aging monarch back to the Emerald Isle, assiduously attempting to court royal favour by sending an album of Irish scenery to Queen Victoria in March 1897.[67] While this gesture did not have the desired effect, he was appeased by the news that her grandson, the Duke of York (later George V), and his wife would visit Ireland in August of that year. Their visit was hailed as a boost to the tourist industry, and they progressed around the country from the vice-regal lodge in Phoenix Park to the residences of various members of the Anglo-Irish community. Many of their hosts were promoting tourism in their own areas and were also involved in the railway companies, with the result that the royal visit was welcomed on a number of levels. However, the crowning glory of the trip, as far as Crossley was concerned, was the fact that the couple travelled on the Shannon Development Company steamer from Killaloe to Banagher. As if this were not exciting enough, he had the distinction of kicking off the duke's hat with his boot as the latter ascended a gangplank to where Crossley was sitting.[68] He was presented with an album of photographs by the journalists who accompanied the royal tour, as well as a silver cigarette case inscribed 'From the ladies of the royal party'.[69] The visit received extensive coverage in the British daily newspapers, with the *Times* forecasting that such visits would turn the country into 'a resort of pleasure-seekers of all classes, and in consequence divert a good deal of English money, which now goes elsewhere – to Scotland, to Switzerland, to Norway – into the Irish pocket'.[70]

As a result of the royal visit, speculation arose again regarding the possibility of abolishing the lord-lieutenancy and appointing York as an apolitical representative of the crown in Ireland.[71] York and his father, the Prince of Wales, were both enthusiastic about the idea, and were supported by the cabinet, but once again the queen objected and the idea was dropped.[72] In September 1900 Queen Victoria returned to Ireland for the last time and stayed in the vice-regal lodge in Phoenix Park. On the last day of her visit she wrote: 'I can never forget the really wild enthusiasm and affectionate loyalty displayed by all in Ireland, and shall ever retain a most grateful remembrance of this warm-hearted and sympathetic people.'[73] However, many of her Irish subjects were not wildly enthusiastic about the visit. A letter to the *Freeman's Journal* from John Parnell, brother of the deceased Charles Stewart Parnell, betrayed an ambivalence that was felt by many: 'We have Royalty here; let us make the most of it for the welfare of the country … Let us do all we can to encourage the visit of her Majesty and of all foreigners to our rich and beautiful country.'[74] This reference to the queen as a foreigner was a growing trend in Irish political discourse, but Parnell also showed his awareness of the need for prosperous tourists to be made welcome in Ireland.

At this time, in common with many others, Crossley was growing exasperated with the attitude of the British administration towards Irish tourism and he castigated the authorities for their lack of commitment to earlier promises of support, accusing them of reneging on the second instalment of £500,000 for tourism development.[75] However, he expressed himself in more conciliatory terms in what was a groundbreaking publication in 1903. His *Concise Guide to Ireland* contained ninety-six pages of text and a list of over one hundred hotels and restaurants. Hotel advertisements featured electric lighting and telephones as great boons, while Sir Horace Plunkett extolled the virtues of Cork city as a holiday centre for those attending the Greater Cork International Exhibition running from June to November. Crossley's editorial to prospective visitors summed up his hopes for their better understanding of the Irish people, in addition to their enjoyment of the country's natural beauty:

> We have also thrown the brief search light of history here and
> there, so that … the tourist might understand in some degree

the nature of the people whose military instincts have been acutely developed owing to the rapid succession of wars, civil and foreign, which form the sad if exciting links of the past. We hope therefore that our tourist-friend leaves us with kinder feelings and a sense, however small, of brighter enlightenment.[76]

The visit of Edward VII to Ireland in July 1903 was once again the occasion of great hopes for an increase in the tourist traffic, despite the cool reception given to the monarch by Irish nationalists, who successfully scuppered plans for a welcome address by Dublin Corporation.[77] By September Crossley was forced to admit that this had not come to pass, but, ever the loyal royalist, he blamed the weather.[78] At this stage he referred to the opposition to tourism encountered in Ireland, and the lack of government financial aid:

> There are people, of course, in this country who do not want foreign visitors here. They would like to raise a big wall all round the island, and put broken glass on top. What is the use of cuddling such crude, obsolete fancies? Let us face the future, and do better next time. Where are the £500,000 we were to receive?[79]

To add to his exasperation, criticism was now encountered from an unexpected source. The former lord mayor of Belfast, W.J. Pirrie, chairman of the Ulster Association, made a speech in London in June 1904 in which he described the tourist movement as an attempt to turn Irishmen into servants of tourists for six months of the year and idlers for the remainder. Crossley vigorously counter-attacked in a letter to the *Irish Times*: 'The leaders of the Ulster Association last year promised to use their influence to further the objects of Irish Tourist Development, which now seems to their new President a damage and calamity to Ireland.'[80] Pirrie attempted to justify his remarks by claiming that he had been quoted out of con-text, and said that if the railway companies devoted as much atten-tion to industry, by offering lower rates for goods, as they had given to the tourist traffic, then they would benefit the country generally.[81] Crossley was unconvinced, as he felt that criticism of the railway companies was unwarranted, and he attacked those who theorised about the difficulties associated with tourism: 'The problem is that Ireland is plagued with a surfeit of lecturers, who make statements and suggestions, which when probed are found to be impracticable and void of reason.' Nevertheless, Pirrie's was not the only voice raised in opposing a tourist invasion. The Gaelic League, founded in 1893 with the aim of halting the anglicisation of Ireland through the restoration of Irish language and culture, was concerned that exposure to foreign influences would degrade the noble soul of the Irish peasant, a notion which drew Crossley's ire:

> Much has been said and written of an Irish Ireland. The Hooligans [sic] of the Irish gutter press having raised their inane heads from their native slush, babble re. an Irish Ireland … (they) won't have foreigners coming to the island which had the honour of being selected for their place of birth … a great league is to be formed for keeping out foreign Englishmen and foreign Scotsmen from Irish Ireland … in the presence of such slavish twaddle, the average intelligent Irishman must feel ashamed unless he is saved by a sense of humour.[82]

This attitude was contested by Sir Horace Plunkett, a unionist and a member of the Gaelic League, at the annual dinner of the Ireland Club in London in July 1904. He said that it would be a mistake to ignore the fact that this apparently non-controversial question aroused conflicting opinions in Ireland and that the best contribution the gathering could make was to try to reconcile the two opposing views. He maintained that the more tourists the railways carried, the greater concessions could be expected and demanded in the transport of agriculture and other produce.[83] Plunkett went on to say that with regard to the issue of anglicising Ireland, and counteracting the work of bodies such as the Gaelic League, he thought Irish people should 'extend their sympathies and feelings to all Englishmen – lay down the basis of the most useful kind of industrial and commercial development for their country'.

In 1905 Crossley could look back with satisfaction on more than twelve years of 'steadfastly arranging Ireland as a great tourist resort', and at this stage he began concentrating his efforts on political action at national and local levels, as he lamented that much still remained to be done, especially with regard to transport. Many of the country's roads were still defective and for this state of affairs he laid the blame squarely upon the local authorities: 'Many county councils still shy at the sight of a steamroller with the unknown terror of a high-spirited mare at its first sight of a motor car.'[84] He had always co-operated with the railway companies in Ireland, who were dependent on tourists and day-trippers for the success of their networks, in promoting their routes and tourist excursions. The companies had come together in 1896 to open a tourist inquiry office at Charing Cross in London, but by 1906 there was a change in the character of the tourist traffic to Ireland, which had once consisted mainly of well-heeled British and American visitors. Now workers from the industrial towns in Yorkshire and Lancashire were arriving in large numbers and they were generally limited to one week's holiday, during which they liked to see as much as possible. Combination tickets were introduced, for which tourists paid in advance for train, steamer, hotel, excursions, etc., and which enabled them to calculate exactly what their holiday would cost.[85] However, many Irish railway companies were not economically viable propositions from the beginning, and Crossley became convinced that the only solution to the problem was the nationalisation of the entire system. As early as 1895, he had begun canvassing for the improvement of the railway service, with better trains, faster services and the introduction of sleeping cars, and he suggested that it would be to the advantage of the railway companies if they were to introduce lower fares. In May 1905 he attended the Seventh International Railway Congress in the United States, along with sixteen other representatives of the Irish railway companies. The congress lasted a week and was followed by a 2,600-mile tour of inspection of North America lasting three weeks, which took in Montreal, Chicago, Boston, St. Louis and Niagara Falls.[86] Such an expedition can only have spurred on Crossley to try to bring about changes in the railway system in Ireland. In February 1906 the *Statist* published a letter in which he pointed out the great savings and improvements that would accrue, with beneficial results to the people of the country and without any loss to shareholders, by the acquisition and management by the state of all Irish railway networks. He stated that the suggestion had met with widespread approval and urged the new government to bow to public opinion.[87] To his delight, his proposition was taken up by the editor, and a debate ensued over the following weeks. However, the debate was not whether something should be done about the railways, but rather which method should be used to resolve the problem. Crossley was confident that some action would be taken, but he could not have foreseen that it would take another forty years before his vision became reality, and that by then the railway network would have shrunk radically.

However, just as the canals had been eclipsed by the railways, by the dawn of the new century it appeared that the latest transport phenomenon, the motor car, might do the same for the railways. The Irish Automobile Club was formed in 1901, and the Automobile Association was introduced into Ireland in 1905 by R.J. Macredy, who anticipated that it would act as a pressure group for road improvements for motorists and cyclists.[88] Crossley foresaw the changes in tourist facilities that would be demanded by the rapid growth in popularity of the sport of motoring, which would bring a new class of tourist. These included the improvement of the roads, petrol and spare parts being made available in every town and village, and crossroads being provided with marking posts. Crossley hailed the opening in 1907 of new premises for the Irish Automobile Club in Dawson Street in Dublin as a symbol of a new era in transport.[89] As that association was to the fore in assuring motorists of special terms and proper accommodation for vehicles at nearly all principal hotels in the country, he was certain that this was the way to cater for the more prosperous tourist. Referring to the 'revolution of the past decade', Crossley assured the readers of the *Irish Tourist* that the motor car was now a principal feature of everyday life, with numbers increasing in Ireland by leaps and bounds. Just as it had replaced the horse-drawn cab and omnibus in British cities, he felt it was destined to play an important part in opening up the remoter parts of Ireland, and he was not shy about advertising his own latest initiative, the provision of a daily service of motor cars along the Antrim coast road from Larne to Cushendall.

At the same time, the vexed question of road improvement and repair was becoming more important on the political agenda. The issue of who should pay for the damage caused by heavy touring vehicles was disputed by local ratepayers, who had to pay for year-round maintenance and who also resented touring visitors on a class basis, as they were often wealthy and chauffeur-driven. The problems caused by the growing number of motorists were reflected in the holding of the First International Congress of Roads in Paris in October 1908, which was attended by 1,600 delegates, including the official representatives of thirty-three nations.[90] This was followed by a road conference convened by the Association of County Councils in London in April 1909, which in turn led to the Irish Road Congress held to coincide with the Royal Dublin Society Spring Show in April 1910. In February 1911 the Executive Committee of the General Council of Irish County Councils, having considered the map of the proposed trunk road scheme for the country prepared by the County Surveyor's Association, was moved to protest that the proposal to allocate only £150,000 to Ireland, out of a total of £1.6 million available in the United Kingdom for the year ending 31 March 1912, was inadequate and inequitable. As Ireland possessed about one quarter of the total mileage of roads in the UK, the burden for road maintenance cast on the Irish ratepayer was three times as great as that borne by Great Britain. The following year, county councils were offered grants by the Roads Board towards the cost of improvement of certain leading roads in each county. The amounts of the grants varied from £1,100 to Wicklow up to £9,750 to Cork, with Donegal, Galway, Antrim, Mayo and Kerry all receiving amounts between £4,000 and £5,200, which would indicate that priority was being given to counties which were recognised tourist areas. At the same time, motoring organisations such as the Automobile Association, the Motor Union and the Royal Irish Automobile Club were authorised to issue international travel permits for Irish motor cars travelling abroad. In addition, it was no longer necessary to pay a fee on the registration of foreign motor cars and motor cycles touring Ireland. Another problem posed by the increase of motor traffic was that of speeding, and by 1912 local authorities were applying to the Local Government Board for permission to impose speed limits under Section 9 (1) of the Motor Car Act, 1903.[91] The board pointed out that it was not possible to make general regulations of this nature, and that the case of each town or village had to be considered on its merits. Moreover, the Automobile Association had offered to supply warning signposts free of charge for erection at the entrances to towns. By March 1914 there were 19,554 motor vehicles registered in Ireland and as more county and urban councils sought speed restrictions during 1914, the radical societal change brought about by the spread of motor vehicles is evident. With the breaking out of war in that year, the board's report for 1914–15 commented that complaints of excessive speed were less frequent than in previous years, owing to restrictions on the supply of petrol and the general curtailment of motor traffic.[92]

In 1909 Crossley finally saw the achievement of a measure for which he had campaigned since becoming involved in Irish tourism. He was convinced that Ireland, in addition to its other disadvantages, was handicapped by virtue of the fact that there were no funds available for the advertising of seaside resorts and scenic districts to a wider audience overseas. He was determined to obtain the necessary legislation to empower Irish local authorities to set aside money from the rates for promoting their districts, claiming that local authorities in English and Scottish towns were able to advertise the merits of their districts with 'striking artistic posters, dainty instructive booklets and in many cases a municipal bureau to give information and advice ... why should not public funds be available to secure this benefit?'[93] In fact, Blackpool was the only resort in England with this power, but Crossley constantly attempted to persuade Irish politicians to lend their support to his efforts in this direction by having legislation passed in Westminster. Kingstown Urban District Council had taken up the matter with Walter Long, a local MP, who offered to introduce a bill into parliament to empower local authorities to strike a small rate for advertising their neighbourhoods subject to the control of the Local Government Board. Crossley felt that if properly supported by local councils, it would stand a good chance of becoming law.[94]

In the summer of 1907, King Edward VII once again visited Ireland, and leading British journals were quick to note the important effect on the tourist traffic. The king stayed in Kingstown on this occasion, a move that Crossley saw as 'directing attention to its multitude of attractions as a holiday and health resort'.[95] Striking while the iron was hot, he wrote at once to Lord Aberdeen, the chief secretary, on the question of municipal advertising of tourist resorts and appealed to him to help remove the existing anomaly *vis-à-vis* similar bodies in Great Britain. Aberdeen agreed on the importance of the subject but said the matter rested with the Treasury, to whom he would forward Crossley's letter, and requested that Crossley ask all local bodies to continue the agitation. This lobbying was eventually to pave the way for the first practical political attempt to do something for the industry in Ireland in a piece of legislation with the esoteric title of the Health Resorts and Watering Places (Ireland) Act, 1909. The act was promoted by the nationalist member of parliament for South Down, Jeremiah MacVeagh, who was a director of the Dublin and South East Railway Company, the Alliance and Dublin Consumers' Gas Company, the Irish British Petroleum Company, Vickers (Ireland) and several light railway companies in Britain. Elected nationalist member of parliament for South Down in February 1902, MacVeagh was a conscientious and active MP, whose family was engaged in hotel-keeping in London. This hotel, together with his financial involvement in the railways, were doubtless significant factors in MacVeagh's interest in Irish tourism.

The first reading of the private member's bill entitled the Health Resorts (Ireland) Bill took place on 31 August 1909. Described as 'A Bill to empower local authorities in Ireland to strike a rate to defray the cost of advertising local health resorts',[96] it became the Health Resorts and Watering-Places (Ireland) Bill on its second reading on 10 September 1909. The act came into being, but proved to be a half-baked piece of legislation, as each municipal body could only act alone. Less than six months after it became law, a proposed scheme to set up a central committee formed of representatives of municipal authorities and various commercial bodies for the purpose of advertising the country as a whole was found to be illegal under the provisions of the act, and had to be abandoned.[97] These provisions were therefore applied only in a piecemeal and uncoordinated fashion, which depended entirely on the enthusiasm and dedication of local representatives. However, by 1914 the legislation was being availed of by at least twenty local authorities. The widespread application of this measure, especially by resorts in the north of the country, demonstrates forcefully how seriously tourism was taken at this time, but also pinpoints the comparative lack of organisation by areas on the western seaboard which had most to gain from tourism.

Regrettably, the glorious prospects for the development of the tourism industry in Ireland were not to be realised. Ireland and Europe were heading for the destruction of the old order and the birth of a new concept of tourism after the havoc of the Great War, the War of Independence and the Civil War. In Ireland many hotels and much of the transport infrastructure of roads, bridges and railway lines were destroyed in the course of political strife, and technological advances were changing the face of professional tourism by the time the government of the independent Irish Free State could accord attention to the industry in the mid-1920s. As for the ubiquitous Mr Crossley, he initially became a very wealthy man on the strength of his tourism enterprises, and married Florence Callow, the daughter of a well-to-do Dublin coach-builder.[98]

During the Great War, Crossley's interest in Irish railways continued unabated, and with R.L. Wigzell he founded a journal entitled *The New Way*, which later became the *Irish Railway Review*. He resigned from the board of the Cork, Bandon and South Coast railway to allow the co-option of a worker representative, and became a member of the National Union of Railwaymen. He later received an award from the union for his services to their cause. In 1917 he proposed to reinvigorate the railways financially by what he called a co-operative recreation system, whereby Irish and British wage-earners would save a portion of their weekly pay for holidays in Irish resorts, thus leading to a closer bond of comradeship among workers. While this suggestion came to nought at the time, it prefigured developments in Ireland during World War Two.

Initially ensconced with his family of nine children in a palatial mansion in Blackrock, where he lived to see his tourism enterprises come to nothing due to the vicissitudes of Irish politics, he disappeared from the tourism arena after the foundation of the Irish Free State, and was declared bankrupt in the 1920s. He died at the age of 84, having converted to Roman Catholicism just two years previously. Crossley's vision of an Ireland replete with tourists was eventually to be fulfilled, but it took over a hundred years from the time that he began his pioneering efforts in the closing years of the nineteenth century.

The Irish Tourist Association 1925–1939

Our country offers exceptional inducements to visitors. It has all the attractions of a pleasure resort. It is full of interest for the students of ancient history or of the evolution of modern states. The Irish people are alive to the cultural and economic advantages to be derived from the influx of visitors from beyond the seas. Every effort is being made to afford improved accommodation and travelling facilities, and all who come can be assured of a hearty welcome.[1]

With these words, William T. Cosgrave, president of the Irish Free State, issued a 'céad míle fáilte' to the readers of the *Times* in the spring of 1926, but his welcome can only be construed as an instructive case of creative writing, as the Ireland of the mid-1920s had few 'exceptional inducements' to attract prospective tourists, except, perhaps, for that of its political evolution. Nor were the majority of its inhabitants in any way alive to the advantages to be derived from such an influx, as they set about adapting to self-government and the demands of political independence. Moreover, such improvement in accommodation and travelling facilities as existed was barely adequate to return the country to its pre-1914 condition.

The events of the ten years beginning in 1914 had a catastrophic effect on the infant tourist industry in Ireland. With the commencement of the Great War, the tourist traffic from Great Britain, the country's main market for visitors, all but dried up. The civil unrest that followed the 1916 rising and persisted into the War of

Independence prolonged the neglect of the transport infrastructure with the blowing up of roads and bridges and the destruction of much of the railway network. The Civil War continued the pattern of depredation on a large scale, and this, coupled with the inability of existing hoteliers to maintain and refurbish their premises, and the lack of any fresh investment in the industry, led to a dispiriting situation for the makers and shakers of the Irish Free State. The legacy of the Civil War was a loss of confidence and disillusionment that were to prevail for many years.[2] Such an environment was not likely to foster an industry such as tourism, which called for a creative and imaginative approach, and which in itself was still in the process of developing. Moreover, the Department of Finance at this time sought to reduce dependence on the banks by minimising borrowing, with an effective veto on new expenditure,[3] and this was to prove a major stumbling block to the development of Irish tourism.

Nevertheless, there were still individuals with a vision of regeneration for the industry, and this was supported to a limited extent by the government that took power in December 1922 under the leadership of W.T. Cosgrave. The first inkling of political interest in the industry comes in a report of the 'director of publicity' of a private conference held by the Tourist Organisation Society in the Shelbourne hotel on 17 January 1924.[4] A growing interest in the development of tourist traffic to Ireland was evinced by editorial articles and correspondence in newspapers stimulated by the programme for the revived Tailteann Games in that year. The Tourist Organisation Society had been in existence since 1915, in which year, owing to the absence of cross-channel tourist traffic, the railway companies and hotels united to encourage the exchange of tourists between the north and south of Ireland. After 1916 the organisation became less active and by 1918 it was decided to suspend activities until such time as their efforts would be more fruitful. There had been small local organisations around the country since the late nineteenth century, but most of them had not survived. One that did last, in a semi-defunct manner, was the West of Ireland Tourism Development Association, which merged with the Tourist Organisation Society in the early 1920s.

The 1924 conference, chaired by Senator James Moran, was the first initiative by the society since the establishment of the state, and followed the formation of the Munster Tourist Development Association in Cork in September 1923, with a membership of eighty members and fifteen directors, including J.C. Foley, a Cork businessman, Alfred Canavan of the United States Shipping Lines,

Barry M. Egan, a jeweller who was also a Cumann na nGaedheal deputy for Cork city and Thomas P. Dowdall, who held a seat there for Fianna Fáil from 1932 to 1943.[5] Of the eighty members, forty-five were hoteliers, (of whom thirteen were women), mostly situated in the Munster region. In June 1924 the Irish Tourist Association, with twenty members, was registered under the Companies Act naming John Patrick O'Brien as secretary, and the following month its membership jumped to ninety-five as the Munster Tourism Development Association was subsumed into it. The meeting in January 1924 included representatives from hotels, railway companies, travel agents and two representatives from the Cork association, J.P. O'Brien and its vice-chairman, Alfred Canavan. Agreement was reached on a number of points, including the fact that there was room for only one organisation for the promotion of tourism in the state, necessitating amalgamation with local societies in Cork, Galway and Bundoran and other smaller towns. It was also agreed to invite the Ulster society, already actively advertising such places as Portrush, the Glens of Antrim and Bangor, to amalgamate, although there was doubt as to the likelihood of this happening. Surprisingly, there seems to have been no intention of looking for direct assistance from the government, 'except such as could be afforded by the Publicity Department in the course of its ordinary work'. However, it was proposed to ask for an increase in the rate for advertisement purposes as provided for in the act of 1909, as the existing rate of a penny in the pound would only raise £17 for places like Bundoran, despite the fact that the village was mainly dependent on summer visitors for its existence. Comparisons were made with the Isle of Man, where the Manx legislature had given unrestricted powers with regard to raising of the rate in 1893. The result of advertising and subsequent development was that the number of visitors to the island had trebled, amounting to 750,000 in 1914.[6] The fact that the monies raised by this method in the Free State could be used for advertisement purposes only, and not for the administration expenses of a tourist society, was discussed and it was agreed that useful work could only be done by the use of a central fund created by the pooling of the funds raised, with expenditure subject to public audit.

The writer of the report felt that a convincing case had been made, and that the ninety-seven local authorities in the state with a direct interest in tourist traffic should be approached with a view to raising the rate. He was impressed by the fact that an average tourist would spend between twenty-five and fifty pounds during a visit, and he claimed that American journalists visiting the

Publicity Department constantly emphasised the tourist possibilities of Ireland. He also reported that negotiations were being carried out with a representative of Hearst's film department with regard to a film, or series of films, to be exhibited in 8,000 picture houses in the United States. However, it was emphasised that no great immediate developments were expected, and a representative of the Great Western Railway declared that although the company was putting out a booklet on Ireland in the spring, 'they were actually hoping that it would not have much effect this year, as they did not regard the country as ripe for an influx of visitors'. The condition of roads and bridges was scarcely safe and rarely comfortable for motorists, and, together with the absence of taxis in Dublin and Cork, the high fares charged by jaunting car-owners and the short-sighted policy of some hotel-keepers and shopkeepers was seen as more of a deterrent than an encouragement to visitors to make a return visit. Several speakers expressed a fear that many visitors to the forthcoming Tailteann Games would be dissatisfied, which would have the effect of generating bad publicity, and a general air of pessimism about the immediate prospects for the industry seemed to pervade the meeting.

Such was the depressing scenario that was presented to the Cosgrave administration, and it would not have been surprising if tourist development had been put on the back burner. However, a conference held at Government Buildings, Dublin, in January 1925, under the presidency of Patrick McGilligan, Minister for Industry and Commerce, saw the establishment of another Irish Tourist Association as a body empowered to contract with local councils for the centralised expenditure of their advertising funds.[7] To enable this body to function, legislation was necessary to amend the provisions of the 1909 act, and this took the form of Section 67 of the Local Government (1925) Act, which became law in March 1925. This provision permitted local authorities, with the approval of the Minister for Local Government and Public Health, to pay contributions as they thought fit to any association formed for the purpose of advertising the advantages and amenities of places in Saorstát Éireann or any part thereof as health or pleasure resorts. It was required to be approved by the Minister for Industry and Commerce and as a condition of his approval to have its accounts audited by an auditor of the Minister for Local Government and Public Health.[8]

One practical aspect of the act was that it defined for the first time what constituted a hotel, namely, 'hotels shall mean any premises with ten bedrooms and upwards, including boarding-

houses as hereinbefore defined, which shall be set apart exclusively for the accommodation of guests'. This was a significant move,
as many inns and public houses throughout the country, not to
mention brothels, dignified themselves with the title of 'hotel'.
Furthermore, the act provided for the amount of the rate to be
raised by councils other than those of counties or county boroughs
to be increased to a maximum of three pence in the pound, thus
entitling resorts such as Killarney, Bray and Tramore to levy a
greater rate than had hitherto been possible. In the event, the only
organisation to receive government approval under the terms of
the 1925 legislation was the new Irish Tourist Association (ITA),
which was incorporated on 28 July 1926. The Cork association was
not, in fact, wound up until 1929, although J.P. O'Brien had been
appointed liquidator in May 1925 and directed to transfer any
remaining funds to the new company.[9]

The president of the ITA was Howard S. Harrington, an
American barrister born of Irish parents who worked in London as
principal counsel for United States shipping interests. On completion of this work in 1921 he decided to make his home in Ireland,
where he resided in Dunloe castle in Killarney.[10] The association
had three vice-presidents: J.C. Foley was proprietor of the Victoria
hotel in Cork and managing director of the Munster and Leinster
bank, besides being a member of the governing body of University
College, Cork and vice-president of the Associated Chambers of
Commerce of the Irish Free State; Dr William Lombard Murphy
was a fellow of the Royal College of Surgeons of Ireland, chairman
of Independent Newspapers Limited and a director of several
transport enterprises and of Clery's department store; Martin
McDonagh, a Cumann na nGaedheal TD, was chairman of Thomas
McDonagh & Sons Limited, of Galway Urban District Council and
also of Galway Harbour Commissioners. All three were supporters
of Cumann na nGaedheal and J.C. Foley was an intimate friend
and supporter of W.T. Cosgrave, who had appointed him as a member of the Electricity Supply Board.[11] As the main animator of these
initiatives, it was he who appointed the man who was to become
the driving force in Irish tourism promotion for the next two
decades, as secretary in name but general manager *de facto* of the
new association.

J.P. O'Brien was a friend of Foley's from Ballyporeen and a
former clerical student, who had been interned in the Curragh
Camp in 1922 as a result of his republican activities. Discussions on
the potential of the Free State led him to consider the exploitation
of its natural resources as a means of attracting foreign currency. A

2.1
David Barry, deputy
manager of the Irish
Tourist Association.

man of great enthusiasm and energy, he was also active in politics,
and he lost no time in employing
former Irish Republican Army
(IRA) colleagues such as David
Barry from north Cork and Seán
Fitzpatrick, a former brigade adjutant of the 3rd Tipperary brigade
and the IRA's head of intelligence
during the War of Independence.[12]
However, O'Brien's best-known
recruit was arguably Christopher
S. (Todd) Andrews, who applied
for a job in 1926 following his
release from internment at the
Curragh in 1924 at the age of 22. In his autobiography Andrews
recalls that the association was housed in a two-roomed basement,
with an outside toilet, leased from Westland Row station at a pep-
percorn rent.[13] This was a squalid start for an organisation hoping
to attract visitors who would savour the beauty of Ireland, but an
interesting indicator of how hard times were and what dedication
would be needed to keep the industry going. Andrews was offered
a job as an accountant, and remarks that he did not personally
appreciate the commercial possibilities of tourism as an invisible
export contributing significantly to the national economy. He
considered it 'a shoddy business … more associated with national
mendicity than with legitimate industry ' and felt no pride or satisfaction in working in tourism development. His was an attitude
that would be held by many politicians and commentators over the
decades, a view that tourism as an industry was not quite
'respectable' and an echoing of earlier fears that it would have the
effect of making the Irish people servile and obsequious. However,
Andrews accepted the offer, and considered that 'the staff might
well have formed the nucleus of a cumann of the newly established
Fianna Fáil party because all four were enthusiastic supporters of
de Valera'. He admired O'Brien, 'a man of unusual appearance,
black-haired and black-visaged with an eagle's nose … a man of
strong personality with considerable nervous energy … with
whom, given the opportunity, I could work harmoniously'.[14]

Andrews describes how O'Brien set about learning how the business had been developed abroad, studying tourist literature and
brochures produced in France, Switzerland and England. He had
ideas for improving hotel facilities, training hotel staff, establishing

schools of catering and providing better amenities at resorts. He believed that it should be a function of government to initiate and support these schemes, even to the extent of building and managing hotels. Andrews also admired the board members, who although unpaid' gave the association as much dedication and service as the board of any of the semi-state companies with which I came to be associated'. Apart from the board and staff, the ITA had an executive committee, a finance committee and a general purposes committee, formed from subscribers who paid five pounds per annum for membership. In addition, subscriptions were sought from transport companies, hotel and restaurant proprietors and individuals interested in promoting tourist attractions in the country. However, in the absence of funding from a government which did not regard tourism as a priority, public monies came from local authorities, of which only six – Arklow, Bundoran, Cork, Dublin, Kerry and Youghal – made a contribution in 1925, and each of those bodies was entitled to nominate a director.[15] O'Brien and Barry went around the country drumming up support, and by the autumn of 1925 over four hundred hotels had enrolled in the association. By 1926 the ITA had an annual income of £10,000 derived from railway companies, shipping lines, hoteliers, shopkeepers and large commercial concerns such as Arthur Guinness & Sons, who contributed £200 in 1925, and the banks, of which the Munster and Leinster gave £100.[16]

The first important initiative was the establishment of *Irish Travel*, the official organ, which was published monthly. The association perceived a need for a publication to act as a medium between its members and the general public, with a view to educating the latter as to the degree of co-operation needed to encourage tourists, while also discussing technical questions of particular interest to those engaged in the catering and transportation industries. Subscription was four shillings per annum, with free copies going to all members of the association and its newly formed Touring Club Department. The September 1925 issue described the association's overly optimistic vision of Ireland as a country that by 1926 would be as well equipped as any country in Europe to cater for visitors.[17] There was also an important propaganda issue to be addressed, as the image of Ireland abroad was a crucial factor in the attraction of visitors, and a preponderance of negative publicity seemed to abound at this time. A letter to the Department of External Affairs from an American barrister stated that New York travel agencies were not favourable to the idea of his visiting Ireland, and that one of them had suggested to him that stray bullets were apt to come from housetops on occasion.[18] The association used the magazine to try to dispel foreigners' fears about the state of unrest in the country:

> Ireland is perhaps the most peaceful country in the world today. It has its own social, political, financial and economic problems to solve, like every other country, but it can be stated truthfully that it is not inhabited by a turbulent, unsettled people … there is practically no crime in Ireland beyond the very ordinary offences that arise out of the conditions of modern civilisation.[19]

In an article entitled 'Is Ireland safe?' in November 1925 the writer poured scorn on 'alarmist reports that are circulated from time to time when news is slack and editors are not over-scrupulous as to the means they employ to gain notoriety'. Quoting George Bernard Shaw, he declared that 'Ireland is probably the safest country in the world for visitors', and continued: 'We hope our readers in other lands will bear this in mind and take the scare stories at their proper value: nothing.' For this reason, the organisation welcomed the establishment of the Irish News Agency under the direction of R.S. Scholefield in December 1925, 'whose duty will be to supply for foreign press accurate news of events and conditions in the country, which will counter the "blood and murder" complex at present in vogue'. However, there is no doubt that intending visitors were put off by the activities of the IRA, which had issued a policy directive that year regarding 'British propaganda films'. Cinema managers were warned that if they showed such films they would be 'drastically dealt with', films were seized and the Masterpiece cinema in Dublin was blown up after the film *Ypres* was shown.[20]

As the new state sought to establish a modern, post-independence identity for itself, it was concerned to create new images to take the place of those that would prove injurious to its new status, such as the 'fighting Irish'.[21] Keown sees this modernity as being at variance with the imagery of a Celtic idyll which nationalists had popularised and which the tourist board had inherited from them. However, this is patently not the case; the images portrayed by the tourist association under O'Brien continued the discourse promulgated by F.W. Crossley, a committed royalist, and contained in countless guidebooks going back to the middle of the nineteenth century, and which tourist interests in Ireland, as in Scotland, saw as being immensely beneficial in attracting visitors to the country. Nor was the government unaware of the importance of presenting a positive image of the country. William Cosgrave, speaking at the AGM of the association in April 1928, emphasised the efforts he had made during his American tour that year to give a true picture of conditions in Ireland. Cosgrave was also being disingenuous in that he chose to ignore the IRA activity which continued in various parts of the country and which had taken the life of the Minister for Justice, Kevin O'Higgins, in July 1927. The sporadic eruptions of violence in Ireland over the following decades would prove a constant irritant to the efforts of tourist bodies to attract visitors, and would be a major factor in the massive decline in numbers in the early 1970s.

Ironically, the association was also to fall victim to a republican snake in its own grass, at the same time as it was attempting to convince foreigners that everything in the garden was lovely. In January 1927 the ITA moved to 14 O'Connell Street, into a suite of offices recently vacated by the American consulate. An enquiry desk was set up, and Andrews took on the editing of *Irish Travel*, engaging Frank Ryan, later a hero of left-wing republicanism in Ireland, as an assistant on the production of brochures and local guidebooks. Andrews is at pains to state that he was unaware that Ryan was still active in the IRA, having been made adjutant for GHQ in 1926 with responsibility for reorganising the Dublin brigade, and that he was actually editing *An tÓglach*, a four-page monthly bulletin, for the organisation while working for the ITA.[22] In October 1928, on the eve of an anti-imperialist rally in Dublin, detectives raided the association's offices and found incriminating IRA documents in Ryan's desk. He was arrested and tried in the Circuit Criminal Court before Judge Cahir Davitt, son of Michael Davitt, founder of the Land League. He was eventually found 'not guilty' by a second jury.[23] Harassment of former republicans, including Andrews, continued, with their frequent detention in the Bridewell without charge. Eventually O'Brien complained to the board of the ITA, and one of its members, Senator P.W. Kenny from Waterford, raised the case with W.T. Cosgrave, upon which the persecution ceased.[24] Andrews left the ITA in 1930 and pursued a career in state-sponsored bodies, eventually becoming chairman of Córas Iompair Éireann and, paradoxically, the person responsible for the closure of many railway lines throughout the country in the 1960s. Ironically, it was his son, Niall Andrews, who organised the repatriation of Frank Ryan's remains to Ireland in 1979.

The ITA's main function was that of handling publicity for the whole country in order to take advantage of the benefits of centralised co-ordination. In September 1925 details of hotel accommodation and charges were incorporated in a *Guide to Ireland*, of which 15,000 copies were distributed free to potential visitors in Britain, North America and other countries. Negotiations were entered into for the setting-up of information bureaux in London and New York, and 100,000 maps of Ireland were issued. At a meeting of the executive committee in October 1925, publicity schemes for the United States and Great Britain were on the agenda,[25] but financial constraints inhibited their putting these into action. When they met McGilligan on 8 June 1926, the ITA requested that Irish Free State representatives abroad should aid in tourist promotion. McGilligan undertook to approach the Minister for External Affairs regarding the use of state offices abroad as agencies for tourist purposes.[26] In July 1926, following negotiations facilitated by the Irish High Commission, a London office was provided for a year free of charge by Great Southern Railways, and its success justified the establishment of an independent operation there in 1928.[27] In the meantime, O'Brien maintained a high profile by getting involved in events such as Dublin Civic Week in September 1927, when he served on the finance and executive committees. The Civic Week was supported by hoteliers and railway companies, and its handbook featured a full-page ITA advertisement exhorting visitors to 'See Ireland NOW!', and another from Great Southern Railways urging them to 'Spend your holidays at the Irish Free State holiday resorts'.[28] The programme included events such as a beauty competition, military tattoo and fireworks display, John McCormack recital, orchestral concerts, lectures by Professor Mary Hayden and Eoin MacNeill, an historical costume ball, the all-Ireland football final and, most bizarrely, visits to Crooksling sanatorium to gaze at early cases of pulmonary tuberculosis being injected and x-rayed!

From the beginning, driven by the ambition of J.P. O'Brien, the association put pressure on the government for an allocation of funds from the exchequer. Deputations from the executive committee and management met government officials on a regular basis seeking action, but generally received only fruitless promises. At a meeting of the executive committee in October 1925 the industry's problems were listed as the shortage of accommodation, improvements and co-ordination of facilities and the standardisation of hotel management on modern lines. These were the themes that would recur on the tourism agenda over the whole of the twentieth century. Most of them were outside the remit of the association, and their inclusion at this early stage was an indication of the determination of O'Brien to turn tourism into a national issue. In the event, it was agreed that the question of organisation in the United States should be deferred pending the return of Patrick McGilligan, who had promised to give the matter his attention during his visit there.[29] It was also hoped to obtain broadcasting facilities for Irish resorts on the Irish radio station, 2RN, which was inaugurated on 1 January 1927.[30]

By 1926 it was generally agreed that annual Irish tourist revenue was in the order of £750,000,[31] and Constantine Curran, writing in *Studies*, cited the example of the Italian national tourist organisation, Ente Nazionale Industrie Turistiche, whose council included politicians, civil servants and representatives of commercial tourism interests, and which received a state endowment of £14,000 annually. Curran pointed out that this small investment had helped Italy to earn £22 million a year from tourism, doubling its home receipts and almost trebling its foreign income within three years, and quoted Benito Mussolini as saying that the industry was a primary element in the restoration of the country's trade balance. In fact, lip service was still being paid to the industry, as when J.P. O'Brien and other representatives of the ITA met Séamus Burke, Minister for Local Government, on 2 February 1926. Writing to O'Brien the following day, Burke assured him of his wholehearted endorsement of the ITA position, and stated: 'In the tourist industry we have a potential reserve of "invisible exports" which, with a minimum expenditure of capital and energy, in development at home and advertisement abroad, holds out promise of a very considerable increase in our income.'[32] However, an emphasis on the word 'minimum', when preceding 'capital', did not bode well for hopes of concrete financial support. The board of the organisation, accompanied by O'Brien, met McGilligan in June 1926 to press for immediate financial assistance to meet greatly increased administrative expenses, and suggested the drawing up of legislation to render the striking of a tourist rate by local authorities compulsory, or alternatively an allocation of a central fund grant for that purpose. O'Brien, like Crossley before him, clearly realised the importance of giving tourism a high profile and he let no opportunity pass for pressing its claims to government ministers. He was also adept at harnessing support at a lower level. The Association of Municipal Authorities recommended the adoption of the tourism rate by their members in 1926, and in 1927 the General Council of Irish County Councils, at O'Brien's behest, urged those councils that had not already struck a rate to do so.[33] The following spring it approved an ITA resolution calling on Séamus Burke to provide grants for road improvements in tourist centres, given the importance of good roads as a means of attracting tourists, and confining such grants to areas that had made specific allocations for tourist advertising purposes.[34] O'Brien's persistence paid off, as those in power began to appreciate the potential of tourism, and this was demonstrated forcefully when the government sanctioned the participation of the Irish minister plenipotentiary at Washington, Professor T.W. Smiddy, in a conference with representatives of the Canadian and British governments on 10 June 1927. Schemes for the development of tourist traffic between North America and the British Isles were discussed, and it was agreed that better publicity methods and the renovation and improvement of hotels were the most important issues.[35] A joint advertising campaign by British railway companies and their Irish counterparts was proposed, but this did not materialise, possibly due to the state's determination to forge a separate identity for itself in North America, as Irish diplomats had been warned against moves by British officials to speak for the Free State abroad.[36]

On 3 January 1928, O'Brien presented General Richard Mulcahy, Minister for Local Government, with a lengthy memorandum detailing activities in other countries and various matters on which the active support of the Irish Free State government was requested in the form of grant-in-aid. The main items were the extension of publicity and bureau work in other countries, the improvement of hotels in Ireland, and the provision of special credit facilities for hotel development on the lines recently provided for the agricultural industry by the establishment of the Agricultural Credit Corporation. Mulcahy, as a good politician should, kicked for touch by promising to bring the whole subject before the Executive Committee 'when a suitable opportunity arose'. However, H.P. Boland, assistant secretary in the Department of Finance, did not regard tourism as a priority for grant aid, fearing that establishing a precedent would lead to constant calls for increasing the amount:

> Tourist traffic as a subject of Government financial aid is entirely a new proposition, and a proposal that breaks new ground inevitably raises the question whether we are to find money for everything … arguments based on the smallness of the grant are all too familiar. Once the principle is admitted there would be no difficulty in making a very good case for increasing it, possibly to many thousands.[37]

By 1928 the ITA intended to distribute over two million pieces of tourist literature, large sums had been spent on press advertising, and information bureaus were operating in London and New York, courtesy of the Great Western Railway Company of Great

Britain, whose directors paid a visit to Ireland during the summer of 1927. W.T. Cosgrave's visit to the United States and Canada earlier that year also provided a boost to North American traffic.[38] On the occasion of the ITA annual general meeting each spring, hoteliers and other tourism interests assembled in force, while government ministers with briefs relevant to the industry were also invited. At the AGM in April 1928, in the presence of Cosgrave, J.C. Foley pleaded for a positive response to the memorandum submitted to Mulcahy. Asserting that £12,000 would be forthcoming in 1928–9, Foley declared that the growth in allocations from local authorities had grown from £2,000 in 1926 to £10,000 in 1928. He compared the lack of financial support by the Irish government with the experience of most other European and Dominion states where large sums, in most instances financed by the state, were spent on tourist development and propaganda. He also mentioned complaints about the shortage of hotel accommodation and high prices, but pointed out that the previous year, despite numerous adverse circumstances, had shown an increase in tourist traffic of more than 15 per cent: 'Next to Great Britain, Americans contribute most to the tourist traffic of Ireland. In 1913, visitors from America numbered 16,560; the number in 1926 was 10,638 and in 1927 12,500 – the highest record for any post-war year.'[39] Cosgrave remarked on the amalgamation of the railways in 1924, when the three main rail networks, the Great Southern and Western, the Midland Great Western and the Dublin and South Eastern, along with twenty-three small railway companies, merged to become the Great Southern Railways Company, with over 2,200 miles of track. He saw this as a development favouring the tourist traffic, especially as the company already possessed hotels in several tourist resorts and was now permitted to operate bus services under the terms of the Railways (Road Motor Services) Act of 1927. Moreover, he supported the point made by many speakers at the conference, and one that would be a constant theme in speeches by Seán Lemass on tourism in Ireland, regarding the Irish holidaymaker's contribution to the industry:

> Not the least important phase of the development of our tourist traffic rests upon the support given by our own people to holiday resorts in Ireland. For a few years at any rate, we might expect an expansion of patriotic enthusiasm for our attractions. The pecuniary advantages to be derived would be far more valuable if we had to a still greater degree the confidence, support and encouragement of our own citizens. Our attractions, our sporting facilities, many places which leading up to

the Treaty and the subsequent period of civil strife were not in favour by holidaymakers, have since been re-opened and give ever-growing opportunity of availing of these facilities.

However, messages of support for the industry were not translated into funding at a time when the Department of Finance held sway in the Cosgrave administration, and in August 1928 McGilligan informed the ITA that the Minister for Finance had vetoed suggestions for a government grant.[40] Undeterred, in October J.P. O'Brien spent six weeks in the United States on a fact-finding and propaganda mission,[41] while, in an effort to lever as much political clout as possible, an ITA committee of elected representatives was formed in December 1928, consisting of ten Dáil deputies and one senator, P.W. Kenny, formerly chairman of Waterford County Council.[42] Possibly, their influence facilitated the allocation of £27,000 from the Roads Fund in January 1929 for special tourist road improvements.[43] The association invited a group of twenty foreign press representatives from Europe, the United States, Japan, Australia, South America and Africa on a visit to the principal centres of tourist interest in October 1929. Accompanied by David Barry, the party was entertained to lunch in the Shelbourne hotel, courtesy of the government, and was addressed by W.T. Cosgrave: 'Visits from the citizens of other countries are particularly encouraging; they promote better understanding and better relations between us and other countries – an object which must be dear to the hearts of all citizens of good will of whatever country.'[44] Efforts continued in persuading the government to foster the growth of tourism by the involvement of its officials abroad. The Dublin Chamber of Commerce, at its meeting on 30 January 1929, referred to the notable improvement in tourist traffic during 1928 and hoped that the enlargement of Free State overseas trade representation would continue to include co-operation with the ITA.[45] Writing in *Better Business*, a trade supplement to *Irish Travel* inaugurated in February 1929, Hanna Sheehy Skeffington, a board member of the ITA representing Rathmines Township, urged: 'Our needs – publicity and again publicity! Every foreign tourist centre should have our literature, and such Irish Consuls and trade representatives as are abroad should be instructed to see that Ireland is put and kept on the map of Europe.'[46]

Nevertheless, the association was left to carry out tourist promotion on a shoestring, co-operating in many schemes with the transport companies. As the disastrous consequences of the American recession began to be felt in Europe in 1930, J.P. O'Brien grew increasingly frustrated by what he perceived as the lackadaisical government attitude to tourism development, and he voiced his opinions at the Congress of Municipal Authorities in Cork:

> In common with all European countries, this state has been sorely affected by the post-war economic slump. Like them, we have discovered the importance of our tourist resources, but if we are to commercialise these resources to the full we must at least keep up with our competitors in the extent and penetration of our propaganda. The annual income of our association from public funds has reached an average of about £10,000 … it is approximately equal to that spent by the Isle of Man, and less than that spent by one English resort – Blackpool. It is fractional by comparison with amounts spent by competing continental countries.

Indeed, by 1930 the defects of the 1925 act had become apparent to the government. The fact that a local authority could choose whether or not to strike a rate for tourist advertising, and if it did, could opt to do its own advertising with these funds, was contrary to government intentions: 'The Minister is satisfied that the most efficient and economic method of conducting tourist propaganda is through a central organisation … every effort should be made to encourage local authorities to centralise tourist expenditure by contributing to such an organisation.'[47] To remedy this fault, McGilligan decided to repeal Section 67 of the 1925 Local Government Act and to draw up legislation to empower local bodies to enter into agreement with the ITA to strike a rate annually during a period not exceeding five years, and to make such an agreement binding on the authority in question. However, speaking at the AGM of the ITA in April 1930, he was quick to point out that the contributions of local authorities far exceeded those of the people who derived the greatest financial benefit from tourism.[48] The Tourist Traffic (Development) Bill, 1931, also provided for the undertaking of projects other than advertising, but although the association had pressed for a compulsory rate by local authorities, this proposal was not adopted. Henceforth local authorities that opted to strike a tourist rate would pay quarterly instalments to the ITA, instead of the former annual payment.[49] Those bodies that opted to administer the monies themselves would find their advertising or other schemes subject to the control of the Minister for Local Government. Interestingly, in the light of future events, Seán Lemass interjected at the committee stage to strike a negative note:

> It is my view that there has been a considerable amount of wasted effort in the organisation of the tourist traffic here. We

have not in this country either the climate or the facilities, or the legislative intention of providing attractions for tourists that are provided in certain Continental countries … if attention were concentrated in getting the Irish people to decide upon spending their holidays in Ireland, and the Irish in America and the Irish people in foreign countries to come home for their holidays to Ireland, much more beneficial results would be secured.[50]

Rebutting these remarks, McGilligan commented that Lemass was giving a very bad advertisement for the ITA and for the country: 'So far as I am concerned, I think this Association is doing very good work, and is well worthy of support both by the members and by the local authorities … the enticement that he (Lemass) offers to Irish-Americans … is that there are no sporting facilities and that the climate is bad.' Stung by Lemass's criticism, he conceded that only the ITA would be approved for tourist development purposes.

The association intensified its efforts during the 1930s, publishing guides, folders and maps, setting up its own photographic and film units, and increasing its drive to promote Ireland's attractions abroad. An excerpt from a guide for visitors to Dublin, published in 1932, illustrates the attempt to present Dublin's social life in an international framework:

> The Silver Slipper, 41 Harcourt Street. The only 'cheerio' spot open in Dublin after eleven or twelve o'clock where you can dance and sup and breakfast and be entertained by a snappy cabaret show, lounge and orchestra. Remodelled dance floor and a hostess who keeps things zipping along! A lively spot to adjourn to after the show is over. (Stiff shirt advised but not essential.)[51]

Offices were provided for the ITA in the premises occupied by the Irish Free State in London in 1932, and J.W. Dulanty, Saorstát high commissioner, gave a reception to introduce the president of the association, T.J.W. Kenny, to a 'distinguished gathering'.[52] Daniel Kelleher, a well-known author of books on Ireland that included *The Glamour of Cork* and *The Glamour of Dublin* in 1919, and *Ireland of the Welcomes* in 1929, was installed in the London office and the process of serious promotion in Britain began. At the same time, the ITA celebrated the fact that the filmmaker Robert Flaherty, renowned for *Nanook of the North,* had arrived on the Aran Islands to make a similar film.[53] During 1933 the ITA opened offices in New York, Chicago and San Francisco, and inaugurated the extension of associate membership of the organisation to the United States.[54]

Officially endorsed by the American Irish Historical Society, a prestigious organisation founded in Boston in 1897 that counted many politicians, clerics, lawyers and businessmen of Irish descent amongst its members, the ITA annual subscription was set at two dollars, with a life membership available for thirty dollars. All in all, the organisation could feel pleased with its publicity efforts during its first years of operation, keeping in mind the limited funds at its disposal, but there was a keen awareness of the necessity to extend their work across a broader canvas, and it was felt that this could never be achieved without state funds.

The transfer of power from Cumann na nGaedheal to Fianna Fáil in the general election of February 1932 was to prove significant for the tourism industry in Ireland, with the appointment of Seán Lemass as Minister for Industry and Commerce and that of John Leydon as secretary of the department. As Daly notes, with Lemass as Minister, Industry and Commerce moved from the periphery to the centre of government policy,[55] and this was a development that would eventually produce the results sought by J.P. O'Brien. This was the period when the system of persuading business interests to commit themselves to financing the Fianna Fáil party was put in place,[56] and as honorary treasurer O'Brien was much involved in the process, which naturally moved him closer to Lemass. At the ITA's AGM in September 1932, with numbers of British visitors up from 317,917 in 1926 to 371,899 in 1931, Lemass assured the association of Fianna Fáil's support for its work and objects, especially in view of the fact that the number employed in the hotel and allied trades had now risen to 47,000.[57] Unusually, attendance at the meeting included four senior officials of the Department of Industry and Commerce, including John Leydon. A former officer of the Department of Finance, Leydon's knowledge of that department's attitude to industrial development would prove crucial in the large-scale development of state-sponsored bodies that took place during the 1930s. The partnership of Lemass and Leydon was an unlikely one, given the former's background as an urban revolutionary from a successful commercial family, while the latter's was that of a rural boy, orphaned early on and later a clerical student at Maynooth. They first met when Leydon served as secretary on the all-party Economic Committee set up in 1929, on which Lemass represented Fianna Fáil and maintained the party preference for protectionism, while Leydon staunchly supported the free trade policy of the government.[58] Nevertheless, Ronan Fanning has described their partnership as 'the most formidable in the history of the state',[59] and O'Brien obviously garnered

IRISH TRAVEL

OFFICIAL ORGAN OF THE IRISH TOURIST ASSOCIATION, DUBLIN.

VOL. 7.　　　　　MAY, 1932.

Irish
"

d in as-
his year
genuine
remem-
heirs of
courtesy
ich has
all the
ory, and
it tradi-
be the
aged in
t.
rue that
ous and
onalism
will en-
ness of

Minister
mmerce,
Associa-
s, April

tha
tha
out
the
thr
ind
"
lan
tou
by
org
ter
ful
ou
ve
ga
exa
wa
Ne
Co
Me
wi
we
the
Or

de
of
tio

leasure in formally opening this National Tourist Bureau which, I hope, will be
spects of holidays in Ireland, but also a storehouse of knowledge from whi
road can learn of the cultural and historical glory of our race."

for Industry and Commerce, on the opening by him of the new I.T.A. I
O'Connell Street, Dublin. With him is shown Mr. T. Kenny, President,

2.2
Seán Lemass,
Minister for Industry
and Commerce,
opening the Irish
Tourist Association's
new offices in
O'Connell St.,
Dublin, in 1932, with
T.J.W. Kenny,
president of the
Association.

the support of both men for his mission of tourism development as the 1930s progressed. Todd Andrews speaks of the close rapport that evolved between O'Brien and Lemass, who did not take easily to people, and the even stranger friendship with Leydon: 'why the rigid, puritanical Leydon should have taken to the gay, extroverted O'Brien is still a mystery to me'.[60] The fact that both O'Brien and Leydon were former students for the priesthood at Maynooth may have engendered an understanding between them, and Leydon's dogged determination to serve the state was certainly equalled by O'Brien's passionate pursuit of the recognition of the importance of the tourism industry. In addition, Leydon was unusual among Irish civil servants in that he travelled abroad extensively on public business, and may have been more open to outside influences, seeing travel as a mind-broadening experience, than many of his more cloistered colleagues. There is no doubt that the triumvirate was responsible for all positive initiatives in the industry between 1935 and 1955. As Minister for Industry and Commerce, Lemass created no fewer than seven state-sponsored bodies in the period between his accession to the post and the outbreak of the Second World War in 1939. The creation of the Irish Tourist Board (ITB) was to have long-lasting implications for tourist development, in an industry that Lemass would probably not have considered as a potential source of economic salvation in the early 1930s. However, John Horgan quotes Lemass on de Valera: 'His interests were primarily political; he was not greatly interested in the details of economic policies.'[61] This lack of engagement with the economic scene by de Valera obviously freed up Lemass to stride ahead in the areas in which he perceived there to be a need, of which tourism became one.

The 1930s saw an enormous rise in the level of unemployment in the state, due to both the recession in the United States, which had the effect of closing off emigration, and the fall-out from the economic war initiated by de Valera. The number of visitors to Ireland in 1932 due to the Eucharistic Congress set a record that would stand for many years, with American liners being moored in Dublin bay in order to provide accommodation for tourists, as there was none available on land. This event boosted the industry in Ireland at a time when most European countries were experiencing a dramatic downturn in tourist numbers following the 1929 Wall Street crash in the United States. The opening of the Free State consulate in Chicago the following year was seen as another opportunity to publicise Ireland's attractions, and the acting consul, Matthew Murphy, in a speech broadcast over the official publicity station of the 1933 Chicago World Fair, did not disappoint:

> The unique scenic beauty of the Emerald Isle is universally known, but notwithstanding this, it is surprising to learn how many Americans pass Ireland on their way to England and the continent … As a result of years of effort on the part of the Irish Tourist Association, the traveller to Ireland will find excellent accommodation facilities and as comfortable hotels as can be found anywhere in Europe … I can give my personal assurance that the roads are everything to be desired.[62]

Lemass confirmed the government's appreciation of the contribution of the industry to the economy at the ITA's AGM in April 1933, stressing that it was just as important to support Irish holidays as it was to support Irish products.[63] At a time when a strict policy of protectionism was being put in place by means of duties and tariffs, and British reprisals were eating into the proceeds of Irish exports, the acquisition of British money through an invisible export such as tourism was a welcome prospect for the exchequer.

Throughout his long tenure in Irish politics, Éamon de Valera was not noted for having any interest in the tourist question, and rarely involved himself in events organised by the industry. However, when he announced in the summer of 1933, immediately after a long state visit to the Continent, that he would take no holiday that year, D.P. Moran, editor of the *Leader*, denounced this insult to the intelligence of the Irish people.[64] Possibly this criticism spurred de Valera into attending the ITA's AGM in 1934, where he congratulated its members on the success of the previous year, and emphasised the importance of Irish holidays for Irish people: 'There is no necessity whatever to go to other countries to see places of natural beauty as long as our own country remains unseen, and I believe it remains unseen by the majority of our people.'[65] From the point of view of natural beauty, the availability of sport and of living well, there was no country that could do better, he continued, and while he was glad to see that the association was devoting attention to the home market, he was also aware that they were leaving no stone unturned to point out to foreigners what a beautiful land this was: 'Ireland is a Motherland, and has children in every country; in the United States alone there are almost twenty million who have some blood relationship with our people.' Unfortunately, de Valera's rhetoric did not acknowledge that the reason that there were Irish descendents in every country was that so many had been forced to emigrate in order to survive, and that in the stringent conditions of the 1930s, many frugal households would not be able to contemplate a holiday. However, Lemass's comments on the day demonstrated that he recognised the straitened financial circumstances of Irish workers, as he recommended the establish-ment of holiday savings clubs organised by the ITA, as such a movement would add thousands to the numbers of Irish holiday makers.[66] Public support for the aims of the ITA was also growing, with the *Irish Times* praising the work of the organisation in a lead-ing article later that year: 'In congratulating our country on this memorable tourist year, we must extend a tribute to the Irish Tourist Association, whose labours have contributed in no small measure to it ... It is a notable achievement in so short a time.'[67]

Lemass continued his campaign for the provision of 'cheap and accessible means and opportunities for our people to secure rest from their ordinary labours, and recreation according to their tastes' at the tenth annual meeting of the ITA in April 1935, stress-ing: 'your work has more than an economic importance ... a value which cannot be fully estimated in terms of cash',[68] and acknowl-edging the organisation's social contribution in addition to its com-mercial one. However, in April 1936 the *Irish Times* wagged an admonishing finger at the government for its application of cus-toms regulations for tourists bringing their cars into the Free State, especially those from Northern Ireland: ' the tourist traffic is of equal value to both areas, and there is no good reason why the Dublin and Belfast Governments should not be able to ... evolve some arrangement whereby visitors to either area should be able to visit the other without the formalities with which the motorist who crosses the Border at present is forced to comply'.[69]

With the inauguration of a scheduled air service between the Free State and Great Britain on 27 May 1936, a new era in tourism was deemed to have commenced. 'The air traveller will appreciate, as never before was possible, the maximum variety of scenery in a minimum of area ... these will be swift and terrible days when, after a few more advances in air speed, the slogan may be "See Ireland in an hour"',[70] prophesied D.L. Kelleher in *Irish Travel*, but political events were to ensure that it would be a long time before air travel to Ireland would have a significant effect on the tourist industry. On the other hand, the number of passengers arriving at Saorstát ports from Great Britain during the months of May to September had almost doubled between 1926 and 1936, and although it was difficult to segregate ordinary business travellers or Irish holiday makers returning from abroad from tourists, it seems logical to assume that increases under these headings were not very substantial and that the major proportion of the increased traffic was attributable to visitors coming to Ireland, either from or through Great Britain.[71] A steady increase had also been maintained in American traffic over the 1926 figures, from 8,127 to 10,820, and discounting the aberration of 1932, when 27,481 Americans disembarked on account of the Eucharistic Congress.[72] At the 1936 AGM, Tom Derrig, Minister for Education, was at pains to point out the government's commitment to the industry: 'The attitude of the government has been and continues to be wholeheartedly sympathetic to the Irish tourist movement ... I believe it is the duty of the government to aid in the development of this very valuable industry by every reasonable means.'[73] Alfie Byrne, lord mayor of Dublin, was equally positive: 'Tourism has now become a major industry in Ireland, and like agriculture, it is one of our basic industries for which no imports of raw material are required. Like agriculture, its benefits are diffused through all parts of the country.' At the same time, J.P. O'Brien received a personal accolade: 'There is no doubt about it that the Irish Tourist Association, under the direction of Mr J.P. O'Brien, has done marvellously good work since it came into being, and has wrought an improvement in the hotels throughout the country that is little short of miraculous.'[74] However, without central funding the association could run publicity campaigns in Britain only with the co-operation of the transport companies.

With the start of the second summer season of air services to Britain on 19 April 1937, and the new airport for Dublin at Collinstown due to come into use in the autumn, hopes were high that the service could be extended to other cities in the country when suitable airports had been constructed.[75] The revival of a moribund annual conference of Irish hotels in May 1937 was welcomed as necessary to bring about cohesion in the industry, and the successful transatlantic passenger flights which took place in August to and from Foynes seemed to presage a brilliant future indeed for Irish tourism. However, the Conditions of Employment Act, which provided for one week's paid holiday for all Irish workers, led to a situation of overcrowding in many Irish resorts in August, and the ITA stressed the need to extend the season.[76] At the same time unsettled international conditions, while giving Ireland an advantage over its continental rivals, were also seen to pose a threat to international tourist traffic. At a time when tourism was expected to attain second place among export industries, and perhaps to challenge agriculture for first place at a later stage, the government at last decided to act. At the 1937 AGM of the association, Lemass hinted at its intentions:

> In some other countries, where the tourist business was a very important source of national income, such activities have been placed under the control of state or semi-state organisations,

and it might eventually be found desirable to adopt the same course here. The government has been giving serious thought to the extent to which the State might usefully intervene to assist the development of holiday resorts, to extend holiday facilities and to formulate a general development policy.[77]

Referring to the fact that in 1938 some 600,000 workers would enjoy a statutory right to annual holidays with pay, Lemass commented that workers should be instructed on how to get the best out of their holidays, and facilities for holidays at cheaper rates should encourage them to patronise home resorts. This somewhat corporatist attitude would be reflected in a startling document produced by J.P. O'Brien at Lemass's request in 1940.

In addition to planning new legislation for the tourist industry during 1938 and 1939, the government considered a number of schemes with a view to gaining recognition of Irish culture in the United States, seeing this as a means of attracting more Americans to Ireland. One was a suggestion by Professor Felix Hackett of University College, Dublin, a founder member of An Óige, the Irish Youth Hostel Association, that an Irish-American foundation be set up to promote cultural relations between the Irish at home and abroad, an idea which finally found fruition in the 1960s. Hackett proposed that a colloquium for Irish-Americans should be held in Dublin during the fortnight preceding the Horse Show, extending over ten days, with lectures in the morning, individual amusements in the afternoon and social functions in the evening, together with excursions to places of archaeological and historical interest. He also suggested that a committee comprising mainly of academics such as Frank Mitchell and Eoin MacNeill, along with Thekla Beere and John O'Donovan of the Department of Finance, should organise accommodation for thirty to forty participants. He envisaged lecturers such as R.A.C. Macalister, Lennox Robinson and Frank O'Connor, to cover Irish archaeology, history, literature and drama.[78] At the same time J.P. Walshe, secretary of the Department of External Affairs, writing to Maurice Moynihan regarding a proposed tour of the United States by Roisín Walsh, chief librarian of Dublin public libraries, suggested that her tour should coincide with that of Séamus Delargy, who was to deliver a series of lectures on folklore in American universities:

> The time has come to interest ourselves in what we might call … cultural propaganda in the United States. Other countries spend quite a lot of money in this form of publicity, and seem to regard it as money well spent. They believe that if they

make their countries interesting to Americans from the cultural point of view, they will eventually profit by an increase in the numbers of tourists and by the general interest created.[79]

Roisín Walsh wrote to de Valera in February 1939, outlining plans for an Irish cultural campaign in the USA: 'These include visits to leading universities and libraries, accompanied by a representative collection of Irish publications ... with a view to arousing interest in Ireland's cultural past and in her present-day achievements.' However, she also quoted a letter from Dr William Warner Bishop, librarian of Michigan University and the leading figure in librarianship in America:

> I wish I could say that I saw signs of a great revival of interest in Irish studies in the US, but candour compels me to tell you that I do not see anything of the sort just now, and I feel ... that one reason is a lack of such facilities as those furnished by the library of information maintained in New York by the government of Great Britain.[80]

Walsh went on to give the results of a poll taken by Dr George Gallup in April 1937 on the question 'Which European country do you like best?', which saw Ireland and Finland sharing fourth place with a vote of 4 per cent each, trailing England with 55 per cent, France with 11 per cent and Germany with 8 per cent. This was depressing news indeed, and strengthened Lemass's determination to secure financial backing from the exchequer for an improvement of existing accommodation and amenities with American visitors in mind. He also wanted to inaugurate a sustained and effective publicity campaign to entice Americans to stay on in the country instead of using Shannon airport merely as a transit stop.

Lemass's decision to break the news of the new legislation for the tourist industry at the 1938 AGM of the ITA was greatly appreciated by that organisation, as it put the imprimatur on their efforts over the previous thirteen years. Declaring that the state had hitherto taken little more than a passive interest in tourist development, and determined to amass as much support as possible for the radical new measures that he proposed, he was accompanied to the meeting by Seán MacEntee, Minister for Finance, and Alfie Byrne. Lemass detailed his plans for a statutory board with substantial funds and powers to register, grade and construct accommodation, improve holiday resorts and engage in publicity work calculated to develop tourist traffic. Remarking that the question of tourist development had been receiving increasing attention in other countries, he proposed to empower the new board to deal with accommodation inadequacies and to assist in providing a scheme for training hotel employees and guides.[81] Thomas Condon, president of the ITA, welcomed the move as 'probably his (Lemass's) greatest gesture to decentralised industry. The tourist industry represented, after agriculture, the greatest individual volume of new wealth among industrial enterprises.' Commenting that government intervention and initiation would do a great deal that had previously been impossible, he pointed out that the full value of any new effort would depend on the maintenance of a spirit of goodwill and voluntary co-operation, and assured Lemass of the enthusiastic support of the ITA. Unfortunately, the vulnerability of that industry was about to be demonstrated yet again, as international events outside Ireland dictated the pace of development over the next ten years and impeded or did away with many of Lemass's carefully considered schemes for the development of tourism in Ireland in the mid-twentieth century.

The Irish Tourist Board: marking time 1939–1945

The tourist industry is one of great potential importance as a factor in the national economy, more particularly from the point of view of its effect upon the balance of international payments … it is apparent that something more must be done if Ireland … is to reap the harvest it might reasonably expect from that rich source of invisible income.[1]

Speaking in April 1939 on the second stage of the Tourist Traffic bill, Seán Lemass was wholeheartedly behind the development of the tourism industry in Ireland, which he estimated to be worth about £2.5 million annually. He could not have foreseen the effects of the cataclysmic conflict that would rip Europe apart in the first half of the next decade, and thus render his hopes for the industry ineffectual. With Ireland's neutrality during the Second World War leading to an isolation which F.S.L. Lyons has compared to a society living in Plato's cave 'with their backs to the fire of life, and deriving their only knowledge of what went on outside from the flickering shadows thrown on the wall before their eyes by the men and women who passed to and fro behind them',[2] tourism in Ireland would revert to the usual response to crisis, the resort to domestic tourism. As the Shop Assistants (Conditions of Employment) Act of February 1938 guaranteed paid holidays to workers in the Irish Free State, there was suddenly a large market available for exploitation, and the Irish Tourist

Association would take advantage of the situation to establish a practice that would become a mainstream habit in Irish society for decades. The newly created tourist board, the repository of Lemass's hopes for a brave new tourist industry, lost its impetus and inspiration, and was left to twiddle its thumbs while Europe burned.

The bill was a radical and imaginative departure in government policy, proposing the establishment of An Bord Cuartaíochta – the Irish Tourist Board (ITB) – with powers of regulation, registration and control in matters relating to tourist traffic. Section 14 also empowered the new body to assist, financially (including by way of loan) or otherwise, in the provision, extension or improvement of accommodation for tourists; to build, establish, equip or operate hotels, guest-houses, holiday hostels, holiday homes, youth hostels and holiday camps; to provide or assist financially in providing services, sports, amusements and other facilities calculated to improve tourist traffic; to improve and maintain amenities and conditions likely to affect tourist traffic; engage in any kind of publicity in connection with tourist traffic; establish or assist in establishing any form of agency in connection with tourist traffic; to provide or assist in providing schemes for the training of persons to do work wholly or mainly connected with tourist traffic; to prepare and publish guidebooks, itineraries, timetables and other publications for the benefit or assistance of tourists.[3] Section 19 allowed for the compulsory purchase of land for the exercise of the above powers, this land to include 'land covered with water and … easements, way-leaves, water-rights, fishing rights, sporting rights and other rights over or in respect of any land or water'. Section 48 gave the minister power to establish 'special areas' in which all boarding houses and other residential accommodation; camping sites; restaurants, cafés and similar establishments; cinemas, theatres, sports grounds, band promenades, premises in which games or entertainment were provided for the public, and local transport services could be made subject to registration by the tourist board. It would also control amenity preservation, provision and licensing of guides, beach guards and attendants at parking places.

These were significant measures indeed, and while there was general consensus on the need for constructive action to assist the tourist industry, the bill's passage through the Oireachtas was not easy. Many deputies were highly critical of the fact that the new body would receive up to £45,000 a year by means of a non-repayable grant, with £600,000 to be made available for works, investments or loans of a profit-earning character, which would be repaid with interest, at a time when agriculture in the country was in a dire state. The fact that the board would consist of only five members, and that a quorum of two would be sufficient for its decisions, was greeted with alarm, and exception was taken to the provision whereby no member of the board could be a member of the Oireachtas at the same time. Amendments tabled by the opposition to provide for representation of the hotel industry on the board were withdrawn after Lemass's forceful dismissal of this idea. Rejecting the call for staff and board appointments to be made by the Local Appointments Commission, he insisted: 'This is a business proposition, to be run by men with the necessary business qualifications … Those appointed will have to conform to certain standards of intelligence, integrity and suitability. They will have to come from a respectable class of the community and they will have to be capable of doing the work of the board.'[4]

Labour's Richard Corish was one of several deputies to query what the position of the ITA would be, as the legislation seemed to remove its main functions of advertising and publishing tourist literature.[5] The ITA had an income of about £18,000, of which £14,000 came from local authorities and the rest from advertisements and subscriptions from hotel and transport interests, but it spent less on publicity than any one of the larger British resorts. Lemass insisted that it would continue its work, with its expenditure being approved by the new body instead of by the Minister for Industry and Commerce, and confirmed that the bill provided for increased contributions from the county boroughs. Gaeltacht deputies were uneasy about the effect of the legislation upon their constituencies and upon the Irish language. However, the stipulation that excited most controversy was that which permitted the board to build, acquire and manage hotels, while at the same time holding power of registration over other establishments, as many deputies feared that this provision would constitute unfair competition to existing hotels. When challenged, Lemass made the point that the new body would build hotels in areas that would not attract private investment, but would be in the national interest: 'Private interests work for profit, and there may be cases where a suitable hotel or other accommodation is desirable in certain localities, but … could not be provided at a profit. The case that occurs to me at once is Rhynana [sic] Airport, in County Clare … I think we should have a good hotel in that vicinity, no matter who provides it.' There was widespread concern about the vagueness of the manner in which the £600,000 available for hotel improvement would be administered. It was not clear if this sum, although designated as repayable advances, would be recouped to the exchequer, as the minister had the power to waive both the interest and capital repayments. Lemass explained that the £600,000 was earmarked for development as follows: £150,000 for loans for extensions and improvements to existing accommodation; £250,000 for loans to, or investments in, new hotels and guest-houses, including provision for hostel accommodation for industrial holiday makers; £150,000 for loans or investments for resort development; and £50,000 for 'sundry investments not included under these three main headings'. However, confining these funds to undertakings of a profit-making nature was deemed to be a retrograde step, as it would not allow local authorities to provide amenities such as promenades in seaside towns. Lemass's prediction that the new body would ultimately derive revenue from its investments seems far-fetched, given the state of the country's finances following the vicissitudes of the economic war against Britain waged by de Valera during the 1930s. General Richard Mulcahy of Fine Gael summed up the misgivings of many: 'The State is going to step into an arena in which it thinks the people have failed; it is going to spend the people's money in a particular kind of way, and enter into certain profit-making occupations. They admit that some of them may not be profit-making, and that they may have to write the money off.' In the Seanad, Professor Michael Tierney of Fine Gael went further, alluding to tourism as 'an entirely problematical pseudo-industry, in regard to which we have no guarantee that any benefits are going to come, except perhaps to a small and relatively unimportant section of the community'.[6] Furthermore, Tierney attacked the close relationship between O'Brien and Lemass: ' … the machinery being set up by this Bill is wildly excessive. You are getting a one-sided development, due to the one-sided energy of one or two people who are more or less professionals in this matter … and have been able to "put it across" on the Minister and the Department.' Throughout the debates Lemass was at pains to present the bill as catering for Irish holidaymakers: 'There is no reference in the Bill to catering for tourists from abroad. The purpose of the Bill is to improve holiday facilities here for our own people.' Furthermore, he argued that 75 per cent of foreign visitors to Ireland had racial associations with the country, and would have no interest in destroying the Irish language or undermining Irish nationality.

At the same time, there were concerns about the effect of political events on tourism in 1939. De Valera's constitution of December 1937 had succeeded in dismantling the remaining provisions of the treaty of 1922. In addition, the Anglo-Irish Agreement of April 1938, which ended the economic war with Britain, had provided for the return of the treaty ports by the British, an event that Lyons sees as fortifying de Valera's contention that Éire was now a genuinely independent state. However, the IRA, which had been declared an illegal organisation by the Fianna Fáil government in June 1936, remained dissatisfied and commenced operations on 16 January 1939, when there were seven major explosions on electrical lines and power stations across Britain. In the following six months over 120 incidents occurred in post offices, banks, hotels and other public places, and on 25 August a bomb exploded in Coventry, killing five people and wounding seventy.[7] The damage caused to Irish tourist promotion was incalculable, as the British public reacted to this campaign of terror, and significant harm was caused by the fact that many British travel agencies refused to display advertisements for Irish resorts. At the same time, Professor John O'Sullivan, Fine Gael deputy for Kerry North and a staunch supporter of that county's tourist interests, referred to cases of notices being painted up in Killarney to discourage visitors.[8] O'Sullivan's report was confirmed by Desmond FitzGerald in the Senate, as he recounted his meeting with a Killarney man: '[He] told me that business was very bad this year; that certain people have been scrawling over their places those remarks about England, and the usual sort of stuff we see in the country supporting outrages in England.'[9] Lemass responded by laying the blame on the people of the area, asserting that the notices were painted by a disgruntled waiter who had lost his job:

> I feel that the people of that district did not make their attitude sufficiently clear. If they are not prepared to co-operate fully in stopping that type of nonsense, I am afraid there is nothing the State can do to help them. There was one aspect of the incident which rather worried me. That was the apparent unwillingness of the community there ... to express their resentment, even though they must have realised how seriously it would affect the main business of that locality.[10]

However, Lemass was being disingenuous, as the government had been informed by the gardaí that the anti-English slogans in question, which included 'England, damn your concessions, we want our country', 'Down with England' and 'We want no uninvited guests', were the work of the IRA. They first appeared in April 1939 and continued up to June, but while those responsible were identified by the gardaí to the Department of Justice, and the facts brought to the attention of the Attorney-General, it was decided not to prosecute:

> partly because the painting was obviously an official IRA job and it was not desired to fire the first shot in a new war

against the IRA (inviting refusals to recognise the court, etc.), and partly (and chiefly) because it was felt that local feeling would not long tolerate a continuance of this particular nuisance which was causing certain financial loss to many inhabitants in Killarney.[11]

By the third week in July the gardaí reported that the slogans had been obliterated and that this activity had ceased. The police had discussed with hotel proprietors the question of falling business, which was said to amount to 50 per cent of normal tourist traffic. Replies indicated that hotel-keepers attributed it partly to the international situation, partly to IRA activity in England, and hardly at all to the slogan-painting. In fact, by the end of June the *Irish Times* correspondent in Killarney reported that the tourist season there had improved considerably, although American visitors were few: 'indications are that August – the peak month – should provide bumper business. A tour of hotels has shown that the flow of visitors, from Great Britain particularly, is normal'.[12] Nevertheless, the effect of the IRA's operations on Irish tourism was raised when Senator Frank MacDermot proposed on 26 July 1939 'That, in the opinion of the Seanad, the country is entitled to an explicit statement from the government as to the justifiability and the expediency of bombing activities in Great Britain by Irish citizens.' Alleging that the Fianna Fáil government and party regarded the bombings with a considerable degree of complacency, MacDermot continued: 'We have lately arranged to spend large sums of money on the encouragement of tourist traffic to this country. What prospect is there of bringing tourists from England … if we make ourselves detested by this kind of deed?' He continued: 'The English have not been pleased by the close-up that has been provided for them … the view of Gaelic civilisation in action. They are far more ready to believe that … there is some racial inferiority about us in the South which makes it reasonable to suggest that the Northern Unionists should never have anything to do with us.'[13] Éamon de Valera, defending his administration, referred to the passing of the Offences Against the State Act on 14 June to curb the actions of the IRA in Ireland, but he did not advert to the bombings in England, nor did he address the matter of the treatment to which Irish people there were being subjected. Irish visitors to England were being refused accommodation in hotels, while Irish workers were suffering a semi-boycott, with a number of them losing their jobs.[14] There was also the haphazard arrest and detention of anyone 'in possession of a brogue',[15] as when the police went through every Irish home in Coventry after the explosion there. As the British applied the provisions of the Prevention of Violence Act and deported suspects, the Irish government established special criminal courts and assumed power to arrest, detain and search suspects on 22 August, and a military tribunal was set up three days later. With the outbreak of war in Europe, and de Valera's declaration of Irish neutrality, it was crucial that the IRA be crushed. A raid on the magazine fort in Phoenix Park in December 1939 occasioned the passing of the Emergency Powers Act in January 1940, and with internment of personnel and no funds at their disposal, the threat of IRA action in Ireland passed for the time being.

The Tourist Traffic Act (1939) became law on 27 July 1939, and Lemass wasted no time in assembling the board of the new body. J.P. O'Brien's closeness to the minister was illustrated by his appointment as chairman, while he also remained as secretary of the ITA for a transition period. At a cabinet meeting on 25 July 1939 Lemass informed the government that his remaining appointees were Thomas Condon, chairman of the ITA; Joseph Gannon, BE; Séamus Ó hEochaidh (An Fear Mór), founder of the Irish college at Ring, Co. Waterford; and Lord Monteagle of Foynes, Co. Limerick.[16] With the exception of O'Brien and Condon, the board members were not men of entrepreneurial experience. Joseph Gannon was a well-known Dublin architect and engineer connected with the construction of Irish beet factories and other large-scale undertakings; Captain Charles Spring Rice (Lord Monteagle) had run a small hotel in Foynes, but his interests lay more in the area of sporting activities such as fishing and shooting; and Séamus Ó hEochaidh was a prominent Irish scholar and a former member of the Senate. The new body acquired premises at 13 Merrion Square in Dublin and began recruiting staff. Among them was Seaghan Ó Briain, assistant secretary of An Óige and secretary of the Gaelic League. As the ITA had provided office space for the hostelling association in O'Connell Street for a number of years, Ó Briain was well known to J.P. O'Brien. Doubtless his involvement in hostelling was advantageous in his appointment as accommodation inspector, but he felt that his standing in the Gaelic League was a more significant factor, given the hostility of many of those fighting to mitigate the influence of foreign culture.[17] O'Brien was extremely conscious of the need to win the support of this faction, especially as tourism was of particular importance to the more disadvantaged areas of the country where agriculture could not be exploited to any great degree, and these areas were also those which members of the Gaelic League saw as being the last repositories of authentic Irish life and tradition and of the Irish language. Another recruit was

Thomas O'Gorman, a former Jesuit clerical student from Clonmel in Co. Tipperary who had been involved in the republican movement.[18] It would appear that the tourist board was fortunate; both men rendered it significant service until they retired, Ó Briain in 1975 and O'Gorman in 1977.

However, the outbreak of war in Europe in September 1939 effectively halted the development of the industry. The board's offices in Merrion Square were handed over to the Irish Red Cross for the duration

3.1
Thomas J. O'Gorman, who began work in the Irish Tourist Board in 1939 and remained there until his retirement in 1977. He retired to Florida, where he died in 2005. *Courtesy of Fáilte Ireland.*

of the 'Emergency' while staff returned to their previous occupations. O'Brien and O'Gorman went back to the ITA,[19] while Ó Briain resumed his work for the Gaelic League and An Óige.[20] As chairman of the new board, O'Brien's position was a full-time salaried occupation, but he chose to draw only half of his salary for the duration of the war. The role of the Irish Tourist Association was changed; henceforth it concentrated on local promotions and the provision of tourist information through local offices. It had a representative on the board of the new semi-state body, and received a subsidy from it. At its AGM in October 1939 the mood was sombre as O'Brien revealed that the government had not yet decided on the extent to which the tourist board would go ahead with its programme of work. An executive committee was appointed to grapple with the problems posed by the situation for the 20,000 people directly employed in the industry, and as the prosperity of other interests such as transport was dependent on holiday traffic, tourism was regarded as playing an important role in the livelihood of a very substantial percentage of the population.[21]

Concurrent with these events in October 1939 was the AGM of the Irish Hotels Federation (IHF), which had been formed two years earlier as a direct response to the Shop Assistants (Conditions of Employment) Bill.[22] This legislation was designed to end the exploitation of shop assistants and other low-paid workers such as hotel employees, by fixing minimum rates of pay and overtime payments, along with the regulation of working hours, employment of juveniles and annual holidays. As it took no account of the irregular nature of hotel work, hoteliers feared that its application to hotel workers would cause wages to soar, with a consequent rise in tariffs. They also saw the need for a trade association to protect their interests, especially with the prospect of registration and grading by the new tourist board. The ITA, with the aid of the Hotel, Catering and Restaurant Association, organised a conference to coincide with the Spring Show in May 1937 and the IHF was established in October of that year, with J.W. (Josie) Mongan being elected president.[23] Born into an hotel family in Carna, Co. Galway, Mongan was a popular Cumann na nGaedheal TD, a native Irish speaker who used only that language when speaking in Dáil debates, and an extremely active member of the ITA since its inception. As the only practising politician in the early days of the IHF, he was an obvious choice as spokesman, and his long experience in the ITA gave him a clear advantage. The IHF held a special meeting in June 1939 to consider the Tourist Traffic Bill, at which Mongan emphasised that although hoteliers did not object to essential state intervention, such involvement should be confined to the minimum, and that the tourist board should not engage in running hotels. To assist it in its aim of disseminating important information on developments likely to affect the hotel industry, the federation commenced publication of a monthly magazine entitled the *Irish Hotel Review* in July 1939. The war put a lot of pressure on hoteliers who had to deal with shortages of essential goods such as soap, meat, butter, alcohol and fuel. As rationing was introduced, they were forced to avail of the black market to obtain stocks of crucial items, and accommodation and meal prices were increased accordingly. In addition, the Aliens Order made by the Minister for Justice in November 1939 necessitated the keeping of visitors' registers with much more information than previously, especially with regard to non-nationals.[24] The federation established branches in Cork, Limerick, Galway and Killarney and went on to register as a trade union in order to obtain negotiation rights with unions representing hotel workers. It initiated close contact with the Irish Tourist Board, who recognised it as the competent body to represent hoteliers in 1950, and the following year the Hotel and Restaurant Association, a smaller, mainly rural group formed in the 1940s, became affiliated. In 1958 the IHF joined the International Hotels Association, and currently represents the Irish hotel industry on many national and international bodies.

As the Second World War continued, it was increasingly the ITA that kept the home fires of tourism burning, while the tourist board languished in a torpid limbo. The provisions for travel permits and transport facilities for British visitors led to the closure of the ITA London bureau and the return to Dublin of its representative there, Daniel Kelleher.[25] At its November meeting, the executive committee decided on a publicity programme to exploit the home holiday traffic. The bombardment of a captive population by intensified newspaper advertising, a new series of holiday publications for all important tourist regions and resorts, and a lecture campaign in principal cities and towns by Kelleher, backed up by window displays, were planned as part of the publicity onslaught. At the same time, an intensive advertising campaign in the Belfast press aimed at persuading northerners to spend Christmas in Dublin was a resounding success, with the Great Northern Railway Company putting on three times the normal number of trains to cope with the rush.[26] As a result, in April 1940 the ITA opened an information bureau in Belfast and Frederick Moran, its chairman, expressed the hope that northerners would visit the south and west in greater numbers.[27] The publicity campaign was reinforced by a twice-weekly series of broadcasts on Radio Éireann entitled 'Irish Holiday', in which prominent personalities gave their impressions of the Irish visitor experience.[28] Contributors included Lord Longford, Seán Ó Faoláin, Lennox Robinson, Seán Keating, Lord Dunsany and Austin Clarke. Speakers at the AGM on 23 October professed themselves generally satisfied with the results of the first 'Emergency' season. Great hopes were held out for the holiday savings clubs scheme, which would require the co-operation of business executives, labour leaders and workers' organisations.[29] Catering for Irish workers' holidays had been neglected in the past, but with its economic importance to resorts, especially those close to the principal industrial areas, this class of traffic was beginning to receive the attention it deserved. In addition, with Irish people in Britain being permitted to make one temporary visit to their homes in both parts of the island every six months, the ITA foresaw a large influx of visitors and recommended that efforts be made to stagger such visits over a long period in order to avoid congestion during the holiday season. One senses a difficulty on the part of many hoteliers accustomed to providing for visitors of a higher social calibre, in having to rely on the vagaries of the 'working class' to maintain their existence. Thomas Condon, a director of the tourist board, hoped to see a time when there would be a holiday fund for everybody engaged in industry in the country, whether farm workers or factory hands, while C.E. Reddin, a former ITA president, spoke of the dullness of the worker's life, and the duty of those catering for his holiday to give him an escape from monotony and lack of variety.[30] These well-meant but condescending comments illustrate the social divide in 1930s Ireland and an attitude that echoed Éamon de Valera's declaration that he only had to look into his own heart to know what the people of Ireland needed. Josie Mongan, now president of the ITA, spoke emphatically on one of the matters closest to the taoiseach's heart – the preservation and renaissance of the Irish language – when he referred to criticism that tourism had a de-nationalising effect on the Irish people, and that its expansion in Gaeltacht areas would hamper the language revival. Deeming it unfair and misinformed, he said that thousands of Irish speakers in the Gaeltacht had had contact for years with visitors and had benefited financially without losing their language or nationality, while in many outlying districts never visited by tourists the language had declined. Commenting on Mongan's speech, an editorial entitled 'Tourism and nationality' in the *Leader* was warmly supportive, stating that he dealt effectively with those myopic people who cherished the notion that the Gaeltacht could be preserved by cutting it off from the rest of the world:

> in Carna, where Mr Mongan resides, the visits of tourists have done no harm whatever to the language … If we had more Gaeltacht businessmen and local leaders of opinion like Mr Mongan, it would be much easier to make the language safe … the more racily Irish our whole life is, the more attractive this country will be to visitors. If that simple and absolute fact were more generally appreciated, we should have an end of all Shoneenism in the tourist industry.[30]

However, the main objective of the association was to capitalise on paid holidays for industrial workers and its major initiative during the war years was the organisation of holiday savings clubs. Work began in the autumn of 1940, and by the end of that year union representatives of Dublin flour millers, coal workers, foundry workers and publishers reported a favourable response to the scheme.[31] Efforts were extended to other urban centres, through contact with union representatives in Galway, Cork and Limerick, and by March 1941 they could report significant progress across the country. Jim Larkin, general secretary of the Workers' Union of Ireland, threw his weight into the campaign and arranged a series of meetings to take place between the union and ITA officials. By the year's end they had addressed 20,000 workers, including over seventy shop stewards of the Irish Women Workers' Union, whose president, Louie Bennett, had enthusiastically supported the scheme since its inception.[32] In December 1943 the ITA announced that a joint committee had been set up representing trade unions, employers, transport companies and the association. The committee included Cathal O'Shannon of the Irish Trade Union Congress,; Patrick Cairns of the Post Office Workers' Union, F.M. Summerfield of the Federation of Irish Manufacturers and J. O'Brien of Federated Employers Limited.[33] The holiday club scheme had an enormous effect on the tourist industry during the 'Emergency', as it filled the gap created by the dearth of British and American visitors, and became an established part of many Irish employees' lives, continuing to function well into the 1960s. As fuel shortages disrupted travel, hiking and biking became the fashion for many young workers, and the provision of eight new hostels during this period by An Óige led to a dramatic growth in membership from 435 to 2,075 between 1932 and 1941. The association increasingly attracted industrial workers as well as the white-collar workers with which it had started. The opening of a hostel in Mountjoy Square in Dublin by Seán Lemass in January 1939 added significantly to the accommodation stock in the capital, as city hotels and guesthouses were often full to capacity with servicemen based in Northern Ireland travelling south in search of relaxation.

In addition to its holiday clubs scheme, the ITA continued its promotional efforts in Northern Ireland, and an advertising campaign carried out in advance of St Patrick's Day in 1941 was an outstanding success, with all the big Dublin hotels occupied by northern visitors. However, such success was tempered by the prospect of widespread unemployment in the country, as the shortage of essential supplies of raw materials for industry began to make itself felt. Senator Patrick Hogan, a former Labour TD and a member of Clare County Council, proposed that representations be made to Seán MacEntee, now minster for industry and commerce, to ensure that the government give special consideration to the urgent need for improvements and extensions of Irish holiday resorts.[34] A deputation was appointed to meet MacEntee and the tourist board. It consisted of Josie Mongan; Fred Crowley of Fianna Fáil, a member of both Kerry County Council and Killarney Urban District Council; Richard Corish, Labour TD for Wexford; Stephen Flynn, Fianna Fáil TD for Leitrim and a member of Leitrim County Council; Senator Patrick Hogan; Senator D.J. Madden, a member of Limerick County Counci, and C. McCluskey of Monaghan County Council. It was significant that such a cross-party and cross-country group was united in its support for tourism at a time when many other pressing economic matters were preoccupying those in power. By the spring of 1942 the rationing of petrol was making

The Government is making plans to bring more Tourists to Eire

*H*e makes plans

to bring them

to *Your* hotel

Mr. T. Chambers, our Hotel Organiser, has an expert knowledge of hotel requirements. His quarter of a century's experience of the hotel furnishing trade is always at your service. MAKE AN APPOINTMENT TO SEE HIM OR ARRANGE FOR HIM TO CALL AND SEE YOU.

Now is the time to consider your plans for the bumper Tourist season that lies ahead. Refurnish to be ready for your guests, but refurnish with method—to a plan calculated to give fullest value for your outlay. Our Hotel Organiser, backed by six furnishing departments, is ready to answer your furnishing problems in the most effective way.

ARNOTTS HOTEL SERVICE *is* PLANNED FURNISHING

1 Mr. Chambers—our Hotel Organiser—with a staff of furnishing experts brings effective solutions to your problems. Your furnishing is planned for effectiveness.

2 Our six furnishing departments are combined into ONE special service. Your furnishing is planned for economy.

3 Arrangements are made for gradual payments. Your furnishing is planned to suit your individual requirements.

ARNOTTS HOTEL SERVICE • HENRY STREET • DUBLIN

86

3.2
Advertisement for Arnotts department store in January 1939 showing their special 'Hotel organiser'. *Courtesy of Arnotts, Dublin.*

transport very difficult, and the ITA suggested that the public be urged to stagger their holidays during the summer and that the management of industrial concerns be approached to spread holidays across the period from May to September.[35]

In the meantime, the tourist board, although dormant, was not dead and in November 1939 its members set off on a tour of the west of Ireland in order to obtain first-hand information on the problems confronting tourism development.[36] Josie Mongan escorted the group to Spiddal, Carraroe, Rosmuc, Carna and Clifden, where J.P. O'Brien addressed a public meeting in the town hall on

'Tourism in Connemara'. Speaking of the significance of the fact that the first public meeting of the ITB should be held in the Connemara Gaeltacht, he said that the board was convinced that the only industry that could benefit the region was tourism. The group visited Lisdoonvarna, Doolin, Lahinch, Spanish Point and Kilkee and met local improvement committees, who put forward their development suggestions. Interestingly, in many places the deputation to meet the group included local clergy. As with most aspects of provincial Irish life, the Catholic Church involved itself in tourism development. Priests were to the fore in the organisation of local committees to promote tourism as early as 1926. In Dungarvan, Canon Furlong was chairman of both the local development association and its active tourism committee. Canon McDonnell, parish priest of Newport, Co. Mayo, was chiefly instrumental in persuading the County Council of the value of tourist advertising. In Clifden, it was the parish priest, Canon Patterson, who presided at O'Brien's address, and Galway County Council met a deputation led by Canon Davis, who succeeded in convincing that body to contribute to the ITA.

In January 1940 the tourist board organised a conference in Dublin for bodies engaged in the industry, including the ITA, the Automobile Association, Aer Lingus, An Óige, the Royal Irish Automobile Club, the IHF, the Restaurant and Catering Association, the railways and travel agents.[37] J.P. O'Brien outlined the ITB's proposed programme of activities and directed discussion on immediate prospects and sources of traffic for 1940. The board's main activity was the continuation of resorts survey and planning begun in 1940, and its annual report for the year ending March 1941 pointed out that conditions at many resorts were unsatisfactory, especially regarding services provided by local authorities such as water supply and sewage systems. As such works required a high proportion of unskilled labour, the tourist board recommended that they should be undertaken by the responsible departments and local authorities during the war. For development works that were within its competence, the board reported that it was formulating plans for twenty resorts, of which nine had been submitted to Industry and Commerce in March 1941, together with an application for £109,500 in the form of repayable advances. It also drew attention to the suitability of such schemes for execution by the Construction Corps, an attempt by the government to provide employment for unskilled men for the duration of the conflict. However, the big news was the decision by the ITB to press ahead with its first large-scale development scheme. It was announced that £40,000 was to be spent on the first stage of the transformation of Tramore, Co. Waterford, into a modern resort.[38] This was not a free grant; every penny was to be paid back to the government with interest by the tourist board, which was a business organisation under the terms of the 1939 act. It was intended that all money invested should be recouped from the commercial development of the area in complete conformity with proper town planning. It was quite an achievement for the tourist board, in the person of J.P. O'Brien, to have wrested the amount of £40,000 from the exchequer in an era of forced austerity and material shortage. The promise of large-scale employment on the venture was a factor, but nevertheless it can only be assumed that his close personal relationships with Lemass and Leydon were also instrumental.

Writing to Lemass in July 1942, de Valera requested that Industry and Commerce should catalogue and examine major projects of national development to which they had been giving consideration before the war, and furnish him with a list of the more important items. Lemass invited the tourist board to prepare development schemes suitable for execution after the war, and the board extended the scope of their survey of resorts to all parts of the country.[39] In December 1942, Lemass listed fifteen industries, amongst which were electricity supply, tourist development, transport, civil aviation, ports and harbours, minerals development, chemical industries and 'general industrial development including an oil refinery'.[40] Referring to tourist projects, he spoke of development schemes for resorts other than Tramore, for which he estimated an aggregate cost of £120,000. He considered these schemes to be especially suitable for execution, as the labour content was high and the quantity of material required to carry them out was comparatively small. However, he admitted that the total of £160,000 provided only for the initial stage of the projects, and that there was as yet no estimate available for the cost of their further development. At a meeting of the Cabinet Committee on Economic Planning in January 1943 it was agreed that plans for the development of tourist resorts under the Tourist Traffic Act 1939 should be completed, and that preliminary work in accordance with such plans should be carried out as far as was practicable.[41] Three months later, Industry and Commerce furnished details of the three resort development schemes already approved, together with the cost of the labour content in each. Of the £40,000 expended at Tramore, the labour content was estimated at £17,000, while development works at Portmarnock and Lisdoonvarna were predicted to cost £64,000 and £6,000 respectively, with labour content running at £24,250 and £2,000 respectively.[42]

The committee considered the contents of the memorandum[43] and six months later requested information on the current position with regard to tourist development. Lemass replied with details of the work carried out in Tramore, and spoke of schemes in hand for developments at Portmarnock, where the cost of acquisition of the necessary property was estimated at £20,000, and at Bundoran, which was estimated to cost £25,000 in total, with site acquisition amounting to £14,000.[44]

During these discussions, Lemass put before the committee an extraordinary document entitled 'Towards an Irish recreation policy' that had been drawn up by J.P. O'Brien at his request, regarding the provision of recreation facilities. What is interesting about the memorandum is the manner in which it demonstrates unequivocally the autocratic tendencies prevalent in Ireland at this time.[45] Running to thirty pages, the report begins by defining recreation as 'the beneficial use of leisure-time', and refers to recent social legislation in many countries guaranteeing the worker's right to such leisure time, with a dire warning on the consequences of such legislation:

> It will not be denied that the natural tendency, particularly with the more hard-working elements of the community, is to use free time for mere idleness and it is equally indispensable that this tendency, if unchecked, will defeat the whole purpose for which leisure-time is ensured ... Recreation is not one of those things that just happens. It must be organised and, particularly in this country where it is a comparatively new concept, the first drive in the work of organisation cannot be expected to come from below and should be started at the top by the formulation of a policy and its active propagation throughout the country under government auspices.

Written in 1943, after four years in which the tourist industry had been sustained by the active participation of Irish workers in the organisation of their leisure time, and particularly by their ready and enthusiastic acceptance of holiday savings clubs, these words seem strangely out of place. They seem to reflect the ideologies of regimes pertaining at that time in some of the countries surveyed and enthusiastically recommended as examples by O'Brien in his report, such as Germany, Italy, Japan and Mexico. O'Brien's plan called for the provision of playing-fields, parish halls, swimming pools and hand-ball alleys in 247 rural parishes at an estimated cost of £1,731,300. He estimated that a government grant of 30.6 per cent, equalling the cost of the labour content, would amount to £531,330, leaving a local authority liability of £139,178. The memorandum concluded that 'adequate facilities for recreation are essential to the health and happiness of our people; existing facilities in rural Ireland are wholly inadequate; it is the duty of the state to intervene for the purpose of improving the position'. While many of O'Brien's arguments in support of physical exercise ring true, the tone of the 1943 document smacks of the totalitarian approach to leisure of many fascist or dictatorial regimes in the 1930s. However, this did not deter the members of the Cabinet Committee on Economic Planning, who considered the memorandum on 2 February 1944, and decided that the Department of Local Government and Public Health would be the appropriate one to bring forward proposals for legislation in the matter.[46] As that department had already prepared a scheme of financial assistance for the erection of village halls, it was decided to request Seán MacEntee, as minister, to state his view of the scheme. It is doubtful if the committee could have anticipated the forcefulness of MacEntee's reaction, which took the unprecedented form of a lengthy memorandum to them outlining his *personal* observations and consisting of a swingeing attack on the proposals and a scathing appraisal of the work of the tourist board. It is possible that MacEntee may have seen an opportunity to belittle Lemass, who had engineered his removal as Minister for Industry and Commerce to the less prestigious Department of Local Government. Lee speaks of tensions between the two men becoming acute during the course of the war,[47] and this may, in part, account for the intemperate attack by MacEntee on O'Brien's work, as he was a known protégé of Lemass. He began by querying the right of the tourist board to turn from its statutory functions to address itself to a subject with which it was only remotely concerned, 'having regard to the fact that, though the Board itself has been in existence for almost five years, its labours so far have been conspicuous only by lack of any practical achievement'.[48] He suggested that instead of amusing itself in drafting 'absurd totalitarian schemes', the tourist board should confine itself to its proper task, justifying its continued existence in a practical way by concentrating its attention on the 'bricks and mortar and bread-and-butter problems with which it was established to deal'. Furthermore, he proposed:

> The members of the board should stick to that work and cure themselves of the delusion that they are competent, out of very little knowledge and experience, to organise the community and the State ... [It] has not only got out of its proper province but also out of its depth; for it is doubtful if its members

appreciate the implications of what they propose. The title ... in fact, is something of a misnomer. 'Towards an Irish Totalitarian State' would be more apt for what is quite a classic exposition of the totalitarian mind ... Those 'on the top' having first driven the people from work, must now 'drive' them to play; whether the driving be done with whips or with laws is immaterial. A considerable step in the creation of the slave state is involved.

MacEntee's sense of outrage was palpable as he denounced O'Brien's document, which he stated was based not only on the false premise that one of the fundamental purposes of the recent holidays-with-pay legislation was to avoid the expansion of opportunities for idleness, but also on a false philosophy. To support his case, he quoted from *The Road to Serfdom*, by economist Dr F.A. Hayek:

> It is no accident that in the totalitarian countries, be it Russia or Germany or Italy, the question of how to organise the people's leisure should have become a problem of planning. The Germans have even invented for this problem the horrible and self-contradictory name of *Freizeit-gestaltung* (literally: the shaping of the use made of the people's free time) as if it were still 'free time' when it has to be spent in the way ordained by authority.

Emphasising that in his view the tourist board 'regards compulsion as synonymous with progress', MacEntee quoted extensively from the enthusiastic review of the Nazi tourist movement in O'Brien's proposal, deconstructing the entire document and dealing in particular with those sections which aggrandised the 'forced' recreation policies of other fascist and authoritarian states such as Italy, Mexico and Japan. MacEntee was at pains to point out that *his* department was giving every encouragement to local authorities that wished to provide recreational facilities in the form of playing-fields, parks and swimming pools for their communities. He could not resist also taking a sideswipe at what was arguably the most popular Irish recreational organisation in the 1940s:

> Forced associations can never be healthy and independent and self-reliant, and any attempt to bring them under State control or to support them by public finances will raise issues which would deeply divide public opinion. Among such issues might be to what extent one form of amusement was to be fostered rather than another, to what extent, say, the Gaelic Athletic Association, with its narrow and bigoted outlook, was

to be supported as against the other football associations which take a more liberal view of their responsibilities.

In conclusion, MacEntee urged that no encouragement be given to the ITB to pursue the matter, and went so far as to suggest that unless its members guaranteed to mind their own business and to devote themselves to the primary purpose for which they were constituted, the board should be dissolved and the members interned as a menace to the peace of the state and to the happiness and contentment of all honest citizens.

It is difficult to assess how seriously one should take this document. On the one hand there is no mistaking the splenetic venom with which it was written, and the sincerity of MacEntee's judicious assessment of fascist tourism policies. It is also intriguing that his seems to have been the only voice raised in opposition to the proposals. Does this indicate that the ruling class in Ireland in the early 1940s possessed the same autocratic outlook as O'Brien and the attitude of politicians like Lemass, who felt that the working classes needed to be directed in their use of leisure time? On the other hand, MacEntee's displeasure may have arisen from what he saw as an attempt by Industry and Commerce, as personified in Lemass, to encroach on the territory of his department, which had a specific brief to care for all aspects of public health, including recreation facilities. In any case, his memorandum, marked 'strictly confidential', was hurriedly circulated to de Valera, Lemass and Seán T. O'Kelly, Minister for Finance. There is no record of their responses.[49] In due course, MacEntee's department presented a more temperate document for the committee's consideration, making no mention of fascist regimes but stressing the work of Irish local authorities in providing recreational facilities and the impossibility of their providing the finance necessary for the tourist board proposals.[50] However, it did inject a pejorative note on the subject of recreation: 'In adopting proposals such as the Irish Tourist Board outline, there is the danger of stressing too much the desire for leisure activities as opposed to work.' It declared that in the current economic situation it would be inappropriate for the government to undertake the provision of recreational facilities, and concluded: 'There is a heavy programme of constructional work to be undertaken after the 'Emergency' and the financing of it will make such demands on the resources of central and local taxation that no encouragement can be given to imposing on local bodies any financial burdens for purposes such as recreation.'[51] In the event, the committee considered the two memoranda at a meeting on 18 July 1944, noted their contents and wisely decided

1. Painting of Bray, Co. Wicklow, in 1862, by Erskine Nichol, showing wide variety of leisure activities. *Courtesy of National Gallery of Ireland.*

2. Poster of Bray for the Lancashire and Yorkshire Railway Company from *That Favourite Resort: The Story of Bray, Co. Wicklow*, by. Mary Davis and publshed by Wordwell Ltd.

4. 'Angling in Ireland' brochure distributed at the 1939 New York World's Fair, probably by the Irish Tourist Association.

3. 'Come to Ulster' poster c. 1930, Ulster Tourist Development Association. *Courtesy of National Museum of Ireland.*

5. Advertisement for Coca-Cola in *Life* magazine in 1943, showing American troops based in Ulster using stereotypical Irish images such as the jaunting car, thatched cottage and winsome colleen along with Nissen huts used to house the troops. The use of the Irish Tourist Board's slogan – Céad Míle Fáilte – with translation for American readers, is interesting. *Courtesy of Coca Cola Company.*

6. Selection of postcards from Bray, Co. Wicklow, up to the 1950s. *Courtesy of Henry Cairns.*

7. Cover of *Northern Ireland gives a great welcome*, published by the Northern Ireland Tourist Board in 1951 and featuring Finn MacCoul, the iconic builder of the Giant's Causeway. *Courtesy of Northern Ireland Tourist Board.*

Poster for the Chairlift.

8. Poster for the aerial chairlift built in 1950 to take visitors to the Eagle's Nest on Bray Head by Eamon Quinn, who also ran the Red Island holiday camp in Skerries, Co. Dublin.

9. Fógra Fáilte poster for An Tóstal, the cultural festival launched in 1953 to attract visitors in the off season.

IRISH TRAVEL   *May, 1939*

MOTOR CARS & GOOD ROADS

bring hungry people nowadays to out-of-the-way places—and even to places not so out-of-the-way but at out-of-the-way hours —looking for a good meal. If the Hotel or Restaurant has installed Electric cooking appliances the visitors will go on their way cheered and refreshed by a good meal and happy in the discovery of a good place to eat.

MODERN TIMES, MODERN WAYS IN IRISH HOTELS, ELECTRICITY PAYS

The following Hotels and Restaurants have recently improved and increased their electrical equipment :—

Bush Hotel, Carrick-on-Shannon.
Cahir House Hotel, Cahir.
Capitol Restaurant, Dublin.
Central Hotel, Exchequer Street, Dublin.
Central Hotel, Roscrea.
Colburn Cafe, Marlboro' Street, Dublin.

Lydon's Cafe, Galway.
Lyons' Cafe, Sligo.
Majestic Hotel, Tramore.
McConnon's Hotel, Blackrock, Dundalk.
Milk Bars, Ltd., Patrick Street, Cork.

to let the issue lie. No more was heard of the controversial proposals, and the tourist board returned to planning for post-war resort development.

In June 1942 the ITA initiated a topographical survey of scenic Ireland, 'a nation-wide perusal of the twenty-six counties, with a view to providing post-war tourists from all over the world with up-to-the-minute information on every aspect of Ireland's holiday life'.[52] The survey was carried out by thirty-three 'officers', who, taking the country parish by parish, were required to list all its antiquities, sporting facilities, accommodation, geological conditions, historic sites and houses, spas, customs, amusements, public services and curiosities. Information was to be gathered on church services, postal and banking facilities, fairs, markets and garages. The co-operation of local archaeological societies, sports clubs and cultural societies was essential to the project, which aimed to enable the ITA to answer the inquiries of tourists while also providing foreign travel agencies and Irish diplomatic offices overseas with information. At an estimated cost of £20,000,[53] this was an extraordinarily ambitious venture, given the transport difficulties of the time. However, by February 1943 a total of thirty-one parishes in County Kerry alone had been surveyed, including the principal

3.3
Advertisement by the Electricity Supply Board in May 1939 extolling the benefits of their appliances for hotels and restaurants catering for motoring holidaymakers. *Courtesy of ESB archives department.*

tourist destinations such as Killarney, Sneem, Kenmare and Killorglin, at a cost of around £440. A perusal of the Wicklow, Clare and Kerry surveys indicates that the gleaners fulfilled their task, amassing a wealth of information on local areas that could also have been of assistance to the government in its social and economic planning for the future. At this time the association was pressing for the implementation of the hotel registration and grading provisions of the 1939 Tourist Traffic Act, and the National Planning Conference was appealing for suggestions for the 1942 National Planning Exhibition.[54] With a figure of 300,000 fewer people in Irish rural areas in thirty years, meaning that 10,000 people had died, emigrated or left country districts every year for urban centres, the conference recognised 'that a great awakening of community thought and effort must precede the discovery of remedies for diseases which are at once deeply seated and of long standing'. Naturally, the ITA saw tourism as a viable remedy for the blight of emigration and stagnation that so affected rural districts, especially in the western parts of the country. The association conceded that the registration and grading of accommodation would take a considerable time, but urged: 'All the more reason why it should be initiated immediately so that when we come to launch our postwar publicity scheme we may be able to boast of better catering services, a fundamental necessity if we expect our own people to "See Ireland first", and if we are to attract a larger volume of overseas tourist traffic to our shores.' Meanwhile, the tourist board was getting its teeth into some real work by means of the Tramore development scheme in 1943. Local labour was used initially and this was later supplemented by a detachment of the Construction Corps.[55] However, difficulties arose in the purchase of properties for the development, and the board's powers of compulsory acquisition under the Tourist Traffic Act had to be invoked. Approval was also received from Industry and Commerce for development schemes at Lisdoonvarna and Portmarnock, although once again legal difficulties with the acquisition of sites prevented the beginning of work during 1942 and 1943.[56] At the same time, the government announced that special ration cards and books would be issued for periods up to six months for temporary visitors to Ireland, to enable them to obtain tea and sugar on the same basis as the native population. The managements of hotels and guesthouses were advised to notify guests from outside the state when confirming their bookings.[57] Irish holidaymakers were also advised to bring their own soap, as catering establishments received no allowance for this commodity.

3.4
Photograph taken by an Irish Tourist Association photographer of a Dublin cycling club. As these clubs invariably headed for well-known beauty spots around the capital, the ITA often despatched photographers to accompany them during the 'Emergency'.

With increasing pressure to implement the registration provisions of the 1939 act to prevent overcharging and other abuses which had become increasingly prevalent during the 1943 holiday season, Lemass made an order fixing 1 April 1944 as the date on which part three would come into force. The board gave notice that the registration of hotels, guest-houses, hostels and holiday camps would take place on 1 March, and that applications for registration should be lodged with them without delay.[58] The ITA immediately suspended publication of the 'Directory of Hotels' that had been a feature of *Irish Travel* since its inception, and by the end of March 1,525 applications had been received.[59] Meanwhile, realisation of the economic potential of the industry was growing, and in September 1944 *Irish Travel* stated that the Commission on Vocational Organisation had allocated an important place to the tourist trade in its report: 'the detailed manner in which it has discussed plans for its development are in themselves a clear indication of the essential part which it plays and must continue to play in the nation's economic life'.[60] However, the board cannot have been pleased with the findings of the commission, which criticised the establishment of a board containing no members representative of the industry, and condemned the fact that the chairman and board members were being paid salaries.[61] Furthermore, the commission viewed the situation whereby the Ministers for Finance and Industry and commerce could set aside the obligation to repay advances as being open to political pressure: 'The consequences of such a power are far-reaching indeed.' Commenting on the report, the *Irish Independent* deplored the fact that hotel organisations were not consulted by the government regarding legislation pertinent to the trade, and that they had no representation on the board: 'This state of things is indefensible, for the Tourist Board has almost dictatorial power over hotels. The public will be curious to know what experience the Inspectors appointed by the Board may have of this trade, and whether they are men or women. Manifestly, their duties are of a type for which women inspectors would be most suitable.'[62]

That these remarks were taken to heart by the industry was clearly reflected in the size of the attendance at the ITA's AGM in October 1944.[63] Almost 300 members and guests heard Lemass deliver a rather pessimistic view of the country's prospects as a self-sufficient and independent entity: 'Our future welfare, the development of our industrial resources and the maintenance of our standards of living can only, in a limited degree, be determined by our own plans and efforts.' Coming from a politician who had worked assiduously to create a system of tariffs and trade barriers to protect Irish industries and eliminate a reliance on imports, this was a significant admission that these methods had not brought about the desired effect, and that an enlarged engagement with the outside world would be necessary in the future. Lemass spoke of the government's hope that work on holiday resorts would provide employment in the difficult period of transition from war to peace. He also mentioned that the next step in connection with registration would be the implementation of the provisions of the 1939 act with regard to the establishment of 'special areas', but theory and practice were not so easily reconciled in this regard. The IHF held its AGM on the same day, and Josie Mongan, referring to the proposed grading of hotels by the tourist board, urged them to go very slowly.

In 1945 Ireland experienced the beginning of what would become a flood of British visitors over the next five years. With war-time rationing continuing in Great Britain, the lifting of transport restrictions to Ireland facilitated the return of the British tourist, not in search of beautiful scenery or hunting, fishing and shooting as heretofore, but simply seeking ample supplies of food, drink and clothing. In the April issue of the *Caterer and Hotel-keeper*, E. Cox wrote:

> During recent days, menu cards and wine lists have been reaching London and elsewhere in England following the

> return from Dublin of people whose business interests had
> caused them to visit the recent Royal Dublin Society annual
> sale of bulls. Only the actual reading of the menu cards and
> wine lists would have convinced many people that today
> Dublin is the best place in Europe for eating and drinking.[64]

Such comments helped to persuade the British public that Ireland
was indeed a land replete with milk, meat and honey, and they
flocked to the country in their thousands. In addition, many
'American and Commonwealth troops who were awaiting ship-
ment home from Britain joined in the rush, with the result that the
ITA had to provide an information bureau for those arriving at Dun
Laoghaire: 'American, Dominion and other troops are availing of it.
Staff are in attendance for the arrival of all steamers from
Holyhead, and their services are much appreciated by men from
the war zones, who are now in most cases making their first visit to
Ireland.'[65] The government joined in the effort to make as much
currency as possible from conditions obtaining in the UK, and did
its utmost to reinforce the notion that Ireland was a friendly and
hospitable destination. British MP Norman Smith interviewed
President Seán T. O'Kelly in October 1945 for *Weekly Illustrated*, a
popular periodical. He quoted O'Kelly's last message to him, 'one
of welcome for the great number of British tourists, who, it is
already very plain, are destined to flock across the Irish Channel in
the few years ahead. "We'll receive them as friends", he said.'[66] On
8 October, the Irish high commissioner, J.W. Dulanty, a staunch supporter of tourist promotion in pre-war years, opened an ITA office
on Regent Street in London.[67] The re-establishment of a travel
bureau in such prestigious surroundings was just what the ITA
needed to celebrate its twenty years of existence, and may well
have prompted the remarks by another British MP, Vernon Bartlett,
in a London newspaper. Proposing a concerted effort for the tourist
trade in Britain, he commented: 'Our neutral friends in Southern
Ireland are to be congratulated on their enterprise in setting going
plans to attract a great luxury tourist trade. But when is British
enterprise going to follow suit?'[68] However, Lemass, speaking at the
ITA's AGM, said he was perturbed at the prospect of too large an
inflow of visitors:

> Not merely are most of the plans for resort development held
> up by difficulties arising out of scarcity of materials, but the
> raising of the standard of hotel accommodation, which is the
> purpose of the registration scheme operated by the tourist
> board, has as yet made insufficient headway … We will be

glad to welcome all visitors who we can accommodate, but we must be on guard to see that we do not sacrifice the ultimate and permanent gain for the immediate benefits.[69]

He revealed that he had asked the tourist board to decide how far it was practicable to raise accommodation standards, and 'to apply ruthlessly, if need be, the conditions which it considers to be practicable for all hotels to attain'. If their existing powers were insufficient, he felt sure that the Dáil would readily agree to expand them. These remarks were not music to the ears of Irish hoteliers, but Lemass was obviously of the opinion that a stern warning was needed in order to galvanise the hotel industry into taking action to remedy their shortcomings. There were now 1,339 hotels registered by the tourist board, many of which were entirely new, while others had been extensively modernised. The number of bedrooms with hot and cold running water, a facility particularly demanded by Americans who were accustomed to rooms with attached bathrooms, had risen from less than one hundred in 1925 to 6,483. In addition, the number of pieces of tourist literature published by the association, which stood at 150,000 in 1925, was now just under two million and the detailed topographic survey begun in 1942 had been completed.

The members of the ITA could feel justly proud of their achievements during the war years. They had successfully initiated a scheme of holiday savings clubs for the country's workers that would thrive for another two decades, until the rising tide of 1960s prosperity obviated its necessity. Substantial traffic from Northern Ireland had been established, and it, too, lasted until the 1970s. The results of the topographical survey would provide material for promotional publications for a long time to come. All in all, for an organisation which appeared at the beginning of the decade to be in danger of being swept under the carpet, the association had become much more widely known and had accomplished the aim assigned to it under the 1939 Act, of bringing Irish tourism to the attention of the Irish public. However, the Irish Tourist Board could only look back ruefully on the war period as a time when the momentum of the Act had been snatched cruelly away, and the enthusiasm for the industry lost through the necessity of dealing with other, more crucial needs during the 'Emergency'. Many members of the hotel industry, poised on the brink of a post-war boom which demanded little more of them than that they should provide plentiful food and drink for war-weary British visitors, were uninterested and unwilling to invest in the modernisation and restoration of their hotels, however, and their resultant neglect of the fabric of the industry would have dismal consequences.

Irish civil aviation and the state

When Orville Wright, the first man to fly an aircraft, took off from Kitty Hawk, North Carolina, in 1903, he could not have envisaged that he had inaugurated a means of transport that would eventually lead to a sense of global shrinkage. Sixteen years later, John Alcock and Arthur Whitten-Brown made the first non-stop trans-atlantic flight, landing in County Galway, and Charles Lindbergh's achievement of the first solo flight across the Atlantic in 1927 was an event that ensured world-wide celebrity for the aviator. The people of the Irish Free State were not immune to the fascination with flying which had gripped the public imagination, and on 24 April 1928, J.C. Foley, president of the Irish Tourist Association, declared when proposing a toast at its third AGM in the presence of W.T. Cosgrave, president of the Executive Council of the Irish Free State:

> The Toast is the New Ireland – I don't refer to the new political Ireland, but the Ireland of new feelings, new aspiration, and new achievement … we must experiment, must take risks within the capacity of the country, in order to reach our goal … It is my proud privilege to congratulate that brave Irishman, Major Fitzmaurice, on the important part which he has played in annihilating space and time, and bringing the outside world closer to us.[1]

The feat to which Foley referred was the first successful east–west crossing of the Atlantic on the 23 April 1928, in which Commandant James C. Fitzmaurice, Commanding Officer of the Irish Air Corps, was co-pilot. His participation focused attention on the potential of this new and exciting mode of transport, but those who, like Fitzmaurice, hoped that the state would seize the initiative in establishing an aviation industry were to be sorely disappointed.

4.1
Major James
Fitzmaurice (*second
from right*) with
Captain Hermann
Koehl and Baron
Ehrenfried von
Huenefeld aboard a
municipal ferry after
their historic landing
in Greenly Island,
Newfoundland on
the first successful
east–west
transatlantic flight in
April 1928. *Courtesy
of South County
Dublin Library.*

The actions of Ernest Blythe in 1926, as Minister for Finance, in cutting the pay of national teachers and gardaí and reducing the old-age pension, were symptomatic of those of an administration suffering from the effects of worldwide economic depression.

The significance of the development of civil aviation to the Irish tourist industry cannot be overstated. At the beginning of the era, visitors to Ireland arrived by sea; the flying machine was seen as an expensive and dangerous private toy or a military tool, and ordinary people could not afford this luxurious mode of travel. Nevertheless, civil aviation in Ireland was seen as an aid to tourism from its earliest years, when representatives of the ITA were members of government advisory committees and board members of Aer Lingus, and the development of the two industries was a parallel one, as they gradually became interdependent. In addition, the development of civil aviation demonstrates the efforts of the fledgling state to bolster its prestige and economic development by the establishment of a national airline, transatlantic and domestic airports and a viable commercial structure to support them. Tension between the departments of Finance and Industry and Commerce, combined with technical advances in flying machines, and, most crucially, the Second World War, forced delays in and abandonment of various development schemes.

In 1928, Patrick McGilligan, Minister for Industry and Commerce, appointed a committee to investigate the possibility of a nationally operated civil aviation service, but its conclusion that such a service would require financial assistance from the state in its early years effectively persuaded the government to take no action. The Department of Finance continued to resist calls from government ministers such as McGilligan and J.J. Walsh, Minister for Posts and Telegraphs, for the development of civil aviation and by January 1930 McGilligan was appealing to the Executive Council regarding the opposition of the Department of Defence to the setting aside of £20,000 of the army air vote for the development of civil aviation. Although the Executive Council did eventually take up the question with the Department of Finance in January 1931, no progress had been made by the time Fianna Fáil took over in 1932, setting a trend that would continue what Fanning calls 'the indifference of the Department of Finance to factors of national prestige when set against their quest for economy'.[2]

Nevertheless, many private interests and local authorities throughout the country were endeavouring to propel Ireland into the aviation age. For the west, Senator Sir John Purser Griffith produced a scheme to promote Galway as a sea and air port, and the Irish Transatlantic Air Corporation was set up in 1931.[3] Despite an assurance of support from Patrick McGilligan and discussions with Seán Lemass in 1932, the scheme did not advance beyond the planning stage. In the south, Cork Harbour Commissioners included a consideration of Cobh as a terminal for transatlantic air services in the Harbour Tribunal of 1927.[4] In Dublin, Hugh Cahill established Ireland's first aircraft operating company, Iona National Airways, in August 1930, providing an air taxi service and a flying school at Kildonan airfield at Finglas. Arthur Cox, a Dublin solicitor, established Irish Airways Limited in 1929 with a view to operating services in Ireland and England, but this plan came to nought. In the end, a Scottish company, Midland and Scottish Air Ferries, began operating the first commercial passenger services between Ireland and Britain on 13 August 1933 with a flight from Hooton, near Liverpool, to Baldonnel.[5] However, this only lasted until 30 September, as the Department of Industry and Commerce decided that an Irish company should operate the service. That same summer Sir Alan Cobham, a renowned British aviator, brought his Air Circus on a tour of the Irish Free State, an event that boosted public confidence in flying as a safe method of public transport. It may also have galvanised the Minister for Industry and Commerce, Seán Lemass, into action. His enthusiasm for aviation had deep roots and Horgan believes that he regarded civil aviation as a crucial national asset: 'Lemass believed it vitally necessary for the country to have national control of its external communications and envisaged the airline as a second line of defence in any emergency.'[6] John Leydon was also enthusiastic. As Roche puts it: 'He saw civil aviation, with its forward thrust and connotation of a new world, as offering Ireland the opportunity of playing a star part in a twentieth-century drama of development, and gladly gave it the exercise of his tremendous capabilities.'[7]

Various schemes were considered by Industry and Commerce during the first two years of the Fianna Fáil administration, but all were dependent on state subsidies of £10,000, an insurmountable obstacle. Early in 1934 a detailed memorandum from Lemass for the Executive Council recommended that 'the aim of government policy should be to secure the development of internal and cross-channel services under the auspices of a nationally-owned company and the utilisation of a Saorstát site as a terminal for the trans-Atlantic route'.[8] There were two native schemes in preparation, one the brainchild of Cork county surveyor, Richard O'Connor, who proposed to service routes emanating from Cork,[9] while Charles Russell was involved in a venture to do likewise from Dublin. In September 1934 a provisional board of the joint Russell–O'Connor scheme, to be known as Aerlingus Éireann, was set up with Russell as chairman and O'Connor and T.J.W. Kenny of the ITA as the other members. Lemass decided to set up an advisory committee before proceeding with the project, and at the beginning of November 1934 the *Irish Times* published an interview with Russell in which he made public details of its brief.[10] Lemass was incensed by this disclosure of confidential matters, and Russell found himself out in the cold as regards further developments.

Lemass appointed W.H. Morton, general manager of Great Southern Railways, Seán Ó hUadhaigh, a Dublin solicitor and chairman of the Irish Aero Club, J.J. O'Leary, founder of the Cahill printing firm, and A.P. Reynolds of the United Dublin Tramway Company as his Air Transport Advisory Committee in May 1935.[11] They agreed provisionally on a proposal by Sir Alan Cobham and a scheme for four separate but related companies, but Lemass decided to proceed with just two companies, a principal holding company which would be 'purely' Saorstát, financed by the exchequer and which would eliminate the possibility of competition from external interests, and an operating company in which the principal company would hold a majority stake. As he was being pressed by British concerns interested in operating cross-channel services during the summer, Lemass visualised such an undertaking as providing valuable experience, and he sought government approval for a twelve-month experimental service beginning early in the summer of 1935.[12] He also proposed that the principal Free State airline should secure a 50 per cent interest in the company operating the experimental service. This company would eventually materialise in the shape of Aer Rianta, while that operating the cross-channel service would become Aer Lingus. Meanwhile, Lemass recommended the acceptance of Cobham's proposal, which he saw as offering the best prospects for the eventual development of services under Irish control and free from association with established British transport interests.[13] This last point was the key to Lemass's actions at this time, when separation from taint by alliance with British concerns was an integral part of Éamon de Valera's policy of economic divorce from Britain.

However, Cobham was unable to proceed and another British concern, Olley Air Services, offered to operate jointly with a Free State company, providing a loan to establish, equip and carry on the Irish company until such time, not later than twelve months from the commencement of operations, as the principal company was in a position to finance its subsidiary. This proposal was approved at an executive council meeting on 20 August 1935[14] and an *ad hoc* board of directors for Aer Lingus was appointed, with Seán Ó hUadhaigh as chairman and the other members of the Advisory Committee as directors. To stimulate public awareness, an Aviation Day was held in Phoenix Park, Dublin, in May 1936, attracting over 4,000 people. The Minister for Defence, Frank Aiken, was introduced to the crowd by Ó hUadhaigh, and the *Irish Times* commented: 'It would be a little unfair to say that the growth of aviation has been ignored. The truth is rather that the growth has been unperceived, and that few people have grasped what it might mean to this country in the future.'[15]

On 22 May 1936 Aer Lingus was incorporated under the Companies Act and held its first board meeting three days later.[16] The inaugural flight took off on 27 May 1936 from Baldonnel aerodrome;[17] regular services began immediately to Bristol, Liverpool and the Isle of Man, and although there were occasionally no bookings, the schedule was maintained as a point of honour. However, one customer who registered his annoyance at the treatment of Aer Lingus passengers arriving in Croydon was Fine Gael TD James Dillon, who described how they were segregated from those arriving by Imperial Airways: 'the sheep from the goats. The sheep, who came by Imperial Airways, were put into a comfortable conveyance and carried into London, while the lone goat was sent to the local railway station and taken on one of those local trains.'[18]

Timothy J. O'Driscoll, former secretary to John Leydon and later director-general of the Irish Tourist Board, drew up the legislation for the establishment of the air companies, the Air Navigation and Transport Act, 1936. With Lemass absent due to illness, it fell to Thomas Derrig, Minister for Education, to introduce the bill in the Dáil. Citing the example of France, Germany and the Netherlands, where state participation in the formation of national air companies had taken place in the 1920s and 1930s, Derrig pointed out the importance of such companies from the point of view of national prestige and commercial and political influence.[19] James Dillon queried whether the investment of £1 million was to be made by way of state socialism or state capitalism, as one or other seemed to characterise almost every activity of Fianna Fáil government.

> Does the government propose to run this enterprise for profit, with a view to contributing that profit to the relief of the Exchequer? … [Or] do they intend to run it as a public service, setting up ideal conditions of employment, regarding solvency as a matter of minor importance, giving extravagant services for the minimum rates, and calling on the Exchequer to make up any deficiency in operating costs?[20]

In fact, the formation of the companies was consistent with Lemass's policy of state intervention in sectors where private enterprise could not or would not become involved, and his combination of idealism and determination was enough to persuade the government. Aer Rianta Teoranta was incorporated in April 1937 with Ó hUadhaigh as chairman and Séamus Fitzgerald of Cork Harbour Commissioners, John Leydon and J.P. O'Brien of the ITA as the other directors. A meeting of the boards of the two companies held in November 1938 formulated an ambitious extension of Aer Lingus routes, including direct services to Paris and Amsterdam within three years. Unfortunately, the outbreak of war in September 1939 put paid to these schemes, and the airline was compelled to retrench, selling off aircraft and cancelling its services to London, Bristol and the Isle of Man.[21]

As early as 1935 Lord Mayor Alfie Byrne had asked Lemass to consider the construction of an airport in Dublin as a relief scheme to ease unemployment in the city, to which Lemass had replied that this was a matter for Dublin Corporation.[22] However, a sense of urgency was injected into the project with the decision to provide temporary transatlantic facilities at Dublin while the airport at Shannon was under construction. Collinstown, Kildonan, Merrion Strand and the Phoenix Park were mentioned as possible sites, this last drawing the ire of the *Irish Times* in April 1936: 'There is a feeling of resentment that there should be even a hint at interfering with the amenities the people now enjoy in the free use of Dublin's great pleasure ground.'[23] Finally, a former RAF aerodrome at Collinstown was chosen to provide an airport by the date planned for the inauguration of transatlantic flights by land planes. It was intended to develop 717 acres at a cost of £150,000, to be divided between the government, Dublin Corporation and Dublin County Council. Desmond FitzGerald, an architect in the Department of Industry and Commerce, designed the terminal building. Described as 'courageously modern and ambitious',[24] his design was awarded the Triennial Gold Medal of the Royal Institute of Architects in Ireland, and the building was completed in 1942. It was August 1939 before the airport was fit for use, and the outbreak of war in September foreshadowed a fallow period for civil aviation. Management of the airport was entrusted to Aer Rianta, and on 19 January 1940 the first Aer Lingus flight took off with little official ceremony. A service was provided between Liverpool and Dublin until April 1944, when it was discontinued at the request of the British government due to air and sea movements preparing for the imminent D-Day invasion.[25]

The Fianna Fáil administration under Éamon de Valera was preoccupied with matters of prestige in foreign affairs, and their success in securing the site of the European terminal for transatlantic flights was a remarkable achievement. John W. Dulanty, Irish high commissioner in London, was confidentially informed in December 1933 by an official in the British Air Ministry that three routes were being considered for transatlantic flights: (a) via Iceland and Greenland to Canada; (b) via Ireland and Newfoundland to Canada; and (c) via the Azores and Bermuda to the United States.[26] Irish diplomats in the United States entered into discussions on the matter with Pan American Airways in 1934.[27] In December Lemass announced that Pan American Airways would establish and maintain its own airbases in the Free State in return for exclusive rights to operate scheduled air services between Ireland and North America for fifteen years. The delicate task of choosing the site of the transatlantic terminal had to be undertaken, as pressure groups from various regions vied with one another to have it sited in their locality. In fact, a party of Irish and British aviation officials had adjudged Kilconry, Co. Clare, and also known as Rineanna, a suitable location in November 1935, but Lemass had delayed the announcement of this choice as he felt 'that on broad grounds of policy he should not expose himself to the criticism that he is dependent solely on the Air Ministry and Imperial Airways for advice'.[28] Accordingly, Charles Lindbergh, the American aviation pioneer, who had already carried out a survey of sites for Pan American during 1933, and Juan Trippe, president of the airline, inspected the Kilconry site in 1936 and endorsed the decision to build the airport there. It was later rumoured that the choice of site might have had something to do with the fact that Éamon de Valera represented that county in the Dáil.[29]

In the meantime, John Leydon and J.P. Walshe, secretary of the Department of Posts and Telegraphs, participated in the Imperial Transatlantic Conference in Ottawa in November 1935, which produced an agreement between the governments of Ireland, the United Kingdom, Canada and Newfoundland on the establishment of an air mail service leading to passenger and freight traffic. A cabinet committee consisting of de Valera, Lemass, MacEntee, Aiken, Gerald Boland and the Attorney-General, Conor Maguire, prepared detailed instructions on every aspect of the proposed service, which would be run by a joint operating company in which Imperial Airways, an Irish national airline and a Canadian airline would be shareholders.[30] Among the requirements of the committee was an obligatory stop at the Free State transatlantic airport for both eastbound and westbound traffic over Irish air space, and the keeping down to an absolute minimum the Irish contribution to the cost of the airport, which would have to be under Irish ownership and control. An agreement was signed in December 1935 which included the former condition and which consented to the establishment of a joint company in which Great Britain would have 51 per cent of the shares, with the remainder divided between the Free State and Canada.[31] Experimental flights beginning in 1936 were to be carried out by Imperial Airways, with Pan American Airways co-operating on an equal basis in the investigation and survey work. A conference on the technical aspects of the proposed airport attended by Irish and British government officials was held in Dublin in July 1936. As a result, Lemass informed the Executive Council that it was estimated that the project would necessitate a £500,000 capital cost and £40,000 per annum maintenance costs, plus £10,000 per annum on wireless and meteorological expenses.[32] It was decided that the Free State should bear the full capital cost of the airport,[33] and a decision on the annual subsidy of the joint operating company was deferred pending negotiations between the Free State and Britain, during which it was to be argued that the burden which the provision of the airport and auxiliary services placed on Irish tax-payers was as great as they could reasonably

be asked to bear. On 14 August 1936 the Executive Council decided that the proposed airport would be built by the Office of Public Works (OPW) and that an interdepartmental Airports Advisory Committee, with representatives from Finance, Industry and Commerce, Posts and Telegraphs and Defence (and later External Affairs) should be established.[34] Meanwhile, the projected cost of the airport rose to £600,000, due to additional construction and dredging work on the flying-boat anchorage area. To complicate the situation further, the debate on the future of land-planes versus seaplanes on the transatlantic route remained unresolved. By the end of November, Lemass was recommending the postponement of the provision of permanent facilities for flying boats at the Shannon airport and the development of the land site there as rapidly as possible, but he did not envisage this happening by September 1937, the date set by the airlines for the inauguration of experimental flights.[35] To ensure the retention of the transatlantic facility by the Free State, he proposed the speedy provision of

4.2
Eamon de Valera, accompanied by Seán Lemass and John Leydon of the Department of Industry and Commerce, greeting the pilot of the first Pan American Airways transatlantic flight to land at Foynes, Co. Limerick, in July 1937. *Courtesy of Foynes Flying Boat Museum.*

temporary facilities at Collinstown. Seán MacEntee disagreed vehemently with this assessment of the situation and conveyed his view to Éamon de Valera in January 1937, enclosing newspaper articles describing the concurrent construction of giant seaplanes by the USA, France, Russia and Germany.[36] However, de Valera was not convinced and his uncertainty reflected that of Charles Lindbergh, Pan American's technical adviser, who revealed the depth of the dilemma to Juan Trippe:

> The Irish are constantly asking me about the future of flying-boats. I have told them frankly that my personal opinion is that the land-plane will be used for transatlantic flying in the future, especially on the Ireland–Newfoundland route … that there is no way of being certain how long the flying-boat would be used and that there was a great division of opinion in regard to the relative advantages of land-planes and flying-boats.[37]

This quandary led Lemass to hedge his bets as construction went ahead during 1937. On 4 July the inaugural Imperial Airways flight arrived at Foynes under the command of Captain A.S. Wilcockson, to be greeted by Éamon de Valera, and two days later Pan American's first flight touched down.[38] In November, Lemass submitted a revised estimate of £535,000 for the Shannon land base alone. At the same time he applied for approval for a partial development of the seaplane facilities, at an estimated cost of £270,000. However, he warned that the OPW had informed him that the nature of the work 'is such that it cannot be asserted with confidence that the actual cost will not materially exceed the estimate'.[39] Meanwhile, work on the land base had commenced in October 1936, and over £200,000 had been expended by the end of 1938. On 19 January 1939, Seán MacEntee, appalled at the spiralling costs, asked Hugo Flinn, his parliamentary secretary, to produce a report on the various seaplane schemes, as he did not feel justified in accepting the recommendation of the Airport Committee without further investigation.[40] To Lemass he made the point that expenditure had been incurred at Collinstown airport to accelerate the provision of facilities for land-planes on experimental transatlantic flights, but that none had taken place, and that he now estimated the cost of the provision of facilities for seaplanes at Shannon at £1,085,000. He proposed the use of Foynes as a permanent flying-boat base and the development of a site such as Askeaton as a base for land-planes. Lemass was not compliant: 'The suggestion cannot seriously be entertained. The site is not nearly so suitable.' Pointing out that £200,000 had already been spent at Shannon, he also registered his frustration at MacEntee's delaying tactics: 'I feel bound to complain that it is not reasonable on your part to hold up my proposals … without bringing either my Department or the Department of Defence into consultation.'[41] To settle the dispute, de Valera met Lemass and Flinn on 22 February 1939 and it was agreed that technical assessors should be asked to advise on the issue of alternative sites. J.P. Candy of the OPW prepared a report on a site at Feenish and this was considered by MacEntee and de Valera on 6 March 1939. It was decided to proceed with the construction of a sea base at Shannon at an estimated cost of £400,000. However, the outbreak of war in September effectively delayed any major expansion. Although some construction of jetties took place at Foynes and it was used during the war, advances in technology rendered the land-plane a superior machine, and both Pan American Airways and Imperial Airways, now renamed the British Overseas Air Corporation (BOAC), declared their intention of phasing out seaplanes.[42] No further construction took place and seaplanes continued to use the Foynes base. Work continued on the land-plane base and the runways were completed; the first aircraft landed on 18 May 1939 and as wartime traffic increased, BOAC began a shuttle service between Shannon and Britain.

In May 1943 there occurred one of those seemingly insignificant but fortuitous incidents that sets in train a series of major events. Éamon de Valera, who had little interest in aviation except from the point of view of national prestige,[43] visited Foynes in May 1943 on a tour of inspection and was appalled to discover that Imperial Airways managed the restaurant there. As a result Brendan O'Regan, then manager of the Stephen's Green Club in Dublin, of which John Leydon was a member, was appointed manager. O'Regan received a contract which his father, a former chairman of Clare County Council and owner of the Old Ground hotel in Ennis, helped him negotiate. It was a most unusual arrangement. There was no board between O'Regan and the civil service, and R.C. Ferguson in Industry and Commerce, who oversaw the drafting of the contract, thought it would never get through Finance, because of the provision that allocated him a specific share of the profits.[44] He was mistaken, and at the age of 26 Brendan O'Regan became 'catering comptroller' at Foynes on a salary of £1,000, plus £200 of the first profit and 25 per cent of any profits after that.[45] While this was an exceptional arrangement in terms of civil service appointments, the fact that Shannon airport was run by Industry and Commerce was equally so, and the ensuing decades were to demonstrate O'Regan's worth to the Shannon area in particular and to Irish tourism in general. He quickly established a good reputation for the Foynes restaurant, with the British newspaper the *People* categorising it as 'the most cosmopolitan publicity yet devised for modern Ireland', and he moved to Rineanna with the opening of the airport restaurant there on 20 April 1944, managing both operations until the former closed down in 1946.

In 1946, in order to maintain the momentum of activity at Shannon, Lemass proposed to establish a free airport to attract goods traffic and develop warehousing and other activities.[46] When this entrepôt trade did not materialise, O'Regan suggested using the airport's status for the enlargement of a kiosk there that sold Irish whiskey, cigarettes, and some souvenirs of dubious quality. Lemass hoped to use the shop as an advertising medium for Irish goods, and to increase the turnover substantially with particular emphasis on dollar sales: 'Dollar takings increased from an average of $1,800 per month in 1948 to $6,000 per month towards the end of 1949. Plans are being considered for the encouragement of sales to tourists of goods duty free.'[47] In 1951 O'Regan obtained approval for stocking souvenirs of continental countries which would not be in competition with Irish souvenirs, with a view to attracting additional dollars. His next proposition was the introduction of a mail-order scheme. Launched in 1954 at a cost of £5,000, the catalogue featured only Irish goods, and with its introduction the profits of the Sales and Catering Department rose from £7,574 in 1951 to £75,298 in 1955.[48] However, there were problems about O'Regan's salary. Under an agreement in 1950 his salary rose to £1,800 a year, plus certain allowances and a commission of 5 per cent on net profits. As a result, his remuneration had increased very rapidly and in 1953/54 amounted to £4,853, and with the development of the mail-order business and the expansion of sales at the airport it would rise further. At an Industry and Commerce conference in 1954 it was conceded that by comparison with the earnings of persons in commercial employment, his entitlement to a high salary could not be disputed.[49] However, O'Regan himself pointed out that if it exceeded £5,000 there would be public criticism. It was decided that no upper limit would be applied, but that the rate of commission would be reduced, as it was desirable to retain the element of incentive. Nevertheless, the Department of Finance was still apprehensive lest O'Regan's salary got out of line with those of others in state and semi-state employment, and suggested an amendment that would lower his salary by about £500. These deliberations give some indication of the esteem in which O'Regan was held by successive administrations and the value put on his services by those who did not wish to lose his contribution to the commercial sector and to the detriment of Shannon airport. De Valera's reaction in 1943 had indeed borne fruit, and O'Regan was to figure as one of the most influential and conscientious protagonists of Irish tourism and the Shannon region for many decades.

As early as 1942, Lemass was planning for the expansion of civil aviation in Ireland in the post-war period and a significant event was the appointment of J.F. Dempsey in January 1943 as general manager of both Aer Lingus and Aer Rianta, and his participation a year later, with John Leydon, in discussions in London initiated by British Airways. Lemass met Lord Winster, the British Minister of Civil Aviation, in London in October 1945,[50] and proposed a bi-lateral air agreement containing a condition regarding the mandatory stop at Shannon of all transatlantic traffic. The agreement was signed on 5 April 1946, and gave Aer Lingus the sole right to operate scheduled services between the two countries for the following ten years. It also involved a financial restructuring of Aer Lingus, with 40 per cent of its share capital being held by BOAC and BEA on a 10:30 per cent basis respectively, while the remaining 60 per cent was held by Aer Rianta. The international aviation conferences in Chicago, Havana and Montreal in 1944 and 1945 had drawn up controls that gave each country authority to restrict the freedom of aircraft using the skies above it. To fly between two countries other than the one in which it was based, a carrier needed what were termed 'fifth freedom rights', and these were to be deliberately restricted. Britain's interest in the bilateral agreement was based on the use of Shannon airport as its gateway to worldwide transport.[51] Under the 1946 agreement, the nominal capital of Aer Lingus was increased from £100,000 to £1 million, and the British would henceforth contribute three of its seven directors.

The decision to inaugurate an Irish transatlantic service came as a result of the first North Atlantic regional conference of the Provisional Civil Aviation Organisation held in Dublin in March 1946.[52] An important achievement from the Irish point of view was the establishment of Shannon as the air traffic control centre despite strong opposition from British delegates, who naturally favoured Prestwick in Scotland. Social, cultural and political links with the USA at a time when Irish-Americans were acquiring affluence and influence there convinced J.F. Dempsey that the time was ripe for an Irish transatlantic service. Leydon and Lemass concurred and in April 1946 an order was placed with Lockheed for five Constellation aircraft for the Atlantic service. It was found necessary to form a new company, Aerlínte Éireann Teoranta, in order to avoid any conflict of interests with the British interests of BOAC, who were still shareholders in Aer Lingus and about to operate through Shannon on the Atlantic route. The first Lockheed Constellation, the *Saint Brigid*, flew into Dublin airport on 27 September 1947. Its arrival created an enormous amount of public interest, with 12,000 people flocking to view the aircraft.[53] It had been hoped to begin the new service in November 1947, but the recruitment and training of 1,000 staff, on both sides of the Atlantic, took over twelve months. The inauguration was finally arranged for 17 March 1948, but Aer Lingus had been expanding its continental routes, overstretching the financial resources of the company, and by the end of 1947 it was obvious that substantial losses were being sustained and that the purchase of the Constellations would be a further burden on Aer Rianta. Moreover, political developments now overtook commercial ones as de Valera, uneasy at the by-election successes of Clann na Poblachta, decided to go to the country. On the hustings in Cork, he stated that he would go on the inaugural flight if re-elected: 'If I go, I shall be able to take in person the greetings of our nation to our friends in the United States of America, whose help throughout dark days was one of the greatest sources of protection to us.'[54] His gamble backfired; in February 1948 Fianna Fáil was returned as the largest party with 68 seats out of 147, but without an overall majority. A coalition composed of Fine Gael, Labour, Clann na Poblachta, Clann na Talmhan and some independents took office. The new Minister for Finance was Patrick McGilligan and the new Minister for Industry and Commerce was Daniel Morrissey, a former Labour party member who had joined Fine Gael. On 28 February it was reported that the government had asked Aerlínte to postpone the inauguration of the transatlantic service. The decision, made at a cabinet meeting the day before, came as a surprise to the company, whose principal officials, including J.F. Dempsey, were in America organising publicity for the service. The *Irish Times* concluded that the government had made a wise decision in the prevailing economic climate, despite the fact that £10,000 had been spent on the acquisition of a New York office and advertising campaigns, not to mention the cost of aircraft and recruitment.[55] The writer also noted, however, that Aerlínte officials had been expecting that many Irish-Americans would use the Irish airline for sentimental reasons, and a telegram received by Taoiseach John Costello from Charles F. Connolly, editor of the *Irish Echo* in New York, summed up the bitter disappointment experienced by those whose pride in the achievement and ambition of their motherland had been boosted by the project: 'News of Government indefinite postponement of Irish air service to United States a great shock to Irish Americans who feel that prestige of Irish nation will suffer if original plans are not carried out stop telegrams being received by *Irish Echo* all parts of United States protesting postponement.'[56] Despite the objections, the government decided on 19 April that they were not justified in allowing Aerlínte Éireann to operate the service owing to the financial commitments involved.[57] The Constellations were put into service on Aer Lingus' European routes, but they were too big; by the summer of 1948, these symbols of a brave new venture had been sold to BOAC. Nevertheless, the inter-party administration did not have a closed mind with regard to a transatlantic service and in July 1949, when Transocean Airlines, an American charter company, proposed to Aerlínte that the two companies operate a joint service to Shannon from April to October 1950, Industry and Commerce felt that it might be possible to conclude a long-term agreement with that company as the basis of a regular transatlantic service from Shannon. At this time they were resisting efforts by the Department of Finance to have Aerlínte wound up in the Air Navigation and Transport Bill being drafted at the time.[58] In the end this project did not get off the ground, but the Department of Finance's efforts to wind up Aerlínte were successfully stymied.

The inter-party government was an uneasy alliance from the beginning, and it could not withstand the controversy caused by the Mother and Child scheme proposed by the Minister for Health, Noel Browne. Fianna Fáil stepped back into power in May 1951, and Seán Lemass took up the reins at Industry and Commerce. He entered into negotiations in 1952 with Seaboard and Western, an American freight airline that had been using Shannon airport since 1947, to lease DC4s to Aerlínte for a transatlantic route. Despite the criticism of opposition members in the Dáil, he proposed to utilise the proceeds of the sale of Aerlínte assets in 1948 to cover initial costs and possible losses. There were also complaints from another source that had to be taken seriously. The British members of the Aer Lingus board protested in December 1952 that they had not been informed of the details of the proposal, and aware that the proposed Aerlínte service might endanger the BOAC operation from Shannon to the USA, they informed the board in March 1953 that they wished to see the arrangements cancelled. They also considered withdrawing from the 1946 bilateral agreement, but it did not come to that; the American Civil Aeronautics Board decided that it would only issue a permit for a two-year leasing period, after

THE Vickers VISCOUNT is the world's first turbo-prop airliner. It's fast ... smooth ... superbly comfortable ... and pressurized to fly high above the weather. Inside the air-conditioned cabin you sit in cushioned, armchair ease. There's just a murmur of sound — no vibration at all from the 4 Rolls-Royce jet propeller turbines. Beneath big windows the world glides by at 300 m.p.h. Surprisingly soon — in well under three-quarters of the time ordinarily taken — you touch down in Dublin. You step out rested, relaxed, fresher than when you started.

No visa is needed for Ireland by British Commonwealth, American or French visitors. Dublin to Shannon air service connects with transatlantic flights. Information and bookings from your travel agent, or BEA or Aer Lingus in London. Telephone : WHItehall 1080.

NO EXTRA COST !

To Dublin from:			Return fares
LONDON	(17-day)	85 mins.	£11.15s. *
MANCHESTER	(17-day)	60 mins.	£6 .16s. †
PARIS	(12-month)	2½ hrs.	£22.10s.
AMSTERDAM	(23-day)	2 hrs. 35 mins.	£22.5s.

*Available Tues., Wed., Thurs. only
† Available Mon., Tues., Wed., Thurs. only

Also Viscount "Dawnflights" on London-Dublin route, £5 single, £10 return. Other Aer Lingus services to Dublin from: Birmingham, Liverpool, Glasgow, Edinburgh, Cardiff, Bristol, Isle of Man and Jersey.

AER LINGUS
IRISH AIR LINES

4.3
Aer Lingus advertisement for their Viscount aircraft in 1953, detailing flight costs and also featuring their 'Dawnflights', early morning services to London at a reduced price. These were later extended to 'Starflights' for evening flights. *Courtesy of Aer Lingus.*

which Aerlínte would have to provide its own aircraft. Given the capital expenditure necessary, there was no prospect of Aerlínte operating successfully, and the proposal foundered.

The rapid expansion of services into Europe and investment for the transatlantic service caused massive financial difficulties for Aer Lingus in the late 1940s. The company had taken on extra staff to do Aerlínte work and, while it was not possible to specify how many redundancies were attributable to the cancellation of the transatlantic service, there was no doubt that at least 250 people had to be let go. Dan Morrissey suggested the establishment of a superannuation scheme to boost morale, as otherwise the companies stood to lose the services of the best and most experienced staff to other airlines.[59] Morrissey proposed a contributory scheme costing the companies about £60,000 per annum, of which British interests would bear almost half because of their participation in Aer Lingus. The Department of Finance protested and a meeting took place on 26 June 1948 attended by Costello, Morrissey, Leydon and McGilligan, at which the latter maintained his objections in view of the losses being incurred by the company. His arguments carried the day and it was agreed to announce that the company would introduce such a scheme when its financial position improved to the point where a subsidy was no longer required.[60] The threat of a pilots' strike in May 1949 prompted Morrissey to agree to the establishment of a provident fund, but once again McGilligan objected, citing falling tourism revenue figures to bolster his argument:

> In inter-departmental discussions this year it was made quite clear by the Department of Industry and Commerce that the prosperity of the air companies depends largely on the tourist traffic … it is relevant to record that the latest official estimate of net income from tourism is £27.5 million for 1949/50, falling to £18 million by 1952/53, as against a net receipt of £35 million in 1948.[61]

Nevertheless, it was agreed that a provident fund would be set up which could be converted into a permanent pension scheme when the operating loss of Aer Lingus fell below £100,000.[62] As it fell to £16,996 in 1949/50, the air companies provided £62,000 in their 1950/51 estimates for the introduction of a full superannuation scheme on 1 April 1950.

The post-war period had seen a gradual decrease in the proportion of tourist revenue to other external revenue, and between 1948 and 1953 this declined from 30 per cent of total receipts from abroad to 20 per cent, with total earnings from tourism £29.9 million In 1953 there was a slump in the tourist trade, with the number of visitors dropping from 2,226,146 in 1952 to 2,048,142.[63] As almost a third of Aer Lingus's passengers were British tourists, the revenue implications were serious. The financial results for Aer Lingus showed a deficit of £83,313 for 1952/53 after having presented surpluses of £72,405 and £14,646 for 1951/52 and 1950/51 respectively.[64] Nevertheless, the number of American visitors arriving by air had superseded the number coming by sea from 1949 onwards. As transatlantic airlines offered a 25 per cent rebate on round trips to Europe between October and May, Brendan O'Regan recommended that promotions be held in co-operation with the airlines to secure off-season tourists to Ireland, especially as out of 160,000 transit passengers arriving at Shannon airport, only 10,000 stayed on in the country. In January 1954 Industry and Commerce informed Aer Lingus that it was not prepared to make provision in the Estimates to cover the Aer Rianta share of Aer Lingus losses in that financial year. There was a loss of £62,663 on the 1953/54 operations, but the following year's report produced a profit of £25,428, and in 1956/57 an operating surplus of £158,548 was achieved. In addition, a new method of financing capital expenditure by means of bank loans conditional on a government guarantee was established, relieving the Minister for Finance of the onus of advancing capital to the airline free of interest. Patrick Lynch, chairman of Aer Lingus, was optimistic about future prospects: 'It is fitting that this degree of maturity should have been reached in the year in which Aer Lingus celebrates its twenty-first birthday; and it is confidently expected that the progressive expansion of business will justify the steps which have been taken.'[65] Lemass was more circumspect in his appraisal: 'For the company, challenge accompanies the congratulations … it seems to me that the choice of occasion is peculiarly appropriate as it marks the emergence of the company as a strong, self-reliant, self-supporting body after those groping years which succeeded the long period of State fosterage.'[66]

The transatlantic service was eventually inaugurated in 1958 by the Fianna Fáil administration, an event regarded as being vital to the country outside the narrow sphere of its air transportation role. As speed was the main ingredient sold by airlines, the introduction of jet aircraft was obviously a necessary component for the success of this service, and Aerlínte began by leasing Lockheed Constellations from Seaboard and Western Airlines while awaiting delivery of jet aircraft rather than invest in piston-engined aeroplanes that would soon be obsolete. The first Boeing operated from Ireland to North America on 14 December 1960, and at the same time it was decided that the two operating airlines, Aer Lingus and Aerlínte, would henceforth be known as Aer Lingus – Irish International Airlines to avoid confusion on that continent. New offices were opened in New York by Erskine Childers, and in 1962 it emerged that Aerlínte had a clear operating surplus in its first full year with its own aircraft at a time when other long-established airlines on the North Atlantic were losing money on what were the world's most competitive route. Traffic on scheduled services went up by 38 per cent and charters by 68 per cent, and Aerlínte's share of 44 per cent of the overall North America to Ireland traffic in that year was a credit to the company's publicity efforts. By 1964 there were ten offices in the United States and two in Canada, and that year also saw the delivery of a Boeing 320, one of the largest commercial aircraft in the world. Three years later there was sufficient confidence in the viability of the transatlantic route for the company to order two Boeing 747s, 'jumbo' jets which would provide increased speed and comfort for passengers, and operating economies for the airline. However, in 1969 the plea by President Lyndon Johnson for Americans to stay at home led to very little growth on the transatlantic route at a time when competition from non-scheduled carriers was increasing. The outdated regulatory framework controlled scheduled fares but not those of charter flights, and this led to a price war in which all carriers were consistently losing money. European governments tried to achieve the domestic operation of charter services through the European Civil Aviation Conference, but felt that the political will to do this was absent in the USA, despite some vast losses by American carriers. The company felt that the result would be the virtual elimination of Aerlínte scheduled services to Ireland and the control of all transport from North America to Ireland by foreign companies. In addition, the increase in violence in Northern Ireland proved disastrous for profits on the route during the 1970s, and it was 1977 before a recovery was to be seen. In fact, the airline board seriously considered the implications of terminating the service in 1975, but decided not to recommend its withdrawal to the government at that stage.

Meanwhile, the bilateral agreement with the USA, an outcome of the 1944 Chicago Civil Aviation Conference, was to have enduring repercussions for Irish aviation and diplomatic relations between the two countries. In Chicago it was soon apparent that the USA and the UK were on a collision course as regards international operating rights. The USA wanted agreements granting the necessary rights with the minimum limitation to airline operators, while the UK advocated an international control of air transport to divide services between nations on an equitable basis and to eliminate undesirable competitive practices. With no reconciliation possible between these opposing viewpoints, the USA hastened to negotiate bilateral agreements with other countries.[67] Three weeks after the conference began, the government approved the Irish delegation's entering into negotiations with the Americans and full operating rights in Ireland were granted to the Americans, while reciprocal rights were granted to Irish operators at USA airports to be specified subsequently. Lemass specifically noted the provision that all USA aircraft operating the direct Atlantic route to and from Europe would land at Shannon airport and stressed: 'This annex in

Paragraph A has what was the most contentious item in the negotiations, namely the above provision.' The agreement was signed
on 3 February 1945 with the proviso that either government might
at any time request consultation with a view to modifying the
agreement, such consultation to take place within sixty days.[68]
However, when the Irish government requested the granting of
landing rights at New York, Boston and Chicago to Aerlínte Éireann
in October 1946 in connection with proposed transatlantic services
in 1947, the Americans replied that it was their understanding that
this would involve a revision of the agreement, and indicated that
they also wished to discuss the question of eliminating the mandatory stop for American aircraft at Shannon, and the right of their
airlines to choose to land either at Dublin or at Shannon. Lemass
feared that the granting of landing rights at Dublin would involve
its substitution for Shannon as the main Irish transatlantic base,
and proposed to defer the discussions until such time as the USA
agreed to designate American airports for Aerlínte. Following discussions in Washington in June 1947, landing rights at Boston,
Chicago and New York were granted to the Irish airline.[69] Talks on
the American demands took place in Washington in January 1948,
attended by John Leydon and other department officials, and by
representatives of the Department of State and of the Civil
Aeronautics Administration, but the American requests were not
acceded to.[70] By 1949 they were clearly frustrated over their lack of
success and in September of that year an American delegation arrived
to confront representatives of Industry and Commerce, Finance and
External Affairs.[71] Discussions went on for three days, and the
American minister in Dublin weighed in by sending two notes to the
Department of External Affairs pressing the American case and
stressing the importance of tourist dollars. The Irish government was
not persuaded. It was acknowledged that there would be additional
dollar income if there were more American tourists, but 'a more
fruitful way of spending money to attract tourists could be found
than by unnecessary airport development'.[72] Dan Morrissey advised
the government that with a capital investment of over £2 million
and an operating loss of £30,000 at Shannon airport, his department could not afford a further drop in revenue if the stop were
abandoned, especially as there were over 1,000 people employed
there. The following month saw the Irish Minister in Washington
at a meeting with George Perkins, Secretary of State for European
Affairs, and representatives of the Dublin delegation, the
Department of State and the Civil Aeronautics Board, but no
progress was made.

With a change of government in May 1951, it was Lemass who had to handle the thorny problem in October 1952 when the American *chargé-d'affaires* raised it on the occasion of the proposed transatlantic service. Lemass informed him that 'if the development of traffic at Shannon continued and the Irish line got started, the Government would reconsider its attitude'.[73] Given that aircraft could now by-pass Irish territory, statistics available to Lemass confirmed that landings at Shannon were almost entirely for operational and commercial reasons, and he proposed to delete the compulsory stop. However, he was not going soft on the principle of denying access to Dublin airport, even at the risk of the USA refusing to allow the operation of the transatlantic service. While External Affairs and Defence concurred with Lemass, MacEntee in Finance submitted a separate memorandum disagreeing with his recommendation. On this occasion he was successful; the stop was retained and the Americans continued to press for its removal. Transatlantic services by Aerlínte Teoranta did not materialise in 1952, and the situation remained static. In the long run it was 1957 before the government agreed to do away with the mandatory stop at Shannon. Another fifteen years passed, and in August 1971 notice was served by the American government on the Irish government that unless settlement was reached on its request for USA carriers to serve Dublin in addition to Shannon, the right of Aerlínte to serve New York would be terminated in August 1972.[74] A settlement was reached in June 1973 that allowed one American airline to operate into Dublin, with the qualification that it had to stop at Shannon in both directions, and Aerlínte was granted permission to serve Chicago via Boston during the six winter months. As the state of Irish tourism improved throughout the 1960s, the air companies experienced similar success and spread their wings in various spheres. The International Air Transport Association (IATA) was founded in Cuba in 1947, with Ireland as a founder member, and in September 1962 the organisation's eighteenth AGM was held in Dublin. The plenary session was attended by President de Valera, Taoiseach Seán Lemass and the Minister for Transport and Power, Erskine Childers. In recognition of his contribution to the organisation, J.F. Dempsey was elected president for the following year. After years of frustrating delays, Cork airport finally opened in the autumn of 1961, with flights to London, Dublin, Paris, Cardiff and Bristol. Two years later, services were inaugurated to Lourdes, Barcelona, Birmingham and Glasgow. Aer Lingus also began an aerial car ferry service in the summer of 1963, but with the coming into operation of marine car ferries in 1965 it was phased out. As part of its educational activities, the Aer Lingus 'Young Scientist' exhibition was inaugurated in Dublin's Mansion House in January 1965. The success of the first year was such that the exhibition moved to the larger venue of the Royal Dublin Society in 1966 and it has remained there ever since. In 1969 the competition was extended to include schools from Northern Ireland and in the mid-1970s teams of up to three students were allowed to enter. In 2000 the event was taken over by British Telecom and continues to be a remarkable forum for students of science.

With the new spirit of enterprise and free-market operation engendered by the First Programme for Economic Expansion in 1958, the airline companies' development of ancillary activities began in July 1960 with investment in the Irish and Inter-Continental Hotel Company, which together with the Gresham Hotel Company planned to build three hotels in Dublin, Cork and Limerick. The hotels opened in 1963, and this was followed by the leasing of Aer Lingus's O'Connell Street premises in Dublin to Gartan Limited for the construction of a hotel that would incorporate a booking-office for the airline. During the 1970s investment in accommodation continued with the building of the London Tara hotel by Aerlínte, and Aer Lingus also ventured into the leisure sphere with the acquisition of the Foxhill hotel and golf complex in Chertsey, outside London. It also acquired a 10 per cent stake in Guinness Peat Aviation, along with the National Catering Organisation, Irish Computer Bureau Services and Sunbound Holidays. By 1974 over £15 million had been invested in schemes designed to cushion the companies against the cyclical swings of the airline industry, and more than half its operating profit was derived from its ancillary activities. However, its aviation-related services were still the prime contributors in this sector: the maintenance and overhaul of engines and aircraft; staff secondment to other airlines; training of flight and cabin crews; the provision of passenger, baggage and freight handling services at airports in Ireland, Britain and North America. In 1975, Peter Barry, Minister for Transport and Power, stated in the Dáil that he would like to encourage the air companies to invest in activities that would provide them with a profit to put against the loss on the North Atlantic route, and in that year they acquired the Dunfey Family Corporation, a well-established American hotel chain with fourteen hotels. By 1977 the revenue from ancillary activities exceeded £50 million, more than double the previous year, encouraging the board of Aer Lingus to advocate the value of the entrepreneurial approach in state-sponsored organisations: 'It is vital for the future of state investment in Ireland that the government and the community recognise the

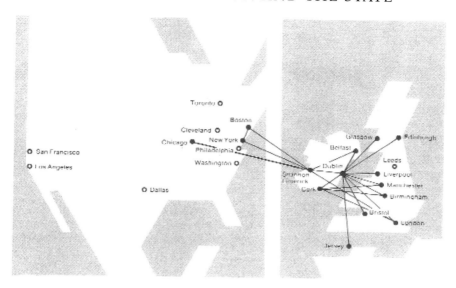

Route and Office System

● ROUTES

○ OFFICES

OFFICES ALSO IN BUENOS AIRES,
HONG KONG AND SYDNEY

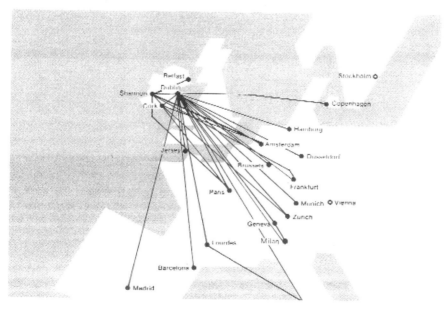

4.4
Aer Lingus route and
office system in 1980.
*Courtesy of Aer
Lingus.*

importance of the development environment which encourages enterprise, courage and innovation.' With profits up to £9.34 million for the sector in 1978, this was an area of the air companies' operations which made a significant contribution to the balance of payments, as over 85 per cent of its revenue came from foreign markets.

In the meantime the airline companies had experienced some trying times, as the troubles in Northern Ireland from 1969 onwards had a negative impact on tourism to the Republic. In 1971/72 the companies recorded their first combined net loss in twelve years to the tune of £2,395,000, due to a combination of the repercussions of continued violence in the North, intense domestic inflation and a sharp slow-down in passenger traffic growth internally.[75] The oil crisis of 1973 pushed the cost of aviation fuel to unprecedented levels, but despite this the companies managed to show a net profit of £1.1 million, while also welcoming a new chief executive, David Kennedy. Aged only 35, he had been actively involved in the companies' ancillary activities and played a major role in the installation of the ASTRAL computer system. The companies maintained a successful charter business until 1974, when regulations for charter traffic were tightened up by the government. With its fuel bill for the following year expected to be 200 per cent higher, there were also concerns about the international hijacking of aircraft, and the Minister for Transport and Power set up a National Civil Aviation Security Committee in 1974.[76] The following year the companies saw their worst-ever operating loss, which was softened somewhat by a $9 million settlement from Trans-Caribbean Airways, and 1976 was also a bad year, with their fourth net loss in a row. However, they returned to profitability in 1977, and in 1978 made a record £4.62 million profit, carrying over two million passengers for the first time, although a 54-day strike by clerical staff was estimated to have cost the company around £5 million and virtually halved its net profit figure for 1978/79.[77] The good news in 1979 was the government's decision to invest a further IR£15 million in Aer Lingus, and 1980 saw another net profit of IR£4 million. In that year just under 2.5 million passengers used the companies' services, with scheduled passenger traffic up 14 per cent on the previous year. The 1980s produced more losses and setbacks for the companies, including a hijacking in 1981 and a pilots' strike in 1985, and the emergence of a rival company in the form of Ryanair, in 1987, was to have far-reaching consequences for the future of Aer Lingus in a manner that could never have been foreseen at the beginning of that decade.

False beginnings
1946–1951

The immediate post-war period brought a tourism boom, generated by an influx of British visitors in search of plentiful food and entertainment. International currency restrictions and the poor state of the transport infrastructure discouraged travel to a Europe devastated by war, and Ireland reaped a huge financial benefit from this situation. However, the government was alarmed at the prospect of losing future potential for the industry due to a shortage of suitable accommodation, as visitors who had an unsatisfactory experience would not be inclined to return. With this in mind, the Department of Industry and Commerce published a Tourist Development Programme in March 1946, seeing the interruption of tourist traffic to the Continent as providing an opportunity for establishing an enlarged tourist trade and identifying the provision of additional accommodation as the most urgent requirement.[1] The proposed solution to this problem, as private enterprise could not be relied upon to meet the increased demand, was the direct intervention of the Irish Tourist Board. It was decided that an interim incorporated company be set up to take over and operate properties which had already been or would be acquired by that body, with a view to the disposal of the board's financial interest in the properties at the earliest possible opportunity. Private enterprise in the provision of adequate accommodation would be encouraged by fixed-term loans to hotel-keepers and others who could not otherwise secure the requisite financial facilities.

The programme also revealed that the estimated cost of resort development schemes already sanctioned in principle exceeded £600,000, with £122,000 having been expended, mainly on the acquisition of properties by the tourist board. Plans for eighteen areas around the country had received approval, and it was calculated that they would cost approximately £1,250,000 over a period of three years. Expenditure on the construction of holiday camps was also being contemplated, in order to cater for the large volume of holiday traffic resulting from the granting of holidays with pay. Accordingly, it was decided that the limit on advances to the tourist board should be increased to £1,250,000, more than double the previous grant of £600,000, but the retention of the stipulation that only schemes certified by the board to be of a profit-earning character were eligible, militated against the successful application of this increase. The document reiterated that the Irish tourist industry would, within a comparatively few years, have to face keen international competition, and that its success would depend 'on the manner in which those engaged in it rise to their opportunity by enterprise, efficiency and the provision of facilities on fair terms for holiday-makers'. The *Irish Times* cautioned its readers that heavy tourist spending would increase living costs by raising the level of already inflated commodity prices, and posed the question: 'Does this mean that tourist expenditure ought to be discouraged?'[2] The answer was in the negative: 'Assuredly not! … When deflationary forces begin to operate and prices begin to fall, tourist revenues may be assets of very real value!' The writer concluded that the solution to the problem was to distribute purchasing power to all sections of the community, to see that visitors left the country with agreeable memories of Irish hospitality, and to lay the foundations of an industry 'whose commercial and cultural values yet are impossible to measure … Dangers lie in hastily-contrived and short-sighted expedients to overcome transient difficulties.'

Short-sighted and hastily contrived as his solutions were, Lemass lost no time in presenting the Tourist Traffic (Amendment) Bill to the Oireachtas, and the debate offers an interesting insight into the mood of deputies at a time when tourism was not seen in the same positive light as it was in 1939. Reacting to negative press comments about the tourist board which suggested that that body 'had avoided to an undue and unreasonable extent publicity in connection with resort development schemes', Lemass explained that due to the delicate nature of negotiations on the acquisition of property, the board was attempting to avoid paying inflated prices by not publicising its schemes for any particular area.[3] Pointing out that the industry was one of major economic importance all over the world, providing a large volume of employment, he also denied that those engaged in it would be degraded by the experience: 'I certainly do not agree that there is any personal humiliation to be experienced in the sale of holiday facilities which would not apply in the sale of other commodities.' Furthermore, although he admitted that the development of hotel, restaurant and recreation facilities, and that of holiday resorts, might be left respectively to private enterprise and to the local authorities, he felt that a central planning and directing authority was necessary for co-ordination and to achieve the best results possible. Referring to press reports objecting to the attraction of tourists while some commodities remained in short supply, he felt that this was not a very strong argument, as only tea, sugar and butter were rationed, and that substantial supplies of other foodstuffs such as meat and eggs existed and were in fact being exported in large quantities: 'It seems to me that it is obviously a much better policy to sell meat and eggs in the form of cooked meals to people coming here from abroad than to export them raw.'

However, deputies on the opposition benches were not slow to attack the legislation's shortcomings. General Richard Mulcahy of Fine Gael criticised the proposals as a complete reversal of Lemass's approach to the tourist industry as indicated by his comments in the Dáil at the time of the 1939 act, particularly in relation to the acquiring, building and carrying on of the hotel business. He proposed that the Dáil decline to give a second reading to the bill until a select committee with powers to send for persons, papers and documents had inquired into and reported on the work already carried out by Bord Fáilte, its further plans for development and those schemes already sanctioned in principle. Further, it should look at the acquisition of properties by the board, the assistance it was giving to stimulate and assist private enterprise, whether it had undertaken or planned to undertake work which should be left to private enterprise and the nature of the administrative machinery established by the board.[4] Other deputies claimed that Lemass and his advisers were experimenting in a totalitarian manner and that the board contained no member who had any training or experience in the hotel trade. Opposition to tourism *per se* was also expressed, as deputies maintained that Irish culture would suffer from it, and veiled references to J.P. O'Brien's 'pull behind the scenes' also featured. Patrick McGilligan made the point that the influx of tourists would have the effect of driving up prices, thus increasing the cost of living. Patrick J. Burke, Fianna Fáil deputy for Dublin County, defended the proposals and refuted Fine Gael allegations that the measures would harm Irish culture and traditions, while also standing up for O'Brien: 'I am very sorry that any deputy should be so ungentlemanly as to attack a man in his absence. The chairman of the tourist board … is an honour to the country and is worthy of the job he holds.'[5] O'Brien had stirred up a hornet's nest by his statement on returning from a visit to the USA in 1946, that his purpose in purchasing the Fáilte Hotels properties was to provide luxury accommodation for American tourists.[6] The press and the opposition parties battened on to the term *luxury*, and what Kevin O'Doherty terms O'Brien's 'vision, imagination, and swashbuckling, buccaneering spirit' in acquiring those holdings was held up to ridicule and opprobrium as the scheme foundered over the following years.

Lemass replied at length to the criticisms levelled at the legislation, declaring that the properties acquired by the tourist board were located in areas where the only hotel business that could be undertaken was a holiday business, and that they would not be catering for the commercial travellers who were the mainstay of many establishments across the country. When challenged on the appointment of the members of the tourist board, he asserted that J.P. O'Brien 'had more experience than any other person of the tourist business' and explained that the reason that no hotel proprietor had been included was to avoid the charge that the board could be influenced in its judgement by persons financially interested in the hotel business. He agreed with complaints that the board had been reluctant to give information concerning its activities and that it had been unduly cautious in its policy, but asserted that he had given the Dáil all the information possible on that body's various operations. He was cautious in his assessment of the work done by the ITB during the war, perhaps signifying his own doubts on the subject:

> Having regard to the limited knowledge we have of the lines on which they have proceeded, I myself would have some hesitation in saying whether they are on sound lines or not, as it is really only in the last twelve months that they have been working on anything more than making plans, and in no case has any single project been brought to the point where judgement on it is possible.

Negative press comment continued, as when a leading article in the *Irish Independent* entitled 'Tourist board and tourists' spelled out the general discontent with the activities of the tourist board and Lemass's apparent acquiescence with their decisions. Stating that his Dáil address was notable for what it omitted, and critical of the fact that no steps would be taken to limit the number of visitors in 1946, the writer declared:

There is not enough hotel accommodation for our own people. Yet the Government intends to permit visitors from other countries to encroach on that accommodation. The Irish people should have first claim on the food and board in this country.[7]

The Tourist Traffic (Amendment) Act became law on 6 June 1946, but it did not succeed in its aims of solving the problem of the accommodation shortfall, as it continued to demand that any finance advanced would only be for projects of a profit-earning nature. Meanwhile, the ITB moved back into Merrion Square with a small staff comprising J.P. O'Brien and his secretary, Kathleen Eason; Tom O'Gorman; Fintan Lalor, secretary; Oliver Ryan, chauffeur; two typists called Una Balfe and Kathleen Brennan; and Grattan Murphy, the treasurer.[8] In 1944 it began to implement its functions under the 1939 act as regards the compulsory registration of hotels and guest-houses. Seaghan Ó Briain and Kitty Kennedy, a domestic economy teacher from Carrickmacross, commenced their inspections, 'armed with notebooks from Woolworths and a couple of pencils' in an ancient pre-war Ford car, on a ration of fuel from the Department of Industry and Commerce which consisted of equal parts of petrol and industrial alcohol. Despite the fact that a scheme for registration and grading had been drawn up by Dublin solicitor Arthur Cox, the tourist board was forced to be realistic. O'Brien's instructions to the inspectors were succinct: 'Clean them up – make sure they have an indoor toilet and a bath with running hot and cold water.' One problem was that hotels and guest-houses, both large and small, did not consider that a guest was entitled to clean bed linen, and most changed it only on Mondays. The owner of a hotel in Tipperary explained to Ó Briain that she had solved the problem by investing in plastic sheets and pillowcases, which only needed a wipe to be clean again, and she was most annoyed when told they had to go. Nylon sheets were similarly unacceptable, a decision which brought the wrath of Cork TDs upon the inspectors, as they were being manufactured in a factory in Bandon. Other universal failings were the appalling state of the kitchens, with minimal standards of cleanliness and hygiene obtaining, and the fact that most Irish hotels seemed to suffer from all-permeating damp. In one dramatic episode, the refusal by Ó Briain and Kennedy to pass the Imperial hotel in Cork led to its being rapidly disposed of by the then owners. Another aspect which caused difficulty was the fact that many hotels throughout the country had never catered for tourists but existed mainly on the trade of commercial travellers, and were indignant at the idea of having to submit to registration and, later, to grading. The fact that hotels had to agree their tariffs with the tourist authorities for publication the following year naturally caused problems, as they could not then exceed them, and this was a totally new departure in practice for them.

By April 1945, 1,192 premises were registered out of a total of 1,774 applications.[9] This provided a total of 14,033 hotel rooms, but the figure of 1,904 guest-house rooms was a source of great disappointment to the tourist board, which ascribed the reluctance of many proprietors to register to their unexpected prosperity in the post-war boom.[10] More than 2,500 inspections were carried out, and the ITB was determined to apply the rigours of the law to those which failed to pass inspection and persisted in calling themselves hotels; by April 1946, twenty-six cases had been taken against proprietors of unregistered premises for the unauthorised display of a hotel sign, of which twenty were proven. In September 1946, Eileen O'Halloran of Kinsale was fined one pound, with thirty-four shillings costs, at Kinsale court, having been prosecuted for contravening Section 33 of the Tourist Traffic Act, 1939, by describing her premises as a hotel.[11] The grading of hotels and guest-houses commenced in 1946, with three categories, A, B, and C, for each. There were 90 Grade A, 261 Grade B and 542 Grade C hotels, with corresponding numbers of 11, 87 and 187 guest-houses.[12] The tourist board expressed disappointment at the low number of guest-houses, but welcomed plans to build holiday camps to cater for families at inexpensive rates. By 1948, the situation had not improved much, with 901 hotels and 288 guest-houses registered, but the addition of the Butlins holiday camp at Mosney was a welcome development, and An Óige's seventeen youth hostels were also included in the list of official accommodation.[13] However, due to continuing criticism of hotel standards, the tourist board decided that those hotels and guest-houses which had previously been given an 'A' grading would be subdivided, as it intended in future to reserve this grade for those premises which approached first-class international standards. A significant problem in this regard was that many proprietors did not see any advantage in raising the standard of their premises, as their regular customers were not the kind of people who would patronise a Grade A establishment.[14]

In 1950 the situation deteriorated even further, with only 875 hotels and 270 guest-houses registered, although the number accommodated in holiday camps was now 3,000.[15] However, the number of bedrooms had risen from 14,033 in 1944 to 16,550, of which 11,300 had running water, an increase of almost 5,000. The original intention of the legislation was that registration and grading fees would cover the expenses incurred in the inspection of premises, but this was never realised. In addition, the cost of print-ing the official accommodation list, of which 60,000 copies were dis-tributed free of charge in 1946, had to be covered by the tourist board. A revision of registration fees in order to meet these costs was already being considered in 1949, as by that time there was a deficit of £2,474 arising from the application of the scheme.[16] By 1951 there was widespread dissatisfaction with it, and with a gen-eral re-organisation of the tourist board being considered, the inspection of premises was carried out on a restricted basis, while the grading of hotels and guest-houses was suspended for 1952, pending the preparation of a revised blueprint for carrying out these tasks.[17]

Meanwhile, the tourist board's incursion into the ownership and management of hotel properties was not faring well. Fáilte Teoranta, the limited company formed to manage and develop the board's properties, was established on 17 May 1946, and its board of directors included J.P. O'Brien and Thomas Condon, another member of the tourist board. Three hoteliers were also appointed directors: James Crowley of the Shelbourne hotel, Dublin; Mary Huggard of the Butler Arms hotel, Waterville, Co. Kerry; and Martin Mortell, of Jury's hotel, Dublin. The company had an alarm-ing number of objectives, which included promoting, establishing, managing and developing accommodation, sports facilities, resort amenities, theatres and cinemas, restaurants and cafés; engaging in 'any kind of publicity' to encourage tourist traffic; providing training schemes for work connected with tourism, and engaging in transport of passengers and goods, among many others.[18] Seaghan Ó Briain, who accompanied J.P. O'Brien on his forays around the country in search of suitable premises, found that they were mainly old private houses in need of conversion and refurbishment before they could operate as hotels.[19] Offices were acquired at Westland Row, Dublin, and a small staff, managed by O'Brien's secretary, Kitty Eason, and a hotelier from Northern Ireland called McIlhenny, set to work. McIlhenny's brief was the hiring of staff and the overall management and supervision of the hotels, which was done on a central basis, as was the provision of supplies. Eason brought in a young architect called Acton who, among other things, oversaw the conversion of Ballinahinch castle, formerly owned by the Martin family and the celebrated Indian cricketer, Ranji Singh. Noel Huggard of the Waterville hotel family was engaged by the Department of Education to train reception staff, waitresses and chambermaids, and the hotels were mainly managed by women.[20] The five properties acquired by the company were Ballinahinch castle, Co. Mayo; the Portmarnock

Country Club, Co. Dublin; An Grianán, Termonfeckin, Co. Louth; the Hydro hotel, Lisdoonvarna, Co. Clare and Courtown House in Co. Wexford, where a smaller house on the property was opened as the Oulart hotel. The operation was plagued with problems from the start, as despite the employment of an army of workmen and the expense of new furniture and fittings, the hotels were only awarded a 'B' grading by Ó Briain, and one of them was refused registration.[21] At the same time, two other hotels, the Commodore in Cobh and the Victoria in Killarney, were acquired in the course of 1947, but they never opened for business.[22]

The Irish Tourist Board, in its annual report for 1948, felt it necessary to explain the failure of the scheme, blaming it on the shortage of building materials for the hotels and the inability of local authorities to provide and improve essential services.[23] The board was at pains to point out that the properties had been purchased with a view to resort development on a large scale, with the hotels being a secondary consideration, and that its direct interest in their operation was of a temporary nature, until they could be sold on satisfactory terms to private enterprise. It was also hoped that they would act as an example in standards for other first-class hotels, but as they had not achieved an 'A' grading from their own inspectors, this was a vain hope. In fact, despite the fact that over one million visitors arrived in Ireland in that year, the Fáilte Teoranta hotels were the only ones not to show a handsome profit in 1947.[24] The company operated at a loss for three years, and it became evident that the hotels would not be regarded as profitable investments by any private concern. In November 1948 all the board members with the exception of O'Brien and Condon resigned, and as they were removed from the ITB in April 1949 by the inter-party administration, they also ceased to be involved.[25] In reply to a Dáil question on 9 March 1949 as to why Ballinahinch castle was being offered for sale, Daniel Morrissey replied: 'The government has taken this decision because it does not consider it any part of its functions to provide state funds for the acquisition and operation of hotels.'[26] Moreover, there were immense accounting complications caused by the relationship between the tourist board, which owned the properties, and Fáilte Teoranta, which managed them. In November 1949 Morrissey informed the government that as the accounts were so overdue as to be of little value, the minimum of time and money would be spent on their preparation, and the company was finally wound up in October 1951.[27]

Another initiative of the tourist board at this time was a scheme for the provision of loans to actual or prospective owners of establishments offering accommodation for visitors. Despite having received the approval of Industry and Commerce in December 1946, the scheme was not attractive to investors, and by 1948 the tourist board was considering its revision: 'It is possible that the conditions that the Board was obliged to insist upon rendered this scheme less attractive to borrowers than loan facilities made available through other sources of credit.' By the following year it was abandoned on the advice of Seán Spillane, the accountant to the tourist board, who considered that there was no point in that body advancing money as they had not been able to negotiate preferential rates from the Irish banks, and would therefore have to apply penal interest to borrowers.[28]

Apart from the provision of accommodation, the main thrust of the 1946 act was the large-scale development of resorts in the postwar years, with the aim of improving facilities and amenities for holidaymakers while also providing employment. In a memorandum to the government in November 1945, Lemass gave details of the programme proposed by the ITB under Section 16 (1) of the Tourist Traffic Act, 1939, with a total estimated cost of £1,137,000.[29] Lemass explained that £75,000 had already been spent on the acquisition of properties and that the board had made loans to the Lisdoonvarna and Rooska Spa Wells Trust and to a company, Gaeleachas Teoranta, which had undertaken to enlarge and expand premises at Garryvoe, Co. Cork, to accommodate persons learning Irish. It is significant that these two developments occurred in areas where Éamon de Valera figured as a crucial player. There had been speculation that the Fianna Fáil determination to keep County Clare sweet for their leader was a factor in the choice of Shannon as the country's transatlantic airport, and the Lisdoonvarna loan, which was never repaid, could be seen in the same light. Similarly, the funding of an Irish holiday school in Cork must have stemmed from de Valera's obsession with the language revival, as it is difficult to see how it would have received approval as a profit-earning project otherwise.

In any case, by 1947 the tourist board had to admit that its large-scale plans for resort development had been severely curtailed, due to the shortage of materials and equipment, and that a radical modification of scale had taken place. However, the board had gone ahead with the formation of an interim development company in Tramore, Traigh Mhóir Teoranta, with a group of local representatives as directors.[30] The Tramore Hydro, with ten hydrotherapy units, hot sea and freshwater baths, a restaurant and other visitor amenities, opened for business in 1948. The ITA devoted a window display to its attractions during Spring Show week in 1949, and *Irish Travel* held it up as an example of the value of specialised catering in Irish holiday resorts.[31] However, this project was also doomed to failure, as the funds necessary for its completion were not forthcoming when the inter-party government took power in 1948 and imposed stringent financial cutbacks on the tourist bodies. The ITB was forced to admit that it had been necessary to apply for further repayable advances from the government to deal with essential maintenance on the properties it had bought, and the last of these was sold, with little or no development having been carried out, in 1952.[32]

One of the radical provisions of the 1939 Tourist Traffic Act was contained in part 4, which dealt with the establishment by the tourist board of Special Areas, in which all business concerns with any connection with the tourist trade were to be inspected and registered with that body. These included boarding houses and other forms of residential accommodation; camp-sites; restaurants, cafés and similar establishments; cinemas, theatres, sports grounds, band promenades, premises in which games or entertainment were provided for the public, any places of public entertainment and local transport services.[33] In addition, the tourist board could apply for powers to preserve the amenities of the area, and could provide and control (and if necessary license) guides, beach guards and attendants at parking places. These wide-sweeping powers could be seen as an extreme example of the state, in the shape of a statutory body, insinuating itself into the social fabric of the country in an unprecedented manner. By June 1943 O'Brien was looking forward to the immediate implementation of the legislation on the termination of the Emergency.[34] However, two years later he conceded that an examination of the requirements for its operation led to the conclusion that the only feasible method of approaching the question was its experimental application to a few areas.[35] Tramore, Bray and Bundoran were selected, but the drafting of necessary regulations had to be agreed with Industry and Commerce before inspections could begin. This did not prove an easy task, as, despite lengthy discussions with Industry and Commerce officials, no ministerial orders had been passed by the time the Fianna Fáil administration left office in 1948. The difficulties concerned the assignment of powers to the tourist board in respect of town planning, which would be resolutely opposed by local authorities fearful of the diminution of their jurisdiction in that respect. Nevertheless, in anticipation of the necessary regulations, the tourist board decided to press ahead with the scheme, and all householders in Bray, Tramore and Bundoran were circularised regarding its provisions.[36] With a view to the future registration of boarding-houses, a preliminary inspection of 1,000 premises was also decided upon. As inspector for hotels and guest-houses, Seaghan Ó Briain was the obvious choice for this task, and he was assigned eight temporary assistants.[37] He set up office in Bray and began work on the town, and in six weeks came back to the tourist board with the information. Tramore was next on the agenda, but the experience there proved to be quite different, as there was massive opposition to the scheme. Ó Briain stayed at the Grand hotel, and was informed by Martin Malone, its proprietor, that protest posters had been appearing regarding the collection of information. A torch-lit demonstration was organised and a large banner stretched across the square with the legend 'Parnell beat the landlords and Tramore will beat O'Brien'. Under the circumstances, Ó Briain and his team quietly left the town. The inspection of Bundoran was abandoned, and the scheme became another abortive venture from the 1939 legislation. However, Lemass kept its provisions in mind, and did not support the revocation of the legislation when the question arose at a departmental conference in December 1951. When informed that his officials considered these powers too drastic, and that more effective results might be achieved by inducement rather than compulsion, he replied that he saw advantage in having the powers in the background, even if they were never used.[38]

A significant development at this time was the appointment of M.K. (Kevin) O'Doherty as secretary of An Bord Cuartaíochta in August 1946. O'Doherty had worked in Industry and Commerce since 1935, becoming private secretary to Seán Lemass in 1942.[39] He saw little prospect of promotion at the end of the war, and decided to leave the civil service. He applied for the position of secretary in Aer Lingus in early 1946, was interviewed by J.P. O'Brien and obviously made a good impression, as the latter subsequently asked him to apply for the post of secretary of An Bord Cuartaíochta. This position was not open to the public, having been advertised solely in Industry and Commerce, at the behest of John Leydon, who wished to have a civil servant in the post. O'Doherty's immediate reaction to his move to the tourist board was one of confusion, although he was not a complete innocent in the field, being familiar with the legislation and the hotels scheme through his civil service work. He admired J.P. O'Brien, finding him a man of great flair and imagination, easy to access and convivial to a fault. Indeed, this last was to prove his downfall. Speaking to O'Doherty in 1946, he prophesied that he had 'ten years left' and he was absolutely correct in this assessment, dying in 1955 at the early age of 56. O'Doherty attended his funeral with Lemass, who had strenuously supported his former comrade to the end.[40] O'Doherty was to find himself in hot water with Industry and Commerce soon after his appointment. Speaking to Bill Taft, later American ambassador to Ireland but at that time employed in the European Co-operation Agency (ECA) office in Dublin, O'Doherty expressed his personal opinion on the issue of landing rights for American airlines at Dublin airport. Having earlier accompanied John Leydon when he went to meet Juan Trippe, chairman of Pan American Airlines, at Shannon, O'Doherty had witnessed the latter's frustration at not being able to fly directly into Dublin, and was himself of the opinion that the restriction, while protecting Shannon airport, was counter-productive to the development of American traffic into Ireland. He said as much to Taft, who quoted his remark to Leydon and Lemass, and O'Doherty was hauled over the coals by Leydon in such a manner as to make him fear the loss of his job. This did not happen, but it was a salutary lesson in diplomacy, and O'Doherty was glad to learn from the experience.

As Minister for Finance in the inter-party administration that came to power in March 1948, Patrick McGilligan immediately set about reducing government spending in an effort to improve the state's economic deficit. At a cabinet meeting on 14 May 1948, he proposed to reduce the grant-in-aid to the Irish Tourist Board to £25,000, a saving of £15,000.[41] Daniel Morrissey, the new Minister for Industry and Commerce, described by Lee as 'hapless',[42] and carrying little weight in cabinet, possessed none of the dynamism of his predecessor and demonstrated little interest in the tourist industry. When Michael Lydon, Fianna Fáil deputy for Galway West, enquired in the Dáil if he would state the government's policy in relation to the tourist industry in July 1948, he was informed that the government was still considering its future policy.[43] Naturally, bearing in mind that he was a staunch Fianna Fáil supporter, J.P. O'Brien was anathema to the new administration. In addition, there was personal animosity between himself and Morrissey,[44] and in any case his performance at this time had deteriorated substantially. Consequently, his services as chairman of the tourist board were dispensed with, and he was succeeded by William F. Quinlan, county manager for Kerry.

Meanwhile, John Costello, head of the inter-party government, wrote to the minister of each department in June 1948 expressing his disappointment at the level of economies achieved in the public service.[45] McGilligan, in his budget speech, announced that the ITB's allocation was to be reduced, while lamenting the fact that the substantial saving resulting from the abandonment of the transatlantic air service would only meet the losses incurred on services in 1947.[46] However, speaking at the AGM of the ITA in October 1948, Morrissey pointed out that in 1947 the nation's earnings from tourism were estimated at £28 million, at a time when cattle exports were worth just over £15.5 million, thus making it a crucial component of the national economy.[47] Referring to the difficulties inherent in establishing accurate tourism figures, Morrissey promised to examine the question of reorganising the statistical services of the country in order to overcome the poverty of economic information regarding the industry.[48]

As the new decade approached, the British invasion of visitors began to wane. Continental countries ravaged by the Second World War were investing heavily in tourist development, and it was obvious that Ireland would have to keep up with the competition or lose the advantage gained in the late 1940s. While the new administration may not have considered tourism a crucial point on its agenda, the introduction of American political influence on the industry could not now be avoided and it came to dominate government thinking on tourism for the foreseeable future. Having been approved in April 1948 for a loan of $10 million for the first three months of the European Recovery Programme under the terms of the Marshall Plan, Ireland found itself in the position of needing to increase its dollar-earning capacity.[49] The first loan agreement was signed on 28 October 1948, and as tourism seemed set to supersede emigrants' remittances as the primary source of dollar income, it was crucial that the government throw its weight behind efforts to develop the industry to its fullest potential. To this end an inter-departmental Working Party on Dollar Earnings was set up by the Minister for Finance in November 1948, with representatives of the Departments of Finance, Agriculture, External Affairs, Industry and Commerce, the Revenue Commissioners and the Central Statistics Office.[50] Its first interim report was devoted to tourism and submitted to the government in November 1949. Tourism was chosen because it was the largest single dollar-earning source, and because 1950, being a holy year, presented the opportunity of attracting pilgrims who were visiting Rome. To this end, Ireland participated in a meeting of the Tourism Committee of the Organisation for European Economic Co-operation held in Paris in October 1949. Colonel Theodore Pozzy, chief of the travel section of the European Co-operation Agency in Paris, which administered Marshall Plan funds in Europe, proposed the organisation of a joint scheme of technical assistance for the tourist industry in countries participating in the European Recovery Programme, with funding to be provided from a special $1 million amount set aside for such projects.[51] Pozzy had visited Ireland during the summer of 1949 at the invitation of Kevin O'Doherty and had toured the country accompanied by William Quinlan.[52] Ireland was nominated to act on the working party set up to consider the suggestion, and met representatives of Austria, Belgium, France, Great Britain and the Netherlands in Paris the following month. It was agreed that there were some problems that could be handled on a joint technical mission to the United States, and a decision from the government regarding the possibility of Ireland's participation in such a scheme was sought.[53]

Morrissey was not impressed by the proposals, feeling that 'the most effective method of obtaining the necessary assistance would be to secure the services of a group of American technicians who would survey conditions in the Irish hotel and allied industries'. However, as ECA officials made constant references to the potential of the industry for obtaining dollars, he concluded: 'It would … be unwise to refuse to participate in the proposed scheme in view of the possibility of adverse reaction on relations with the ECA, adverse criticism in OEEC [Organisation for European Economic Co-operation] and perhaps, also, in the USA, where the fact that Ireland was not participating might be specially noticed.' McGilligan agreed, suggesting that one Irish representative, preferably from the hotel sector, should be despatched, and that Ireland should insist that each country should be responsible for the expenses of its own delegate, as they would not be covered by the ECA.

In 1949 Morrissey announced that the Central Statistics Office had been instructed to undertake a special enquiry into expenditure by visitors to and from the country, as Ireland's income from dollar sources in 1948 was estimated to amount to only $7 million.[54] Seán MacBride maintained that in order to sustain the country's current dollar earnings from tourism, it would be necessary to increase them by 44 per cent. Both men emphasised that the profits made by hoteliers in the preceding years should be ploughed back into improvements and extensions of their premises in order to cater for an influx of American tourists, but that there was no need to aspire to luxury in this regard. In fact, Joseph E. Carrigan, chief of the ECA mission to Ireland, had expressed the same sentiments when addressing the Publicity Club in Dublin: 'What they want is good, clean accommodation. They like showers, but I don't think it is necessary to have a shower or bath connected with every room.'[55]

As far back as the 1890s Frederick Crossley had brought up the question of training staff for Irish hotels, and this was an issue that would surface continually during the twentieth century. In 1926 J.C. Foley went before the Technical Education Committee of the Department of Education and stressed the need for the provision of catering training. He pointed out the importance of the hotel industry, as it employed 5,000 people nationwide and, citing the model of the Westminster School in Britain, he called for the establishment of catering colleges in Dublin and Cork.[56] As regards the management of Irish hotels, Foley reported that he had headed a group of thirty hotel proprietors, accompanied by George Fletcher, assistant secretary at the Department of Education, who undertook an extensive tour of French resorts in May 1927.[57] By 1935 the ITA was actively campaigning for a school of hotel management in Ireland, but no progress in this direction could come about without the political determination to stimulate it, and it was obvious by 1939 that steps had to be taken to redress the lack of proficient staff. One of the provisions of the 1939 act was 'to provide or assist in schemes in providing schemes for the training of persons to do work which is wholly or mainly connected with tourist traffic'. With no structured training schemes in place, most hotel workers had to learn through what Corr calls 'the sitting next to Nellie' principle.[58] Early in 1940, IHF officers held discussions with the Dublin Vocational Education Committee on the training of hotel workers and laid the groundwork for what was eventually to become the Dublin College of Catering.[59] At the same time, officials of the Department of Education met a deputation from the Irish Technical Education Association,[60] and it was agreed that three con- current courses of action were needed: institutional training for hotels, which could be operated in the new college; management training for guest-houses by means of winter courses in three centres situated in tourist areas in the south and west of the country, involving close co-operation between local vocational education committees, the ITB and local hotels; and training in local centres of Irish-speaking workers for employment in hotels and guest- houses. On 16 June 1940, St Mary's College of Domestic Science in Cathal Brugha Street, 'Dublin's latest, most modern school', was opened by the Minister for Education, Thomas Derrig, and blessed by Dr John Charles McQuaid, the Catholic archbishop of Dublin.[61] Meanwhile, the *Irish Times* pointed out that 'the determination with which Scotland is facing the tourist problems of the post-war period makes it increasingly clear that that country will be Ireland's principal rival'.[62] The similar appeal of the two countries and the work beginning in Scotland to improve the standard of hotel accommodation, cuisine and service were mentioned, and the establishment of a school of hotel management there, in advance of any such development in Ireland, was seen as a grave disadvantage: 'It is patently absurd that, for a business which calls for such wide, and at the same time, such specialised knowledge, no proper training should be offered in this country.'

As the war ended and Ireland was engulfed by British tourists, the ITB set up some training courses outside Dublin. Running in hotels such as Kelly's in Rosslare, they took place in the slack season and generated some welcome funds for the establishments concerned.[63] However, these were only sporadic occurrences and could not hope to solve the nationwide problem of staff shortages and incompetence. The tourist board organised for representatives of the IHF, the Hotel and Restaurant Association and the catering branch of the Irish Transport and General Workers' Union to visit training centres in Switzerland and the UK during 1947 to examine teaching methods and curricula there.[64] As a result an agreement was signed between the Irish and Swiss governments on 14 March 1949, under which nationals of both countries could be exchanged for training.[65] The ITB entered into negotiations with Swiss hotel authorities, and it was hoped that the scheme would be fully availed of by Irish hotel and restaurant owners. By the following year, arrangements had also been made with the French government for a similar arrangement, but difficulties in the operation of that scheme prevented Irish nationals from working in France, although some did go to Switzerland, and a number of stagiaires from both countries came to Ireland.[66] Difficulties also arose in Ireland with regard to the granting of employment permits for foreign hotel workers, and at a meeting between trade union and Industry and Commerce officials in June 1950, union representatives made it clear that they intended to delay the issuing of permits by dilatory action, as they had a consultative role in the process.[67]

Meanwhile, Brendan O'Regan had been busy at Shannon airport, arranging staff exchanges with the KLM restaurant at Schiphol airport in Amsterdam and the TWA flight kitchens in Paris during 1949.[68] In 1951 he proposed an ambitious training scheme for staff at Shannon airport to Industry and Commerce, with instructors' fees being paid by Clare County Council. The fees would be £10 per month for sixteen trainees, and he foresaw no financial loss to the airport. Industry and Commerce were of the opinion that 'this was probably not an over-optimistic view because any loss would adversely affect his own earnings.' They suggested that the ITB and the IHF should be asked to collaborate and contribute towards the scheme, but O'Regan was not enthusiastic, and the scheme went ahead without any outside financial aid.[69] The Shannon Airport Catering Service Staff Training and Advancement Scheme came into being on 16 July 1951, and it provided daily classes and exchanges with Swiss hotels. Out of 98 applicants, 20 were chosen for the course, which included foreign languages as well as hotel and catering management skills. This was the first coherent approach to the problem of staff training in the country and was a revolutionary initiative in a sector of the tourism industry which had previously been dominated by the practice of family-owned and managed hotels. It eventually culminated in the establishment of the Shannon Hotel Management School, the first of its kind in the country.

At the same time, the tourist board awarded eight scholarships at a total cost of £840 for courses at St Mary's College in Cathal Brugha Street, Dublin, for 1952.[70] The following year it stepped up its support by awarding twenty-eight scholarships in Dublin, while allocating £5,000 to the college for the purchase of special restaurant and catering equipment. As the Shannon airport school commenced its second year of operation in the autumn of 1952, the tourist board contributed certain essential equipment for the course, and by 1954 it also provided a technical advisory service for hotels, as it employed experienced hotel operators to visit hotels and vocational schools to show training films, lectures on the running of bars, restaurants, reception areas and housekeeping, while also advising on the question of organisation and equipment. However, this piecemeal approach to the problem was totally inadequate to the needs of the industry, as the number of tourists visiting Ireland increased in the late 1950s. By 1958, the tourist board was spending £21,000 annually on training,[71] but courses were poorly constructed and standards uneven. A working group was set up in 1960 to advise on the structure of a training council for the industry, and the result was the Council for Education, Recruitment and Training (CERT). This was established in November 1963 and funded by Bord Fáilte Éireann to the tune of £14,849 in its first year.[72] In 2003 it merged with Bord Fáilte to form Fáilte Ireland, a new tourism body for the third millennium.

During the autumn of 1949 the ITB submitted proposals to Daniel Morrissey for the restructuring of the organisation. They were based on a scheme formulated by Roger Greene, a solicitor and a member of the board, at the minister's request, and had received the approval of Colonel Pozzy of the ECA. However, as time passed and no action appeared to be forthcoming, Greene resigned his seat on the board as a protest in June 1950.[73] Morrissey presented his conclusions to the government in February 1950, and as a result a Committee on Tourism consisting of the taoiseach and the ministers for external affairs, agriculture, finance, and the parliamentary secretary to the Minister for Industry and Commerce, was established. The need for such a committee was doubtless prompted by the reaction of Patrick McGilligan, who opposed Morrissey's plans in no uncertain terms: 'The remedying of existing defects is primarily a matter for those engaged in the industry … they have ample resources to finance improvements which would serve to maintain the greatly increased prosperity they have enjoyed in recent years.'[74] Castigating the board for submitting a reorganisation scheme based on the premise that higher salaries and more staff were a condition of the formulation of general policy, he continued: 'The Board's proposals are not a basis on which the Minister would consider it justifiable to agree to place £3 million at its free disposal, as is recommended by the Minister for Industry and Commerce, even if no problem of financing grants of such magnitude existed.' McGilligan also pointed out that although dollar earnings from tourism were important, they constituted only one-tenth of total tourism income, and were likely to remain of secondary importance in relation to revenue derived from British visitors. At the same time, a note addressed to John Costello on the subject of tourism from within his own department was brutally honest in its appraisal:

> The memo submitted by the present Tourist Board is a deplorable document. A new board should be appointed … the salaries proposed by the existing Board seem altogether too high, even by commercial standards, for a body which has failed to provide the Government with any useful guidance and advice on the future of the tourist industry … most of the present tourist 'literature' is abominable.[75]

In the meantime, the Central Statistics Office confirmed that tourists to Ireland had spent £34 million in 1948, while Irish nationals holidaying abroad spent £6 million.[76] Interestingly, the research they undertook at ports and railway termini showed that movements between Britain and Ireland, to and from jobs, was of much greater frequency than hitherto supposed, and many of those passengers formerly counted as tourists were now correctly categorised as 'revolving' emigrants. Liam Cosgrave, parliamentary secretary to Morrissey, speaking at the annual dinner of the Wicklow Chamber of Commerce early in 1950, made the point that in 1948 tourism had accounted for a quarter of the country's total income from abroad, and was second only to merchandise exports on the income side of the balance of payments.[77] Furthermore, he said that its importance was even more fully demonstrated by the fact that tourism receipts were the highest from any single export category. These facts should have strengthened the determination of the inter-party government to do something meaningful for tourism, despite their traditional aversion to the industry on mainly political grounds, but this was not the case. When the Committee on Tourism presented its report in June 1950, it made thirty-four recommendations ranging over subjects as diverse as the improvement of landing facilities at Cobh and the avoiding of the 'caubeen and pipe' type of advertisement, in addition to the usual one of the urgent need for provision of better accommodation for tourists. It also commented on the membership and staffing of the tourist board, and on the desirability of unifying the functions of that body and those of the ITA, but concluded that a merging of the two bodies would not be feasible in the near future.[78] A meeting of the cabinet on 23 June 1950 considered the report and two appendices, one a memorandum entitled 'The Irish Tourist Board and tourist publicity' drawn up by Kevin O'Doherty, and the other a document on 'The Irish Hotelier' by T.J. Sheehy. They approved the immediate putting into effect of recommendations regarding provisions for sale of Irish goods at airports, including a permanent display of Irish-made goods at Shannon; the production of a leaflet explaining customs procedures for visitors, which were a source of much irritation; and the production of sets of Irish stamps and books on fishing in Ireland. However, as these were but minor details in the tourism field, it is evident that no serious immediate attempt was being made to address the basic problems besetting the industry.

Richard Beamish of the Cork brewing family and a member of the tourist board, pulled no punches when writing to John Costello at this time, insisting that no real progress in developing the industry could be made until hotel accommodation was substantially improved, and that the hotel industry would not respond unless some state aid was forthcoming.[79] Whether or not Beamish's letter had any effect on government policy is not clear, but in the face of unanimous dissatisfaction with the membership of the board, it was dissolved and a new board held its first meeting on 4 October 1950. Beamish alone retained his membership; the chairman was James Nugent, a director of the Irish Life Assurance Company; other members were Noel Huggard of Ashford Castle hotel in Cong; A.J.

5.1
Kevin O'Doherty,
former private
secretary to Seán
Lemass and
General Manager of
the Irish Tourist
Board from 1950 to
1956. *Courtesy of
Fáilte Ireland.*

McClafferty, manager of the Royal Marine hotel in Dun Laoghaire; and S.J. Muldowney, a chartered accountant. However, a significant development was the appointment of Kevin O'Doherty as general manager of the ITB. He was interviewed for the post by Patrick Lynch, economic adviser to John Costello, but who also knew O'Doherty well from his stint in Industry and Commerce, and who told him that he had recommended him to Costello as 'the only candidate who knew anything about tourism'.[80]

O'Doherty's observations on the new appointees to the Irish Tourist Board demonstrate the degree of dysfunction that obtained in the tourism sphere as the new decade dawned. James Nugent, a director of the Irish Life Insurance Company, knew nothing about tourism but was a very close friend of James Dillon, Minister for Agriculture at the time. A.J. (Tony) MacClafferty had served in the army with Liam Cosgrave, and O'Doherty believed that Cosgrave was responsible for his appointment. Noel Huggard was deeply involved in the family hotel business and rarely appeared for board meetings. Richard Beamish was another occasional presence, and according to O'Doherty, 'if he did come, he changed his mind three or four times in the course of one meeting'. Lastly, S.J. Muldowney had no experience in the tourism arena. O'Doherty contends that the attitude of the inter-party administration towards tourism was quite negative, and the catchphrase 'that matter is in abeyance' summed up their lack of commitment. The board appointed in 1950 categorically refused to meet representatives of the hotel industry, despite repeated requests, thereby scotching efforts by O'Doherty and other employees of the organisation to maintain good public relations with hoteliers. A strike of hotel workers began in Dublin in October 1951, and their committee felt constrained to complain to Lemass, and to de Valera, about the behaviour of McClafferty, who, they felt, had ridiculed their actions: 'As tax-payers we believe this man should not be allowed to use his position to criticise workers with whom he has a trade dispute and we demand his removal from the Board.'[81] However, no action was taken and the board held tenure for its five-year term, except for Noel Huggard, who resigned for business reasons in 1951.

Meanwhile, Ireland's participation in the international tourism sphere was firmly secured thanks to O'Doherty's efforts at this time. While still finding his feet as secretary of the ITB, he was despatched to Paris in 1947 by J.P. O'Brien to attend the foundation of a European tourism organisation,[82] and the contacts made at that time resulted in O'Doherty becoming vice-chairman of the European Travel Commission in 1948. He also developed very cordial relations with British tourism interests at this time, to the extent that the British offered to stock Irish tourist literature in their offices around the world, but this overture was stymied by the Ulster Tourist Development Association. In August 1950 the Executive Committee of the International Union of Official Travel Organisations (IUOTO) held a meeting in Dublin.[83] Founded in The Hague in 1925 and re-organised on a worldwide basis in 1947, this association represented thirty-nine countries around the world, and enjoyed consultative status with the United Nations. Delegates from the USA, Britain, Greece, Italy, South Africa, Australia, Switzerland and Denmark were guests at a dinner hosted by Daniel Morrissey and attended by Colonel Pozzy and William Quinlan. Following their meeting, the party embarked on a tour of Cork and Kerry as guests of the tourist board, and the result was quite a coup for the Irish officials, as it was agreed that the sixteenth General Assembly of the organisation would be held in Dublin in October 1950.[84] This event received great media attention as nearly a hundred delegates from all over the world discussed tourism in an international framework, and it certainly focussed public attention on the potential of the industry. Liam Cosgrave, deputising for Morrissey at a banquet in Dublin castle, made the point that tourism was now the state's biggest dollar earner.[85]

However, when the counting was done in 1950 it emerged that tourism receipts were in all probability going to fall to £28 million.[86] The honeymoon was over, and stringent press criticism of the tourist board was the order of the day, complete with allegations of incompetence and neglect on the part of members of the board. Hilgrove McCormick, in a series of articles in the *Irish Press* entitled 'The future of Irish tourism', laid the blame for a downturn in the tourist trade squarely on the shoulders of the tourist body, ' [due to] lack of leadership and organisation, with the Irish Tourist Board the arch-villain of the piece'.[87] It fell to Liam Cosgrave, on

Morrissey's behalf, to spell out the bad news to the ITA at their AGM in October 1950.[88] The anticipated rise in American visitors due to the Holy Year had not materialised; in fact, he foresaw a reduction in the overall number of visitors due to that event. Addressing the meeting, Paul Miller of the ECA office in Dublin expressed his support for the proposed quarterly report form for hoteliers, prepared by the Central Statistics Office, which would list visitors by nationality and expenditure, thus enabling the Irish government to compute more accurately the country's financial returns from tourism, while at the same time assisting in their compliance with the statistical requirements of the OEEC Tourism Committee. He also confirmed that his organisation's interest in tourism was solely concerned with closing the dollar gap. It was a strong hint to the government to get on with the job, but it was only with the submission of a detailed memorandum on policy proposals and a reorganisation scheme, with estimates, to Morrissey on 12 December 1950 that some action was taken.

This took the form of the Tourist Traffic (Amendment) Bill, which was introduced in the Dáil on 14 February 1951, but following the return to power of Fianna Fáil in May 1951, this bill was not proceeded with. Instead, it was Seán Lemass, once more in the driving seat at Industry and Commerce, who set out to change the statutory organisational structures of the industry in a manner which belies his reputation as a pragmatic, hard-headed politician but which illustrates instead his deep sense of personal loyalty to former comrades. As for the immediate post-war years in Ireland, it was truly an era of false beginnings, as almost all those brave new schemes provided for in the pre-war legislation came to nought, and left the promoters of tourism with an uphill task to be undertaken in the grim economic environment of the early 1950s.

North of the border 1922–1980

While acknowledging that Northern Ireland would never be a primary world destination like London, Amsterdam or Rome, and that jumbo jets would be unlikely to use Aldergrove airport except as a stopover for transatlantic traffic, it has to be remembered that tourism provides over 8,000 permanent jobs and 3,000 seasonal jobs. Revenues from tourism raise incomes generally across the Province, particularly west of the Bann, where they represent a substantial injection of money for hard-pressed regional economies … Tourism involves a friendly mixing of people of different races, colours and religions; for Northern Ireland, this is a process which must surely be of special help in the community.

Written in the annual report of the Northern Ireland Tourist Board for the year ending 31 December 1977, at a time when terrorist activities had all but stopped tourism expansion, it is clear that these words are addressed to the people of Northern Ireland. The report goes on to explain that expenditure by government and district councils on tourist schemes and projects had brought immediate benefits to the people of Northern Ireland in terms of employment, in the form of carparks, picnic areas, lay-bys, toilet blocks, marinas, slipways, jetties and harbour facilities, hire cruisers, day and sea angling boats, scenic paths, play areas, caravan sites and campsites, bowling greens, tennis courts, information and visitor centres, and accommodation and catering facilities. In the absence of tourists, it was the people of Northern Ireland who gained immediate and permanent benefit from them. The NITB must have found it difficult to justify spending on tourism projects when

6.1
Group of tourists at
the Giant's
Causeway, Co.
Antrim, in the 1880s.
Taken from *Old
Portrush, Bushmills
and the Giant's
Causeway, courtesy of
Stenlake Publishing.*

hotels and leisure facilities were being destroyed on a continuous basis, but a belief that all this would end some day, and perhaps soon, demanded an optimistic outlook.

As with other parts of the country, work had begun in the 1880s to take advantage of the province's natural beauty, along the coastline and in the Glens of Antrim and the lake-lands of Fermanagh. The railways were a prime factor in this development, with various companies building their own hotels and linking up with ferry services to Scotland and England. The railway companies pushed tourism because, with little industry in Ireland outside of Cork, Dublin and Belfast, there was very little freight traffic, the mainstay of normal railway operation. Steamers were going from Belfast to Liverpool from 1824, and from the 1860s there were also services to Barrow-on-Furness, Glasgow and Ardrossan. Hotels on the coast were centres of recreational excellence where guests played golf, tennis and lacrosse, bathed and yachted, toured the Mountains of Mourne, the Antrim coast and the Donegal highlands and enjoyed a lively social life. Large numbers of well-heeled visitors came from Britain to mix with business and professional upper classes from the North of Ireland. Within the province, day-trips and home-based holidays developed Bangor, Newcastle, Larne, Whitehead, Ballycastle, Portrush and Portstewart as popular resorts for the general public. Henry McNeill of Larne was a pioneer of the package tour, using long cars and jaunting cars in the 1880s to convey visitors to the Antrim coast and glens. They arrived at Larne, stayed a week or a fortnight, and enjoyed a planned programme of tours. However, the disruption of the First World War and political turmoil in Ireland itself forced tourism in the North to take a back seat until the 1920s.

With self-rule conferred on the six northern counties in 1921, a voluntary tourist development organisation was established in 1924 by eighteen of the province's most prominent businessmen as a result of a conference held during 1923 at the instigation of the Ulster Association.[1] Representatives of local councils, seaside resorts, chambers of commerce and transport companies attended, and this led to the establishment of the Ulster Tourist Development Association, a limited company whose council comprised 'men of means and influence', including Sir Frederick Cleaver of Robinson Cleaver department stores, and Robert Baillie, a well-known tour operator. Voluntary contributions were sought from local authorities, business concerns and private individuals. Financed by a gift of £500 from a local organisation, the association became a limited company on 25 February 1924. Its first offices were at Donegall Square in Belfast and within three months it organised a visit by a group of English and Scottish journalists, who toured the coasts and countryside of Down and Antrim. The first *Ulster Guide* was also published in that year and included over 100 scenic views, detailed promotional copy, a travel section and specific information on activities and special interests. Its first annual report ended on a positive note: 'The Council desires to emphasise the bright future which lies before Ulster in the tourist world, provided all interests combine to make it a success.'[2]

Representatives of the association travelled to London to promote the province there and efforts were made to increase tourist traffic by means of press visits, promotional folders and financial support for international sporting events such as the Ulster Grand Prix. Local artists were commissioned to design an annual Ulster poster. In 1928 a significant advance was the achievement of the redesignation of the Travel Association of Great Britain to include Northern Ireland in its title, and the appointment of the chairman of the UTDA to the executive of that body. It was also the year in which the organisation received the imprimatur of the Northern Ireland government when the prime minister, Lord Craigavon, visited its offices. Fifty-six golf clubs and forty-four hotels recommended by the Belfast and North of Ireland Hotels Association were listed in the organisation's 1928 publication *Ulster For Your Holidays*, and attention was drawn to the fact that 'Northern Ireland, or Ulster, as it is generally known, is part of Great Britain and consequently there are no restrictions regarding customs while travelling in the North of Ireland.'[3] The London, Midland and Scottish Railway company presented its summer programme, including a seven-day conducted tour for £4.16.6d with visitors staying at the Laharna hotel, Larne, 'the largest tourist hotel in Ireland', with tours to 'the world famous Giants Causeway, Portrush, Antrim Coast, Glens of Antrim, Gobbins Cliffs, Blackhead, Sallagh Braes, Lough Neagh and Belfast'. The Belfast Omnibus Company advertised its Daimler low chassis all-weather, pneumatic-tyred vehicles, with drop windows and comfortable seated accommodation for tours throughout Ireland, 'hail, rain or shine – comfort all the time'. McNeill's hotel in Larne promoted Antrim coast tours running from May to September at a cost of £4.16.6d for seven days and six nights, with 'three excellent meals each day'. Edited by Alexander Riddell, the publication acknowledged the work of playwright and novelist St John Ervine, 'who by his brilliant pen has kept Ulster prominently before the public and from whose book *Ulster* (published by the UTDA in 1926) prolific extracts have been taken for this work'. The Ulster Tourist Trophy car race was the event that more than any other placed Northern Ireland on the international tourist map. Starting in the 1920s and continuing every year until its abrupt end in 1937 after the Newtownards disaster in which several people were killed, the race attracted top international drivers and crowds of enthusiasts from far and near.[4]

The association moved to more prestigious offices at Royal Avenue in 1929, and within a year the number of enquiries had more than doubled at its information bureau. Local communities in the province were encouraged to set up their own tourist associations, the British Holiday Fellowship Association established its first Northern Ireland branch at Corrymeela, and efforts were made to attract conference traffic to Belfast. By 1930 every county council in Ulster was subscribing to the association, but even so, as in the Free State, regular representations were made to the government with a view to obtaining an annual grant. However, despite the logic of promoting Ireland as an entity, co-operation on an all-Ireland basis was not something that northern tourist interests were seeking. The UTDA was mainly controlled by unionists, who did not wish to have any meaningful truck with their nationalist counterparts in the South, while Free State diplomats abroad stoutly denied the existence of a separate northern state by alluding to themselves as representatives of Ireland, a practice that the British Foreign Office found unacceptable.[5] Nevertheless, expressions of goodwill from both associations continued to characterise their relationship. In 1930, Viscount Craigavon, addressing the AGM of the UTDA, expressed himself delighted to hear of the cordial relations between the two associations: 'Ulster was glad to pass on her tourists to the Free State, and he was sure that the Free State was equally glad to pass hers to the Six Counties.' In the event, the northern association was the first to achieve success in its lobbying for central funding. In 1935 the Northern Ireland government agreed to contribute to its funds on the basis of one pound for every pound collected from voluntary subscriptions, up to a ceiling of £4,000.

Tourism acquired more importance in the inter-war years as the ability of all classes to go on holidays or short breaks and the rapid growth of motor transport created an increasing demand for popular recreation facilities and accommodation. Hoteliers and caterers saw the need for more organisation and co-ordination in order to make the most of the tourist growth and expanding interest from across the sea, and by expatriates from America and the Commonwealth. Various tourist bodies emerged during this period, such as the Northern Ireland Hotels and Caterers Association, and with the transport companies and tour operators this body lobbied the government for the establishment of a statutory tourist body. Speaking in the House of Commons in March 1938, the northern Minister of Commerce, John Milne Barbour, paid tribute to the industry for accruing £1.5 million to the province in 1937, and estimated an increase of £250,000 in 1938. At the same time, a government committee was set up to consider accommodation, amenities and facilities for tourism, as a result of recommendations by the UTDA that the potential of the industry should be closely and officially investigated.[6] Some of its members were appointed to the committee, and its findings were delivered to the government in 1939. However, the province was soon to find itself at war, and all new development was suspended for the duration of the conflict.

It is interesting to note the continuing participation by northern tourist concerns in developments in the South during the 'Emergency'. At the opening of the ITA office in Belfast in April 1940, W.A.E. Withers of Belfast, responding to a toast to 'the press', hoped that the lead given by the ITA would result in the establishment of a UTDA office in Dublin.[7] Given that Northern Ireland, as part of the United Kingdom, was at war, it was unlikely to experience a rush by southerners to visit the province, but it is clear that cordial relations did exist between the two associations. With conflict in Europe leading to a declaration of neutrality from Éamon de

Valera, it might have been expected that northern tourist interests would no longer seek to fraternise with their southern non-combatant brothers, but that was certainly not the case. All the annual functions of the ITA and the IHF up to the end of the war were attended by representatives of the northern tourist association and its hotel association. Rosemary Owens, manageress of the Union hotel in Belfast, was one of the few northerners to join the southern association. She also became a member of the IHF when it was set up, and became vice-chairman of that organisation in 1940. Walter McCleary, president of the Northern Ireland Hotel Association, was a regular guest, as was Fred Storey, chairman of the UTDA.

In the face of restricted travel between Great Britain and Northern Ireland during the war, the UTDA concentrated on internal tourist traffic and visitors from the Free State.[8] A new range of literature was produced for Ulster-based troops, including a special publication for the Americans, and presentations were held in barracks around the province. Another innovation was the circulation of colour posters showing Ulster's scenic views to army units and to air-raid shelters in London, to keep the province in the minds of potential post-war visitors. At the same time, the government discouraged travel because they wanted people to save their money for the war effort. With food and clothing rationed, excursions were the thing, and people went to traditional resorts.[9] However, many people also went to the South on holidays and to obtain commodities like ham and tinned fruit that were unavailable in the North.

By 1942 the UTDA was planning for Ulster's post-war traffic, and the Ministry of Home Affairs set up a Planning Advisory Board for Northern Ireland with a tourist committee headed by Storey. Naturally, the committee's suggestions included the establishment of a statutory tourist organisation, and this was acknowledged by Sir Basil Brooke, prime minister of Northern Ireland, at the association's AGM in 1945, when he pledged government support and assistance.[10] The end of hostilities brought problems, as all forms of transportation had been adversely affected by the war; there were severe food shortages, and a sharp decline in members' and associates' contributions. To make things worse, the government withdrew its pound-for-pound backing and restricted its grant to a flat £2,000. However, the government was aware of the need to give a cohesive direction to tourist development, and the Northern Ireland Tourist Board was finally established under the Development of Tourism Traffic Act in 1948.

The board was an autonomous body empowered to inspect, register and grade accommodation, and to provide grant aid to local authorities and private enterprise wishing to invest in tourism development. Its functions were to promote Ulster as a distinct holiday destination; to co-operate with hoteliers, guest-house owners and caterers in the expansion and improvement of accommodation and standards; to inspect and register all catering establishments; to conduct tourist research and make proposals for the better marketing of Northern Ireland tourism; and to investigate, stimulate and co-operate with local authorities, government agencies, carriers and tourist developers to determine how suitable new facilities and attractions and services should be developed to create a broader and more lucrative tourist infrastructure. As the rest of the United Kingdom did not possess these powers until 1969, it can be taken as a measure of the view taken by the Northern Ireland and British governments of the opportunity presented by tourism to bolster the economy in post-war Ulster. The NITB was directly responsible to the Minister of Commerce, who appointed a chairman and members for four-year terms of office from a cross-section of travel, catering, business and civic interests. The board in turn appointed a general manager and other staff to implement the policies devised to fulfil the board's remit. These included organising the industry to afford maximum employment and stimulation of trade, catering not only for the well-to-do but also for the millions of newcomers on holidays with pay, and ensuring that overseas tourists would return to their own countries as ambassadors of goodwill.[11] The chairman of the new body was J. Nelson McMillen and the board included Fred Storey of the UTDA and Professor E. Estyn Evans. As the body initially had no staff and no accommodation, temporary officials and accommodation were provided by the Ministry for Commerce for the first five months. Staffing levels were modest, with around a dozen employees, relatively small for the amount of work being done at home and abroad.

A system of co-ordination and amalgamation was agreed with the UTDA, in order to maintain the goodwill, voluntary assistance and experience of that body. Covering a trial period of one year, it gave the association an opportunity to discuss suggestions for projects that the board might undertake, and the association effectively became the Advertising Committee and 'parliament' of the industry, with the board providing executive authority and personnel.[12] Offices were obtained at Royal Avenue in Belfast, though these soon proved inadequate for the purpose of administering a complex state organisation and providing a tourist information centre. The staff of the

UTDA was subsumed into the board, and C.W. Magill, its organising secretary, was appointed secretary to the NITB in June 1948 and promoted to general manager in January 1949. Clerical staff and 'outside representatives' were engaged on a probationary basis. Using reports from the UTDA's monthly meetings with local authorities, trade and voluntary organisations and private individuals interested in tourist development, the board hoped to create a two-way traffic of information and suggestions upon which a coherent development policy could be formulated. The board's income was fixed at £25,000 per annum, and it was empowered to recommend the provision of loans to local authorities towards the cost of tourist amenities, and also for the provision and improvement of accommodation.[13] Fred Storey was appointed chairman of the Finance Committee with responsibility for applications for grants and loans to catering establishments. The main emphasis of the NITB's work in the early years was promotion within the UK, while promotion to international markets was done by the British Travel Association.

In its first year of operation grants paid included those to the Ulster Motor Cycle Club for 'starting' money for foreign competitors in the Grand Prix de Europe; a contribution towards the cost of entertaining delegates to the International Geological Congress and payment to the Travel Association of Great Britain and Northern Ireland for overseas publicity. Applications approved for payment in 1949 included that to Estyn Evans for expenses incurred during a lecture tour of North American on behalf of the NITB; another to the Ulster Angling Federation for restocking Ulster rivers; and one to the Belfast and District Trade Union Congress towards the cost of a sightseeing excursion for delegates to the Irish Trades Union Congress. Discussions were held with local authorities in Cushendall, Newcastle, Warrenpoint and Larne on the provision of swimming pools, promenades and tennis courts, and with Antrim County Council on the possibility of developing a road racing circuit. In a rather outmoded form of administration, committees were formed to deal with advertising, transport and registration.

Preparation for the registration of accommodation providers proved an onerous task for the board, as its limited staff had to evaluate thousands of applications. Over 3,500 calls were made, as the first year was spent educating caterers in their legal obligations under the 1948 act, and 1,702 premises were eventually registered, netting a sum of £5,574 collected as a levy by the board and passed to the Treasury in the form of stamp duty. A catering education scheme was also mooted at this point, with the proviso that it should be co-ordinated between the board, the industry and the Ministries of Education and Labour.[14] At the same time, close collaboration with the Building Control division of the Ministry of Finance was established by the board to guarantee that all requests for building licences from catering establishments and tourist organisations were referred to the board for examination, with fifty-six permits being issued for building improvements during the year. Applications ranged from hoteliers to proprietors of small cafés, the bulk being owners of boarding-houses. However, despite publicising the availability of loans under Section 33 of the act, few applications were received and only one was approved, but it was anticipated that activity would increase rapidly as capital expenditure became easier and raw materials became available. Food rationing was seen as the greatest obstruction in wooing prospective visitors: 'While caterers suffer serious restrictions in Northern Ireland, as part of the United Kingdom, in the type, variety and quantity of food which can be provided, competitive holiday areas must have a prime appeal to British travellers.' This was a veiled reference to the tourism boom in the southern part of the island, stimulated by reports of plentiful supplies of food and drink. The effectiveness of advertising was another concern for the fledgling body, requiring as it did the co-operation of tourist authorities and individual establishments.[15]

Over the next three years the bulk of the board's expenditure was on publicity. Out of its income of £25,000, grants were made available each year to the tune of £10,000, split 4:1 between the British Travel and Holidays Association and the UDTA, with the latter body also expending its own funds on publicity. A representative was installed in the Ulster Office in London to assist intending tourists, and inspectors were sent to organise publicity in Scotland, northern England and the Republic during the winter months, establishing connections with agents and holiday organisers, clubs and organisations, distributing literature, giving talks and slide shows and showing films as they became available. Meanwhile, a group of coastal hotels and the Ulster Transport Authority, in collaboration with local authorities and shipping companies, developed a thriving tour business, based on Bangor, Whitehead, Larne, Ballycastle and Portrush. In addition, useful 'feature programmes' on the province were broadcast by the BBC. A photographic library was established, and the board co-operated with the Ministry of Education and the County Antrim Technical Education Committee in the establishment of a catering college at Portrush in 1950.

However, difficulties in obtaining realistic statistics continued to present problems. It was estimated that the gross revenue from tourism was between £6 million and £10 million in 1951–52, and not less than £10 million in 1952–53, but such vague figures could not help in planning future development, and this uncertainty was mirrored in the lack of information on visitor numbers, with no attempt being made to present even a conjectural figure. Initially, registration of premises lagged behind supposed eligibility, but 2,030 registered by 1952, when practically full registration was achieved.[16] No grading was considered possible due to continuing materials shortages and difficulties with major capital expenditure. Improvements to 303 existing premises were estimated to have cost £537,080, while thirty-eight loans amounting to a figure in excess of £60,000 were sanctioned between 1951 and 1953. Grants to local authorities towards the capital cost of facility improvement schemes came to £71,000 during this period, and funds were also advanced for the provision of entertainment and sporting events. An accommodation and information service was provided in connection with the Festival of Britain in Belfast, but difficulties with cross-channel transport peaking in July and August continued, with twice the average monthly traffic obtaining in those months, especially after the lifting of travel restrictions in 1952. The shipping service after the war was inadequate by any standards, using ships that had seen war service and been refurbished. Packaged coach tours were the holiday of choice for the majority of British visitors at this time, driven by Northern Ireland tour operators who spent six months each year seeking business throughout Scotland and a wide area of England. At the same time, British operators were also including the North in tours of England, Scotland or 'Eire', thus ensuring additional publicity in these companies' publications. In the mid-1950s, the Belfast Steamship Company was bringing in upwards of 2,000 passengers daily on each of its services from Glasgow, Ardrossan, Liverpool and Heysham during the summer period, with a consequent logistical problem of their dispersal.[17] They were staggered to arrive over Thursday, Friday and Saturday to avoid having everybody travelling on the one night. Another complicating factor was through-traffic to the Republic, with people *en route* to Donegal or Cavan or peripheral border areas as opposed to visiting Northern Ireland.

By 1954 Robert J. Frizell was general manager of the tourist board, which was receiving a government grant of £60,000, along with an extra £5,000 for international motor racing at the Dundrod circuit.[18] Frizell took a paternalistic attitude towards his staff, and after he hired Robert Blair to work in the despatch department in 1959, he ordered him to attend night school in order to better himself. Blair later expressed an interest in photography, and ended up attending the College of Art in Belfast for four years at the NITB's expense, after which he worked as a photographer for the board for almost four decades.[19] As in the South, most of the people who were employed in the tourist board regarded it as a job for life, and dedicated their lives to it.

In 1954 the bureaucratic machinery delayed grants to local authorities significantly and the board sought the simplification of this process in order to hasten the work of bringing resort areas 'up to a standard which will make them really competitive with other areas', presumably south of the border. It was also hoped to initiate an international publicity campaign directly controlled by the board, as opposed to that provided by BTHA, which promoted the United Kingdom as a whole. Conference traffic was sought but was hampered by the dearth of suitable accommodation in Belfast, the favourite destination. As air traffic increased, the introduction of a 'de luxe' air service by Viscount aircraft in November 1953 was seen as a step in the right direction.

Rather belatedly, a realisation of the value of tourist traffic in enhancing the prestige of a country was dawning and the attitude of successive Westminster governments was changing. With constant communication between the voluntary organisations north and south of the border in Ireland during the war years, northerners were familiar with what was a much more structured and coherent model of development in the Republic than that pertaining in the United Kingdom, where there was still no statutory body to organise the industry on a nationwide basis. Although the system of government grant to the NITB changed from a fixed sum of £25,000 per annum in 1952 to an amount based on detailed annual estimates submitted by the board, by 1955 this had only increased to £65,000. At the same time, with the realisation of changes in holiday patterns, the board was proposing an alteration in the shape, type and size of accommodation formerly designed to cater for whole families, to make provision for an increasing number of motoring visitors. It was stressed that advertising policy should emphasise that which was unique in Ulster, and it was also felt that the erroneous impression of endemic bad weather needed to be countered vigorously. Cultural and 'almost aesthetic' special interests such as bird-watching, archaeology, folklore, folk-dancing and folk music were to be exploited, as were hiking and climbing, coarse fishing and the study of agricultural methods.[20] There is something a little quaint about the idea of holidaymakers from industrial Britain being attracted by the possibility of studying agricultural methods. On the accommodation and catering front, the news was not good, with a drop of seventy-three in the number of premises. Loan facilities for improvements were not being availed of, because the terms of the loans were not sufficiently attractive and those premises that did carry out alterations were immediately subject to revaluation and faced with increased rates in addition to the capital expenditure that they had incurred. However, on the publicity front the governor of Northern Ireland contributed by giving lectures and film presentations overseas, and the tour of Australia and New Zealand by the prime minister, Lord Brookeborough, was seen as being of immense value in raising the profile of the province there. A start was made on filmmaking with the board's production of *The Northern Ireland Coast* and *Letter from Northern Ireland*, a BTHA production, being completed in 1955. A stand was taken at the Dublin Horse Show in co-operation with the Ulster Transport Authority and the Great Northern Railway, and proved successful, 'although only limited space was available in one of the secondary halls'. The lack of adequate signposting was lamented, as the board was under the impression that 'the twenty-six Southern Counties of Ireland have been elaborately equipped'. Unlike the ITB, the northern body was not empowered to erect either road signs or those directing tourists to ancient monuments, and this was seen as an enormous deterrent to the growing number of motoring visitors from Britain and 'Southern Ireland'. As in the South, there was constant dissatisfaction with the dearth of qualified catering staff. Education and training was seen as the 'Cinderella' in the field of general education for the vast number of young people 'who finally go to Britain or overseas'. Transport improvements were to be seen in the inauguration of several new air routes and new ships on sea routes, along with improved facilities at ferry terminals, but the need for new railway rolling stock was paramount.

A glance at a 1954 publication, *Northern Ireland Gives a Great Welcome*, gives a flavour of the type of publicity emanating from the tourist bodies there. A flamboyant and highly coloured front cover features a virile Finn Mac Coul (sic), while the back cover shows transport routes from the United Kingdom but none from the Republic. Only the northern portion of the island is visible on the map.[21] The 'Introduction to Northern Ireland' is at pains to explain the political reality of a divided Ireland, pointing out that although the province of Ulster comprised nine counties, that traditional name had now become synonymous with the self-governing

144

six-county area created by the 1920 Government of Ireland Act and that the three most important facts for the tourist to remember in those days of austerity were:

> There are no customs barriers between Britain and Ulster; you need no passport or permit for your journey, and there are no currency restrictions – you can take as much money as you like to Ulster! It is part of Great Britain, and Sir Winston Churchill made this perfectly clear when, paying tribute to Ulster's part in the Second World War, he said: 'But for the loyalty of Northern Ireland we should have been confronted with slavery and death, and the light which now shines so strongly throughout the world would have been quenched.'[22]

These words were to reappear repeatedly in northern tourist publications, much to the chagrin of Bord Fáilte, and were a source of some confrontation between the two bodies.[23]

In 1956 an analysis of the tourist trade concluded that England remained the main source of business, as Ulster's geographical situation outside the orbit of international tourist traffic, due to not being a terminal point of transatlantic air and shipping services, was an obvious deterrent. About 30,000 North Americans were estimated to pass through Ulster – 'rather swiftly' – every year, and there was a growing interest in historical features, family origins and other research studies. Visitors from the British Commonwealth were apt to stay longer, and travel more widely, while 'foreign' and Asiatic visitors were more specialised, with the majority having academic and educational motives linked with holiday enjoyment. Plans were being mooted for an Ulster folk museum and a planetarium at Armagh, together with an annual Ulster Festival embracing the whole province. A report on the hotel situation throughout Ulster was commissioned by the board in collaboration with the Ulster Development Council and was presented to the government. Passenger numbers were up 44 per cent to 62,000, and the drive to extend the season saw June traffic up 27 per cent and September up 7 per cent on the previous year. A quirky method of gauging the number of international visitors was the evidence of clothing 'obviously from other countries and the sound of foreign languages, noticeable chiefly in Belfast'.[24] The issue of coach tours was a fraught one in the late 1950s, as British coaches were still prohibited from entering Northern Ireland, although by this stage they operated with comparative freedom in the Republic, where they had provided an enormous boost to the tourist trade. British operators had to hire Ulster Transport Authority vehicles, while a

145

reciprocal arrangement north and south of the border permitted coaches from each part of the island to function in the other's territory.[25]

The following year was a bad one for Irish tourism generally, as Irish Republican Army terrorist activity on the border was given worldwide publicity and also stopped much movement between the North and the South. In the North, improvements by caterers and holiday schemes were either deferred or prohibited by the British credit squeeze, while the Suez Crisis leading to petrol restrictions almost killed early season bookings for motoring traffic.[26] The ratio of air-to-sea traffic increased from 6 per cent in 1948 to 18 per cent in 1957, while passenger arrivals increased by 80 per cent in that time. In 1958 the first post-war direct link with North America was provided from Belfast via Glasgow and Reykjavik to New York, but the major deficiencies of Nutt's Corner airport were deplored and the NITB pressed for a city air terminal. An Ulster Festival featuring cultural events got local support and external publicity in 1957 but did not warrant continuation in 1958, although the NITB considered that a worthwhile event of special 'Ulster' significance could succeed. Meanwhile, it was conferring with county, rural and government departments on the problem of better access to the Giant's Causeway, and its conclusion was that this, the major tourist attraction in Northern Ireland, should be acquired in the national interest and developed to meet the needs of the modern tourist.[27] It was felt that a scheme involving heavy capital expenditure from central funds was necessary: 'the modern tourist seeks at this point transport and provisions for his comfort similar to that which he finds at other world famous tourist venues. Today the Causeway is in almost the same condition as when it was first opened to the public.'

Under the Food and Drugs (Northern Ireland) Act of 1958, government policy on food hygiene was outlined, but the NITB felt that the achievement of these standards demanded a much larger expenditure than the catering industry could yet afford: 'It must be evolved slowly by encouragement, example and a generous provision of every possible form of assistance and advice.'[28] The board also reported that loan facilities on offer had received a very poor response, with hoteliers complaining that they did not compare favourably with special facilities provided in other countries. Accommodation continued to be a problem in Belfast and other parts of the North, where no hotels or restaurants existed. Amendment of the licensing laws, while providing for uniformity of hours, did nothing to address the complaints of tourists, 'particularly those who seek refreshment in licensed premises on

Sundays'. On the question of publicity, in the absence of a very considerable special grant-in-aid, a direct sales campaign in overseas markets was not feasible.

The 1960s saw a new era develop in Northern Ireland tourism as the subject came up for intensive discussion in the House of Commons, where it was accepted that tourism should be recognised as an industry. An investigation of the board's affairs was undertaken by the Organisation and Methods division of the Ministry of Finance, comprising a scientific examination of the industry and its potential, and the attending problems of the extension of the holiday season, staggering of holidays and lengthening of the period of 'summer time'. Despite the dislocation of internal road transport and shipping services by strikes in July and August, British coaches appeared for the first time on northern roads, along with the first pleasure boat on the Erne for many generations.[29] However, a realistic appraisal of the shortcomings of the tourist offering in the province was articulated in 1961: 'the climate, a shortage of capital, the absence of a strong catering and hotel management tradition, and Ulster's position on the perimeter of the European tourist area, are all handicaps which the province is slowly overcoming'.[30] At the same time, attempts to bolster local interest in tourism development could be disappointing. Robert Blair manned a one-day public meeting organised by the board in Enniskillen town hall in 1962, complete with film and brochures, but virtually nobody came, and local people laughed at the idea of Fermanagh as a tourist destination.[31] The story was different in Bangor, Co. Down, where the borough council employed three tourism officers responsible for promotional activities, special events and advertising. Major Jock Affleck began working for the council in 1951, at a time when the majority of visitors came during the traditional Glasgow fair, the last fortnight in July, and the Lancashire wakes, the week's holiday allowed to workers in the industrial towns there. As that traffic declined in the 1960s, Affleck promoted Bangor in Dublin, with the help of Bord Fáilte personnel there, mounting exhibitions in Brown Thomas's department store and raising the amount of Irish currency in circulation in Bangor by over 30 per cent.[32] However, this sort of collaboration went against the political grain at the time, so he had to be very discreet. His assessment of general promotion at the time was that there was no clearly defined tourism product being sold, with the UTDA thinking that baking soda bread and giving a good breakfast would bring the visitors in, while the NITB was visualising jumbo jets decanting 500 tourists on a regular basis, both of which were a long way from reality: 'Tourism changed because you had a generation that was not prepared to sit on a cold beach in semi-arctic conditions.'

In 1963 the board appointed Max Beeton, brother of the famous designer Cecil Beeton, as its representative in Dublin. At the same time, the Belfast Regional Survey published in the Matthew report of 1963 contained many propositions for the tourist industry, and the NITB hoped that the needs of the tourist, whether Ulster resident or visitor, would be catered for in planning being undertaken for reconstruction, improvement and preservation.[33] In the transport field, passenger shipping plans for the future were concentrated on the car, which appeared to be defining and shaping the siting, type, quality and capacity of catering services, hotel accommodation and the many supplementary tourist facilities which motorists required.[34] As the Caravan Act began to function in 1964, county councils commenced licensing and certifying sites, and thirty-seven caravan parks and several campsites were approved. In 1965 the development of a planetarium at Armagh was under way, and its advent under the direction of Patrick Moore was regarded as a most valuable tourist attraction.

By 1966 it was evident that enormous changes were taking place in the holiday and recreation fields. Recent reports on leisure and the countryside showed that space and recreation would be at a premium in Britain by the following decade:

> In Britain today 44 per cent of the population is under thirty, and by 1980 the proportion will be up to 47 per cent. Active holidays are increasingly being demanded. As increasing affluence brings greater leisure, the number of people who can afford two holidays a year will grow, and it may become customary to take half somewhere in the sun, and the remainder as a contrast following some recreational pursuits in which our island excels.[35]

Changing tourist habits included the increase of motoring holidays, with visitors not staying more than two or three days in one place; the decline in popularity of the traditional seaside holiday; the growing tendency of visitors to regard Ireland as a geographical unit, made easier with the removal of cross-border restrictions on private cars; the growing demand for high standards of accommodation; the increased interest in particular activities such as walking, cruising, fishing, golf; a greater demand for caravan sites and campsites and a mounting appreciation of open- air amenities and special attractions, such as forest parks and the Ulster Folk Museum.

The shortage of adequate funds for publicity and marketing was a constant headache for the NITB. Resulting from the recommendations in the Hall report on the economy of Northern Ireland of 1962 being accepted by the government, the board was given greater resources for the extension of its publicity programme. One immediate and novel result was the 'Ulster Cavalcade', a team of tourism and transport officials together with Ulster singers and dancers who toured Britain on co-ordinated tourist drives in 1963 and 1964. This involved press advertising, travel trade displays and public exhibitions, film shows and musical concerts. It travelled in a convoy of decorated vehicles from Stranraer to Carlisle to London and back, covering a population area of 27 million people. In 1963 over 21,000 attended entertainments and information shows and the following year the campaign was extended to the Clyde valley in Scotland. However, there were those at Stormont who looked askance at this scheme, as Irish traditional music and dance were perceived as nationalist culture. Catholic schools included Irish cultural traditions in their education while state schools and Protestant schools did not, so they became identified with nationalists, and thus politicised and polarised, and those in power took no pride or interest in them. Similarly, there were problems about promoting Londonderry, as the political establishment there consisted mainly of unionists, who regarded Gaelic culture as belonging to the Catholic population, thereby rendering them averse to promoting it.[36] In any case, the cavalcade lasted only two years and while the publicity acquired through press, television, radio and travel interests was effective, the advertising policy of the board, based on a small-space repetitive technique to create literature requests, generated unavoidable comparisons with the methods used by rival areas, presumably those of the Republic: 'Northern Ireland advertisements are not so prominent as others, and represent approximately ten per cent of a rival budget investment.'[37]

In 1965 the board's first press officer, Desmond McGimpsey, was appointed to handle public relations and liaise with the press, television, radio, travel writers and publishing channels. He was a journalist who had worked in Belfast and London and would be responsible for some interesting initiatives during his years with the NITB.[38] Another development was that of 'Ulster Weeks' in Britain, during which northern commercial and tourism interests invaded a specific city or town for a week to promote Ulster goods and tourism, while also dispelling ignorance about Northern Ireland in other parts of the UK. Terence O'Neill, the prime minister, travelled to the town in question to launch the trade week each year, beginning with Nottingham in 1964. The *Belfast Telegraph* reported that 'shops all over Nottingham had signs proclaiming the event, and Ulster flags were on display in all shops. Captain O'Neill made a tour of local shops, and was interviewed on television. Thousands of Nottingham people turned out to see the Premier.'[39] In the USA and Canada, promotional work for a project on the ancestral homes of American presidents in Ulster was begun by the Marquis of Hamilton, who carried out a number of press, radio and television engagements arranged by the NITB. At the same time, the Belfast Festival at Queen's, the brainchild of an Englishman called Michael Emerson, was inaugurated, with Desmond McGimpsey handling all publicity and public relations, and introducing the *Guardian* journalist Mary Holland, who later became a strong supporter of the nationalist population, to the province.[40]

However, the most dramatic development in 1965 was the initiation of collaboration with Bord Fáilte. From the time that Seán Lemass became taoiseach in 1959, cross-border co-operation with Northern Ireland was one of his priorities. In his 1959 speech on the estimates for his department, he spoke of the need for co-operation with the North and mentioned tourism as a suitable vehicle.[41] The Minister for Transport and Power, Erskine Childers, was equally keen, seeing co-operation with the NITB as a means of securing the collaboration of BTHA for worldwide publicity. However, an approach to Lord Mabane, chairman of that organisation, to visit Dublin in August 1962 was referred to the NITB, and Robert Frizell replied: 'We have, and hope to maintain, the friendliest possible relations [with the ITB], but joint promotion in overseas markets is not even under consideration at this time.' It seemed that political considerations overruled practical proposals, and Thekla Beere, Secretary of the Department of Transport and Power, noted that this attitude was due to the personal prejudices of a few members of the northern tourist board.[42] The 1962 NITB annual report was anxious to make the position clear. While expressing 'the most cordial and friendly relationship and joint consultation on matters of mutual interest' with Bord Fáilte, it added a caveat on the subject of joint promotion: 'The Board is aware of opinions expressed in favour of joint all-Ireland promotion, but believes that in Northern Ireland this is not entirely a matter for the Board. It must be remembered that Ulster has its own special traditional pattern of tourist trade and is in competition with other areas of the UK to win British visitors.'[43] Childers continued to press for some form of co-operation, and in 1964 T.J. O'Driscoll of Bord Fáilte called for

cross-border tourism co-operation, seemingly to no avail. However, later that year Brian Faulkner, the northern Minister for Commerce, indicated that he would be prepared to meet Jack Lynch, the Republic's Minister for Industry and Commerce, to discuss cross-border trade, and on 14 January 1967 the first meeting of the northern and southern prime ministers took place at Stormont, with Lemass looking specifically for the abolition of barriers to tourism.[44]

Following this meeting and those of Faulkner and Childers on 4 February 1965, discussions between the NITB and Bord Fáilte took place in Dublin in May. These were the first official meetings of the two tourism bodies and many facets of joint co-operation were discussed. Capital schemes on or near the border in which both bodies were involved were the subject of research, and joint publicity between local tourism bodies was also contemplated.[45] Regular conferences were held during the year between the tourist organisations of Fermanagh and adjacent Bord Fáilte regions, and surveys of potential joint developments carried out. A major initiative was the collaboration of the two boards in the organisation of a conducted visit of the British Broadcasting Corporation's most popular radio show, 'The Archers', around the entire island. It arose initially from a suggestion by the Guinness brewery in Dublin, and Northern Ireland's participation in it was due to collaboration between Desmond McGimpsey, who participated in the programme, and Aidan O'Hanlon, his counterpart in Bord Fáilte.[46]

6.2
T.J. O'Driscoll, Director-General of Bord Fáilte; W.L. Stephens, Chairman of the Northern Ireland Tourist Board; Brendan O'Regan, Chairman of Bord Fáilte and R.J. Frizell, General Manager of the Northern Ireland Tourist Board, at the first joint discussions on cross-border collaboration in Dublin in May 1965.

6.3
Brendan O'Regan,
Chairman of Bord
Fáilte; Brian
Faulkner, Northern
Ireland Minister of
Commerce; Lord
Geddes, Chairman
of the British Travel
Association and
W.L. Stephens,
Chairman of the
Northern Ireland
Tourist Board, at a
meeting in Belfast in
1968. *Courtesy of the
Northern Ireland
Tourist Board.*

This unusual publicity project also included the co-operation of Radio Éireann, the Farmers' Union and the Ministry of Agriculture. Discussions continued throughout 1966 on closer collaboration between the two bodies on the production of a joint folder prepared by Bord Fáilte, the NITB and BTHA for distribution in North America. There were some difficulties in finding a formula agreeable to all, especially with regard to the representation of the border on maps and the naming of the two states, but with major obstacles overcome, the folder was set to appear in 1967.[47] Consultation on the co-ordination of all-Ireland promotional touring parties also took place, along with discussions on further publicity material for the whole island, with BTHA as the third partner. On the technical side, there was much exchange of information, particularly with regard to hotel grading, and co-operation was extended in research work, information services and press and public relations. The Northwest and Midland Regional Tourism Organisations in the Republic were keenly interested in an Erne–Shannon canal link for pleasure boats, and the airport at St Angelo in County Fermanagh, with much discussion of both taking place in 1967. On 11 December 1967 Jack Lynch, Lemass's successor, travelled to meet O'Neill in Belfast. They and their officials agreed that the second joint promotional folder needed to be better than the first, as it had been described in Dublin as 'a real hash – Northern Ireland encroaches on Donegal! The Mountains of Mourne are everywhere except in their right place.'[48] Another significant initiative was the

152

6.4
A party from
Northern Ireland,
led by Sir William
Geddis, Lord Mayor
of Belfast, setting
off on the inaugural
Aer Lingus direct
flight from Belfast
to New York in
1968. *Courtesy of the
Northern Ireland
Tourist Board.*

establishment of a joint information point on the border between
Newry and Dundalk for the 1969 season.[49]

Meanwhile, a reorganisation of the tourist board, including the
establishment of development and marketing divisions, was completed in 1968. The Development Divison, under manager I.M.
Williams, initiated tourist schemes by local authorities, extension of
accommodation and catering, and collaboration with local tourist
development associations. The marketing division, under John H.
Quinn, was responsible for co-ordinating promotional campaigns,
exhibitions, package holidays, educational visits, research, advertising and publicity. Ernest Sandford, an experienced journalist, was
appointed publicity officer, responsible for publicity, advertising,
literature, presentation and supervision of information services.[50]
That year, the long hot summer and restricted foreign currency
allowances for British holidaymakers was good for Northern
Ireland, but motorists complained about the signposting, which
was inadequate and confusing, and this was considerably strengthened when the motoring correspondents of reputable British
national newspapers added their weight. The NITB called on the
Ministry of Development and other bodies responsible for signs to
think more imaginatively about them, as their greatest weakness
seemed to be a lack of co-ordination and consistency: 'We appear
to think that our visitors have swotted up on their Ulster geography before they come here, and can therefore decipher at a glance
abbreviations such as C'burn and P'down.'

By 1969 the violence on Northern Ireland streets was already affecting visitor numbers, and John Williams, deputy general manager of the NITB, explained on a visit to London that tourism there had been 'badly mauled by disturbances in recent weeks' and that they would be lucky to achieve the same revenue, £28.5 million, as they had in 1968.[51] Nevertheless, collaboration continued with the ITB and BTHA to sell Ireland as a single holiday unit to overseas visitors, and Desmond McGimpsey undertook an extensive public relations tour of Canada with the aim of presenting events in Ulster in perspective. An unusual experiment was the introduction of twelve 'personality girls' on Irish Sea ferries, a co-operative venture with the shipping companies: 'These Ulster girls, most of whom were graduates or university students, were specially chosen for personality – their intelligence and good looks spoke well for our young women in general.'[52] The NITB also co-operated in the setting up of the first-ever fleadh ceol in west Belfast in 1969. Desmond McGimpsey worked with Paddy Devlin of the Northern Ireland Labour Party on publicity and public relations for the event, which was designed to decrease tension in the area, and received a mention in the House of Commons for his work.[53] The three tourist boards met in Dublin in July 1969 to report on how each had benefited from four years of collaboration, and agreed to extend their joint promotion to Australia. The NITB felt that Northern Ireland was now less isolated on the world scene owing to this close collaboration, benefiting from the joint selling of holidays by BTHA and Bord Fáilte at major international promotions, and their treatment of Ireland as one holiday country in their overseas offices. Results could be seen in groups of international travel agents coming to both parts of the island on briefing tours and overseas parties of visitors crossing the border.

The year 1970 marked many new departures in tourism development in Northern Ireland. A new chief executive, Robert C.C. Hall, was appointed and the board was reduced from eleven to seven members. Hall came from the oil industry and was not popular within the industry because of his demanding approach.[54] He wanted to break away from BTHA and sell Northern Ireland on a worldwide scale independently, and he also wanted to do away with the UTDA. A Research and Planning Department was created, reporting directly to Hall and acting in an advisory capacity to all the other departments. A major priority for the department was to develop longer-term economic planning, and to collect and collate data necessary for the preparation of a five-year plan during 1971. A full programme of research was devised to operate in 1971, the main objective being to establish a continuous and comprehensive knowledge of visitors to Northern Ireland. A study was undertaken of the viability of existing hire cruiser operations and prospects for expansion, along with another into the economic conditions necessary for establishing a fleet of sea angling boats suitable for the development of package holidays, and of possible locations for marina development. A major analysis of the role of financial incentive schemes in the development of accommodation was commissioned. The feasibility of establishing a computerised accommodation reservation system for the province was examined, and market research continued on the demand for camping and caravan holidays. Surveys of tourist habits in the Republic and within the province were also commissioned and a considerable amount of research material was obtained from Bord Fáilte and BTHA.[55]

However, the tourist board felt that certain problems persisted in negating their efforts. Northern Ireland was receiving continuous and extremely bad publicity abroad as a result of civil disturbances, often exaggerated by foreign news media. The board attempted to present a balanced picture by inviting overseas journalists and travel trade executives to see for themselves that outside of small areas in Belfast and Londonderry, Ulster was mainly peaceful, and had many superb attractions. In addition, there was considerable misunderstanding in Northern Ireland about tourism and its vital contribution to employment and the economy of the province. Lastly, both government and private investment in Ulster's tourism had been running at a relatively low level historically compared both to revenues earned and the intensive efforts being mounted by most other developed countries of the world. Nevertheless, it held the view that with the reorganisation and modernisation process being undertaken, tourist revenue of £35 million, with 35,000 people employed in the industry, was not an unreasonable target for 1975. The five-year plan to run from 1972 to 1977 concentrated on broad strategies and established long-term estimates of investment, income, visitor numbers, holiday demands and leisure trends: 'This economic blueprint must now be backed up by a physical plan incorporating everything from isolated picnic tables to the multi-purpose recreation complex.'[56] In previous collaboration with the Ministry of Development, the board's long-term views had been represented in the various area plans prepared for the sub-regions of Northern Ireland. The five-year plan would seek to develop and co-ordinate the tourist content of each area plan. During 1971, provision was also made to expand development staff so that the board would be able to assume a leading role in this planning for the future.[57]

With civil disturbances escalating over the course of the 1970s, Northern Ireland continued to be difficult to sell as a holiday destination, conference business suffered and many organisations postponed or discarded plans for public entertainments. By 1973 no major advertising was being undertaken, as marketing activity concentrated on maintaining contact with the travel trade, tour operators and transport companies. A new home holidays scheme was launched in co-operation with the Northern Ireland Hotels and Caterers Association at a cost of £25,000. It appeared to be successful: £95 million was spent by Northern Ireland people on home holidays, despite the sharp increase in cheap holidays to Spain.[58] Another original scheme in 1974 consisted of the board's marketing staff approaching major industrial companies with large workforces in Northern Ireland and suggesting that social and sport committees should invite groups from their sister plants in Britain to visit Northern Ireland for active holiday weekends. It was estimated that about 1,000 bed nights were sold as a result.[59]

In 1975 there were signs of increasing traffic from continental Europe, and the NITB felt that it was 'one of very few agencies which continues to work constantly to present some balance to the popular picture of Northern Ireland – bombs, bullets and smoking ruins'. It saw this activity as corporate public relations work on behalf of the province, with the principal task being to convince Ulster people that they had a beautiful country that was attractive to foreigners and to convince foreigners that it was not in a state of civil war.[60] With civil disturbances wreaking havoc on the streets of the province, in 1975 it was decided that the five-year plan would be pushed back to 1980, with roughly the same target of 1.1 million tourists. It was calculated that it would take four years from the time civil normality was restored to increase the accommodation stock by 3,000 bedrooms and build up catering facilities.[61]

By 1978 the tourist board was optimistic about future prospects. A special study undertaken by the University of Surrey, the foremost academic institution in the UK specialising in tourism, had concluded that of all the nationally significant economic options open to the UK, none offered a greater potential contribution than the planned development of tourism services, which would expand the wealth-creating sectors of the community, generate employment, create growth in real personal disposable incomes and conserve the natural and physical environment. The British prime minister, James Callaghan, opening the Brighton Conference

Exhibition Centre, reflected that a record number of over ten million overseas visitors to the UK in 1976 brought something like £2,000 million, while British holidaymakers spent another £2,200 million, making £4 billion altogether. He estimated that there were 1.5 million jobs dependent on tourism, or industries and services closely connected with it, but pointed out that the real need was for professionalism in the industry.

His words had more relevance in Northern Ireland than in other parts of the UK, as it had the highest unemployment rates and a comparatively low level of tourism. For the first time since 1969, as terrorist violence in Ulster declined, tourism figures improved significantly, with the number of visitors up 12 per cent on 1976 and tourist spending up 20 per cent, far in excess of inflation rates. However, marketing was still difficult, though in 1977 the board decided to expand its operations in North America, while intensifying efforts to develop a first-class US heritage trail. Research in the Republic showed that despite substantial improvements in the civil situation, a very large proportion of people there were reluctant to consider a holiday in the North. Meanwhile, the NITB put its faith in press visits as one of the most important and effective means of making people aware that Northern Ireland was a beautiful, friendly country, with civil violence really no greater than in many other countries of the world! A change was also agreed with BTHA, placing that relationship on a commercial basis, with the board paying for a range of specific services, and putting its own area managers for North America and Europe in BTHA offices in New York and Frankfurt respectively.[62] In 1978 Northern Ireland had its best visitor figures for many years, with a 27 per cent increase generating a 34 per cent increase in revenue, but the year ended with other problems looming, such as the energy crisis that had already had a depressing effect upon tourism in the Republic. Publicity and marketing efforts continued, as the 1980s showed every sign of continuing the violent trends of the 1970s. Robert Hall moved the NITB into twelfth-floor offices at River House in Belfast to lessen the threat of terrorist action against the organisation, and also felt that he personally was a target.[63] A 3 per cent fall in business in 1980 was due to diverse factors such as the exchange rate between the pound sterling and the Irish punt and the worldwide recession that hit all tourist travel to Europe. Moreover, home holidays were out of favour and people found it cheaper to go South: 'It was brought home to us this year that many Northern Ireland people do not feel they are 'on holiday' unless they have got on a boat, caught a plane or crossed a border.'[64] The following year a renewal of unfavourable publicity from the IRA hunger strike at the Maze prison in late spring and early summer was a severe setback, made worse by a still deepening recession.[65] The 1981 annual report of the NITB remarked that a map in its conference room was dotted with green pins marking individual places where good publicity followed a visit by a local travel journalist to Northern Ireland, and the comment on the annual report said it all: 'could be more.'[66] Nevertheless, the NITB remained positive about future prospects, but in the long run, continuing disturbances in the province over the following decades delayed significant progress in tourism in Northern Ireland until the beginning of the third millennium.

Taking tourism seriously 1951–1960

By 1951 the realisation of the importance of the tourism industry was growing in Ireland. It had replaced emigrants' remittances as the country's largest source of dollars, an important factor in view of the Marshall Aid received by Ireland, and an increasing number of people were finding employment in the sector. In addition, the failure of the various schemes provided for in the 1939 Tourist Traffic Act had forced the inter-party government to reconsider the needs of the industry and contemplate new legislation. Its fall from power left the Fianna Fáil administration with these proposals, but Seán Lemass delayed the enactment of new legislation for another year. However, the decrease in tourist numbers stimulated an awareness of the need for a properly organised and financed publicity pro-gramme as the 1950s loomed. In 1949 the prospects for a good tourist season were encouraging. Aer Lingus reported that it had carried 180,470 passengers during 1948, an increase of almost 50,000 over the previous year;[1] motoring visitors were now entitled to a three months' ration of petrol for use during their holidays and CIE announced that it was resuming coach tours. In Tipperary, the South Riding County Council had decided to double its contribu-tion to the ITA, from £300 to £600, and in Dun Laoghaire the first of two enlarged types of mail boat was expected to begin services in April 1949.[2] The Fáilte hotels around the country were open for business, and Butlins holiday camp at Mosney was promising 'In all Ireland, no better holiday value. Really good food, comfortable accommodation, facilities for all sports … first class entertainment

7.1
The advertisement for Butlins Holiday Camp, Mosney, that appeared in the June 1949 issue of *Irish Travel*, described by Thomas Bodkin in his *Report on the Arts in Ireland* as the 'very nadir of ill-drawn vulgarity'. Note that all the potential clients are women, both single and married. *Courtesy of Butlins.*

... dancing in Ireland's loveliest ballroom to Ireland's best dance band'.[3] Tourism was becoming respectable, and the need to amass dollar earnings was to become the overriding preoccupation of those who saw the long-term potential of the industry.

With a dearth of suitable accommodation and facilities for tourists, there had been no rush to instigate a large-scale publicity campaign in the immediate post-war period. However, the need for an effective publicity policy was a concern of Irish tourist bodies and it was agreed that the ITB would subsidise expenditure by the ITA in that context, as it was not considered necessary to set up another active publicity organisation.[4] In 1948 the association received just under £25,000 to cover the cost of its publicity efforts during the previous two years,[5] but the association's funding by local authorities had not increased in the previous ten years, while costs of administration and printing had more than doubled. The ITB covered the maintenance of a tourist bureau set up in New York in 1947 in association with Aer Lingus, which came to just over £4,500 per annum, but the overall amount spent on publicity in 1948 dwindled to £17,000, which included the ITA subvention.[6] The president of that body, P.C. O'Hara, speaking in October 1949, referred to its expenditure in the previous year as representing 'a puerile and farcical effort to maintain and extend a source of income which reached a figure of £28 million in 1947 and £33 million in 1948', while pointing out that England was spending £250,000 a year on publicity. With the acceptance of Marshall Aid funds and the need for dollar repayments, however, an effective publicity campaign in the USA was essential if Ireland was to exploit its advantages there. When the Committee on Tourism presented its findings to the government in June 1950, one of its recommendations concerned the avoidance of the 'caubeen and pipe' advertisement. To add fuel to the fire, Thomas Bodkin, former director of the National Gallery of Ireland, submitted a report on the arts in Ireland to Costello in 1950 which was scathing in its assessment of advertising intended to develop tourist traffic.[7] Bodkin castigated the ITA for its 'lamentably inartistic' publications, singling out a folder entitled 'Kingdom of Kerry' for 'its unpleasant type, clumsy layout, blurred illustrations and peculiarly ugly brilliant blue ink'. Similarly, while allowing that its official organ, *Irish Travel*, contained a good deal of interesting and informative matter, he declared: 'If its managers attached importance to good design, such things as the advertisement for Butlins holiday village which appeared in its issue for July 1949 would certainly have been rejected as the very nadir of ill-drawn vulgarity.' Bodkin conceded that the

ITA experienced difficulty in producing good material because all their printing had to be done in Ireland, with a consequent 'dead level of mediocrity', and also arising from their obligation to obtain prior sanction for their publications from the tourist board. Furthermore, he remarked that the displays of the Irish and Ulster tourist boards' respective premises in London 'often suggest, erroneously, that Art is thought more of in the six north-eastern counties of Ireland than in the country as a whole'. At a departmental conference on 20 February 1950, Bodkin's report was considered, and it was agreed that the Industrial Development Authority should be asked to implement his recommendations.[8] However, the quality of ITA productions does not seem to have improved appreciably. In September 1951, Lemass was back in Industry and Commerce, and he demanded to see samples of that body's colour posters, which had been prepared for distribution in Britain and America, as well as Shannon airport.[9] He pronounced them unworthy of being published with the aid of state funds, or of being exhibited at the airport, and decided that the matter should be referred to Fógra Fáilte, the newly created tourist publicity organisation. In any case, Bodkin's criticisms were not news to the ITA. In April 1949, J.C. Coleman, assistant secretary of the organisation, prepared a general report on publicity in the tourist industry that anticipated the points made by Bodkin. In a detailed analysis of publicity material, he covered publications, advertising, posters, display material, visual aids in the form of photographs and films, and radio and press relations.[10] Coleman expounded on the problems caused by outdated printing and advertising methods and the crucial necessity for availing of new technological advances, while also urging the adaptation of a public relations scheme. He suggested the abolition of *Irish Travel*, as he felt it had long outlived its usefulness, and proposed the publication of a bi-monthly or quarterly glossy magazine with a higher price tag and targeted subscription market to take its place. Pointing out that publicity had become a highly technical profession, attracting personnel with imagination and skill, he deemed it essential that qualified staff be assembled and made familiar with the product – Ireland. Management should have opportunities to meet representatives of tourist bodies in other countries to ascertain new methods of publicity techniques and tools. Moreover, he sounded a warning note on the importance of matters not directly controlled by the tourist bodies, such as transport, care of ancient buildings and the cleanliness of Irish towns and people, as being crucial. Coleman submitted his report to the ITB in April 1949, but as that body was in a state of flux at this time no action was taken on his proposals, although some were implemented later in the course of the 1950s. The following year, Kevin O'Doherty, general manager of the ITB, penned a short document on tourist publicity in the USA, focussing on the Irish-American market there. He asserted that as most American publicity experts responsible for selling Ireland were not familiar with the country, they were not always successful in hitting the right note in their advertising campaigns, and he alluded to the Gimbals' store slogan 'Good ould Gimbals loves good ould Ireland', carried in each of twenty-eight window displays featuring Irish goods, and a programme sponsored by the Westinghouse company on 6 February 1950, 'The loud red Patrick', which he found 'in the very worst tradition of the objectionable stage Irishman'. O'Doherty's point was that American publicity directors and publishers would welcome a consultant from Ireland with a broad cultural background and an understanding of American publicity. Having had informal discussions with publishing interests in the USA, he contended that such a service would be of great benefit to Irish tourism development. His proposals included the exploitation of Irish native charm and character, legends, antiquities, language and dress, but all these were to be subordinate to the image of a modern, progressive outlook and sophisticated side of Irish life in an effort to eliminate the 'lazy leprechaun' idea of Ireland. He considered it of paramount importance to lead American public opinion away from the conception that dirt, inefficiency and ignorance were synonymous with Ireland. O'Doherty submitted his memorandum to the ITB board, the relevant government departments and Aer Lingus, but again no action was taken.[11] An advertising campaign costing £13,000 was carried out by the ITB in the summer of 1951 in nineteen British newspapers and 165 magazines and periodicals with a view to developing off-season traffic, and as a result an increase of 22,500 inward passenger movements over the previous year from Great Britain and Northern Ireland was reported.[12] At the same time, the board undertook a publicity campaign to emphasise the value of tourism in the local economy, with 27,000 copies of a booklet entitled 'What does tourism mean to you?' being widely distributed in Ireland, while its exhibition at the 1951 Spring Show was based on the same theme.

As part of the European Recovery Programme set up to administer Marshall Aid, a Technical Assistance Programme in travel, hotel and allied activities was operated by the European Co-operation Agency. Under its aegis, various groups involved in Irish tourism participated in a joint tourism mission to the USA sponsored by the

Organisation for European Economic Co-operation early in 1950. They submitted reports with recommendations for improvements in the administration and development of the industry. Members of the Irish delegation included O'Doherty and Kevin Barry from the ITB, Brendan O'Regan of Shannon airport, and Patrick F. Dornan, manager of the Great Southern hotel, Parknasilla. However, this group found it impossible to agree on their findings and two separate reports were submitted to the government.[13] An Irish Hotels Federation delegation visited the USA separately and presented its conclusions, and a Tourism Survey Group from the USA, led by Robert K. Christenberry, visited Ireland in July and August 1950 and did likewise. The amalgamation of this intelligence, to be known as 'The Christenberry Report' for reasons of convenience, was published by the government in July 1951 under the title *Synthesis of Reports on Tourism 1950–1951*,[14] and established the main areas of concern. These were:

1. Official organisation
2. Ireland's tourist areas
3. Accommodation
4. Hotel operation
5. Publicity and advertising
6. Transport facilities
7. Miscellaneous

The reports generally agreed that the situation whereby two separate bodies administered the development and promotion of Irish tourism was most unsatisfactory, asserting that they were completely inadequate to handle their mission of actively promoting tourism to Ireland from abroad. They recommended the integration of the two bodies, with a new board consisting of members with practical experience of the industry. The augmentation of the range of activities of the board, with a consequent increase in state financial aid, was considered essential if the industry was to realise its full potential. The section dealing with Ireland's tourist areas divided the country into seven regions, with an emphasis on the perimeter. Almost the entire midland area from Cashel to the Northern Ireland border was excluded, save for parts of Tipperary and Kilkenny. Considered totally from an American point of view, the report dismissed most of the east coast, except for Dublin, as unattractive, and regarded the southern and western parts of the country as being most suitable for promotion. On tourist accommodation, the report cited the figure of 20,000 American visitors to Ireland in 1949, and estimated that this number could be increased to 40,000 in 1951, 55,000 in 1952 and 70,000 by 1953 if definite steps were taken to put a publicity and promotion campaign into effect in the USA without further delay. It recommended the expansion of hotel and guest-house accommodation, with the construction of new hotels and the modernisation and rehabilitation of existing ones in strategically important areas, and spoke of the need to overhaul the registration and grading systems. On hotel operation, it singled out sanitation and hygiene as being deficient on a countrywide scale, and recommended staff training schemes for both management and lower grades of workers. The need for development of accountancy skills was also highlighted, and this section ended with a summary of suggestions on 'what American travellers want'.

Mooting a budget of $200,000 for tourism promotion in the USA alone, the section dealing with publicity and advertising stressed the need for educating the Irish public on the economic value of tourism, suggested that factors of appeal to the Irish-American market should be investigated, and that promotion by individual hotels was an option to be considered. The IHF pointed out that of the £33 million earned in 1948 from tourism, £31,761, less than one-tenth of 1 per cent, was spent by the ITA under all headings, while the British Travel Association spent £297,663 in that year on overseas publicity alone. Quoting the Wimble Report on European Recovery and the Tourist Industry, they gave a figure of £350,000 as the amount of grant aid received by the British Tourist and Holidays Board from the British government for 1947/48, while Italy made an appropriation of 60 million lire for tourist promotion, Norway expended $27,000 on its New York office alone, and Denmark spent $21,000 in the USA exclusive of the cost of tourist literature, which was printed in Denmark.[15]

The report submitted by O'Regan and Dornan made the point that as 90 per cent of overseas travel by Americans was purchased through travel agents, they needed to be constantly briefed by Irish promotional agencies, and the expansion in off-season traffic, particularly by Irish-Americans, was also emphasised. The section on transport facilities alluded to the unsatisfactory landing conditions at Cobh and Dun Laoghaire and the possibility of persuading more Americans passing through Shannon airport to spend time in Ireland before journeying on, and suggested a need for car-hiring facilities, deeming Irish roads satisfactory apart from their signposting. The last section consisted of comments on places of historic interest; evening entertainment; problems with tipping, water shortages, postal and telephone services; hotel signs and

7.2
Irish Tourist Board staff and board members outside premises in Lea House, Ballsbridge, in 1953. L–R, *back row* Jack Coleman, Niall Sheridan; *centre row* A.J. McClafferty, unknown, Thomas Condon; *front row* Fred Moran, Kitty Eason, J.P. O'Brien, Richard Beamish. *Courtesy of Fáilte Ireland.*

food, all considered to be important in the overall provision of a satisfactory tourist package for the American visitor.

The initial government response to the reports was cautious, with Daniel Morrissey recommending that they should not be published, as government policy on the tourism question had not yet been established, and proposing instead that information should be disseminated by way of lectures to meetings of hoteliers and other interested parties.[16] Seán MacBride, who as Minister for External Affairs took an active interest in tourism matters, suggested that interest-free loans for the building of hotels by private individuals and low-rate loans for substantial extensions of existing hotels should be made available.[17] He further proposed the construction of five hundred ten-bedroom units of the type utilised at Shannon airport for overnight transit visitors: 'these units to contain adequate bathrooms, showers and to be fully furnished and decorated … could then be sold, hire purchased or leased to existing hotels as extensions … could also be used for the purpose of enabling country houses to accommodate tourists.' The cabinet kicked this suggestion into touch at a meeting held on 9 May 1950, deciding instead that a committee called 'The Dollar Exports Advisory Committee' should be established to advise on the promotion of commodity exports to the dollar area.[18] Paul Miller, chief of the ECA mission in Dublin, advocated the development of a unified programme by the ITA and the tourist board, 'so that they could be mutually helpful to each other' at the ITA's annual general meeting in October.[19]

On 17 July 1951, Seán Lemass, once again Minister for Industry and Commerce and still loyal to his old comrade-in-arms, J.P. O'Brien, obtained the informal approval of the cabinet for the latter's appointment to fill the vacancy on the board of the Irish Tourist Board caused by the resignation of Noel Huggard, 'in the event of the Board's not accepting a suggestion of the Minister that O'Brien be appointed by the Board to a specified whole-time technical post on their staff'.[20] The ITB was evidently not disposed to employ O'Brien, despite his years of dedicated service to the industry, and he became a member of the board. Interestingly, the record of the cabinet meeting includes the note 'No formal record to be made by us, that is, no decision of the Government to be conveyed and no record to be introduced in the minutes', which suggests that the cabinet was not keen to be associated with the appointment.

In December 1951, Lemass introduced another Tourist Traffic Bill to legislate for changes that he had already made. In October he had announced the establishment of a new organisation, Fógra Fáilte, with J.P. O'Brien as general manager, to combine the publicity functions of the ITB and the ITA, and on 3 July 1952 An Bord Fáilte came into being as the new statutory body with responsibility for development of accommodation, amenities and facilities for tourists.[21] Speaking at the second stage of the bill, Lemass stressed the importance of the industry to the national economy; overall earnings from tourism were second only to earnings from agricultural exports and represented the largest single item in dollar earnings. During 1950 gross receipts from tourism were estimated at just under £33 million, exceeding by about £3 million the gross receipts from all livestock exports, and falling short of receipts from all agricultural exports by only £12 million: 'It would be no exaggeration to describe it as a corner stone of the national economy … Certainly on the success or failure of our efforts to expand tourist revenue will depend whether we can maintain, much less improve, the present standard of living of our people.'[22] With a balance of payments deficit of £66 million in 1951, Lemass saw the only solution

to the nation's economic problems as being an increase in both production and exports and believed that tourism 'offers an opportunity of expansion and the prospect of a quicker return than any
other trade'. With only 260 copies of the Christenberry Report sold
out of a total print run of 2,500 copies, he expressed his disappointment at the failure of the accommodation sector to take advantage
of the expert opinions contained therein, seeing this as a sign that
the government had not yet succeeded in arousing sufficient interest in the potential of the tourist trade.

While broadly maintaining the functions given to it in the 1939 act,
the new tourist board was given two more – the power to protect and
maintain historic buildings, and the provision of signposting. As
Fógra Fáilte was to have responsibility for publicity, An Bord Fáilte
would relinquish its power in that regard, and also that of building
and operating hotels. Deputies of all parties concurred in their
agreement that radical action was needed to galvanise the industry,
but concerns were expressed about some aspects of the proposed
legislation, such as the future of the ITA, which henceforth would
be reduced to being an agent of Fógra Fáilte, providing tourist
bureaux in Ireland. As these initiatives ran contrary to the recommendations of the Christenberry Report, in that there would now
be three bodies engaged in tourism work instead of a single cohesive unit, some deputies were bold enough to suggest that Lemass
was engineering a post for his old friend, J.P. O'Brien, with independent deputy Jack McQuillan accusing him of acting with his
heart and not his head.[23] However, the main provisions of the bill
allowed for a programme of state-guaranteed loans up to a limit of
£3 million for the improvement of hotels and guest-houses, with
grants from the tourist board to cover the interest charges for the
first three years (later extended to five years), and this move was
almost unanimously welcomed.

The most dramatic illustration of the commitment of Lemass to
the cause of tourism development during the early 1950s was An
Tóstal, a springtime cultural festival designed mainly to attract
American tourists in the off-peak season. In 1951, Juan Trippe, president of Pan American Airlines, suggested to Lemass that a 'Come
Back to Erin' festival aimed at Irish-Americans could prove a solution to the dollar problem and presented him with a lengthy memorandum on the subject.[24] The comprehensive proposal was to put
into place a programme of sporting and cultural events with the
support of the Irish media and the churches. The idea appealed to
Lemass and he entered into discussions with the ITB, but that body
considered that a more orthodox approach to the American tourist

business would be more beneficial in the long term.[25] Lemass felt that it would be 'unwise to disagree with their [Pan American Airways] approach on commercial grounds' and demanded that the tourist board consider the publicity aspects of the scheme. In February 1952 the *Irish Press* announced that a national festival would be held in 1953, organised by the ITB.[26] No state funds would be forthcoming, and commercial and other interests would be called upon to raise the necessary finance. It was decided that the festival would be called An Tóstal, meaning a pageant, muster or array, but that its English rendering would be 'Ireland at Home'.[27] The ITB explained that it was meant as an expression of Ireland's national life, presenting an opportunity to project widely 'our spiritual and cultural place in the modern world', and stressed that while it would be mainly based in Dublin, it was hoped that all parts of the country would participate. There was some negative reaction to the proposed festival. The *Irish Times* asked:

> How seriously are we expected to take the proposal for a festival of Dublin next year? ... Nobody could regard it as anything more than an extravagant joke ... We make these comments not with any notion of dashing cold water on the concept of a festival of Dublin, but rather in hope of persuading people who are in charge of it to take a fittingly modest view of their responsibilities and not to lead visitors to expect too much.[28]

It was an ambitious proposition, and perhaps Seán Lemass was the only politician in Ireland at this time with the courage and vision to consider such a large-scale enterprise. Major-General Hugo Hyacinth MacNeill, a retired army officer, was appointed national co-ordinator, and tourist board staff toured the country advising local and church authorities as well as sporting, cultural and social organisations. The Catholic Church was brought on board, with the announcement that a mass to mark the festival's opening would be celebrated in the Pro-Cathedral in Dublin on Easter Monday 1953. By June 1952, Industry and Commerce was totally committed to ensuring government participation in the festival, concurring with the ITB's proposal that the opening ceremony should be performed by the president, Seán T. O'Kelly, outside the General Post Office. Stands would be erected in O'Connell Street to accommodate distinguished guests, and at an appropriate point in the ceremony the official Tóstal flag would be hoisted.[29] Opening ceremonies would be held simultaneously in selected provincial centres, and government ministers, senators or parliamentary secretaries would be requested to perform them. By October 1952, Hugo MacNeill was in New York outlining the aims and scope of the festival to consular staff there. Their role was to assist in the formation of committees of Irish-Americans in cities and towns throughout the USA in preparation for the festival.[30]

What is remarkable is that the entire cabinet was convinced by the vision and determination of Lemass to throw its weight behind the festival. The Department of Local Government was no exception, and the minister proposed to include provisions in a local government bill being prepared to empower borough corporations, urban district councils and town commissioners to spend money on decoration up to a limit of three pence in the pound.[31] He also sought government approval to notify all local authorities that they could incur expenditure in connection with An Tóstal in anticipation of the necessary covering legislation, a significant indicator of the realisation that the cities and towns of Ireland in the early 1950s were drab and depressing places. The Minister for Posts and Telegraphs, on being approached by Finance regarding the use of An Tóstal seals, being produced by Fógra Fáilte, by all government departments on their outgoing mail, expressed no objection but pointed out that as his department was proposing to issue a special stamp to commemorate the festival, use of the seals would have to be discontinued when the stamp came into use.[32] The Department of Defence had, of course, been heavily involved in the organisation of the festival from the beginning, and the army would form a significant part of the opening parade in O'Connell Street. Special messages of encouragement to the Irish people from Taoiseach Éamon de Valera figured in newspaper pages, stressing the need for public participation in addition to that of state, local authorities and cultural organisations: 'Those who have not been in Ireland before will find a land of many surprises, a welcome without limit, and a people glad to be host to her home-coming children and their friends.'[33] De Valera also decided to attend the opening ceremonies in Cork and participate in some of the events there.

However, there were those who did not welcome suggestions in the press that licensing regulations would be relaxed during the festival in order to allow for longer drinking hours. The Reverend William Fletcher, temperance agent of the Presbyterian Church in Dublin, felt constrained to write to de Valera stating that body's objections: 'It would, I think, be a pity, when we want to be at our best, to demean ourselves by allowing over-indulgence in harmful drinking. Our tourists will not demand extra facilities ... we should respect them more than to think that they will find Eire's chief attraction the "ever open door" of the public house.'[34] Fletcher was supported by the Women's Christian Total Abstinence Union, who passed a resolution strongly deprecating the possibility of allowing public houses to stay open until midnight, preferring that visitors should consider Ireland as a country 'where true hospitality and friendship may be enjoyed without having recourse to indulgence in strong drink … the roads should be kept as safe as possible for visiting motorists, as statistics show that very many accidents are caused by drink, especially in the early hours of the morning'.[35]

Across the thirty-two counties, 172 centres organised programmes and a voluntary corps of student guides drawn from the universities was formed to meet trains, ships and aircraft to distribute badges and programmes to incoming visitors. Permits to utilise the Tóstal emblem on their products were issued to 159 firms by the tourist board, in the hope that it would serve as an incentive for Irish commercial interests to produce souvenirs of the highest possible standard. The board also saw the festival as benefiting the Irish people in a non-material manner, in that it would develop a better sense of civic spirit, an increase in public interest in cultural affairs and a stimulus to Gaelic activities. However, it did stress that the successful organisation and promotion of the festival was to be regarded as a long-term project, and that the experience gained in the first year would enable the adjustment of its plans over the following years.

An Tóstal was officially launched by Seán T. O'Kelly on Easter Sunday 5 April 1953, but the first year could not be deemed an outstanding success, due to a shortage of events of national and international standard. Newspaper coverage of the event in some English newspapers was negative in the extreme, portraying precisely the opposite image of the country to that desired by the government and the tourist board. The *Daily Mirror* described the opening ceremony as a near riot and went on to lampoon the 'Bowl of Light', an artistic endeavour on O'Connell Bridge that was eventually thrown into the River Liffey by students from Trinity College:

> The Irish are running a festival called An Tóstal. Literally translated it means At Home and is a welcome to all visitors to see Eire with all its hospitality and charm. It has started with a bang. Just before the opening 3,000 Dubliners gathered near O'Connell Bridge and started pelting each other with flowers. Then with flowers in pots. Then with rocks and bottles. Shop windows were smashed. Cars were overturned and decorations were ripped down and smashed. Twelve people were

arrested. Four went to hospital. That's what I call a real At Home.[36]

…

There are traffic jams in O'Connell Street as hundreds cram the bridge trying to see the Tóstal Bowl of Light, which looks like something out of an ice-cream parlour. It stands fifteen feet high in what appears to be a half-sunken submarine with fountains playing in it – and is the biggest joke of the festival. So six Civic Guards stand around to protect it![37]

Criticism was not confined to overseas publications: The *Irish Times*, in a leading article, lamented the lack of the spirit of the festival in Dublin suburbs: 'So far as this country is concerned there are only two tourist areas. One is the heart of Dublin; the other is the "scenic" region of the West; and beyond these two there is no recognition of anything else that might be deserving of attention.'[38] Not slow to take advantage of the government's embarrassment in the matter, John A. Costello, leader of the opposition, tabled a parliamentary question enquiring of the taoiseach 'whether An Comhairle Ealaíon (The Arts Council) was consulted as to the design of the recent erections on O'Connell Bridge before they were designed or erected'.[39] The answer was patently 'no'; and it was J.P. O'Brien who galloped into the fray, issuing a statement of support for the festival which the *Irish Times* printed under the heading 'Was it for this …?' Incensed by the criticism, he proclaimed that thanks to the organisers and the universal enthusiasm invoked, there were 'tawdry contraptions' all over Ireland, and that if the Tóstal councils concerned had called in cultural consultants, most of their funds would have been spent on consultants' fees, delaying the festival until 1954: 'In spite of the hooligans, heartachers [sic] and humbugs, the first Tóstal started in triumph and dignity. The brave adventure will finish its voyage with becoming pride and with due gratitude to the thousands of voluntary workers all over Ireland who made it possible.'[40] Éamon de Valera, speaking at the concluding ceremonies organised by Ennis Tóstal Council, typically professed himself pleased with the festival's achievements in the area of community co-operation: 'The thing … which pleases me most is not so much the advertising of the good things we can offer visitors, but the effect it has upon ourselves … It has thrown us back very largely upon ourselves, making us think of the things of the past and realising the treasures we really possess.'[41] These were not words calculated to gladden the heart of Lemass, who was striving to wrench the Irish people out of their obsession with the past and to make them confront the harsh economic realities of the mid-twentieth century, and he cannot have been impressed to hear de Valera publicly confess his ignorance of the economic situation in the country: 'I myself was greatly surprised back in 1946–47 to find that tourism promised to be one of the biggest of our industries. It had worked out at an average of thirty million pounds for a number of years.' To learn that the leader of the government, a politician in power at that time for over fourteen years, had been totally unaware of tourism's importance in the economic sphere towards the end of his first long period in government must have galled his second-in-command, who had put so much effort into the development of the industry. To be damned by the faint praise of the *Evening Herald* was no consolation: 'An Tóstal won the admiration and support of the country in general as a notable gesture. We regret to have to affirm that in our opinion it was no more than that! It was obvious that the amount spent abroad on advertising and organisation was greater than the total receipts from foreign visitors.'[42] However, the writer did concede that a start had been made in awakening local consciousness and pride, and concluded: 'The realisation on the part of residents in many country towns that they are a corporate community, with a local history and background of identity, and ... a future of endeavour and prosperity, may be counted as an achievement.'

Unfortunately, the anticipated increase in tourists in the off-season period did not materialise, and the overall figure for visitors for the year actually decreased. The ITB concluded that material assistance by way of grants and guarantees against financial loss was necessary to encourage the organisation of major events of general, sporting and cultural character.[43] James Nugent, chairman of the board, presided over a special conference held in Dublin on 29 September 1953, and attended by representatives of Irish transport companies, hotel and catering interests, travel agencies and automobile associations, to consider the organisation of the 1954 festival.[44] The consensus of opinion was that the festival was held too early in the year, and that the 1954 Tóstal should be held two weeks later. Representing Fógra Fáilte, J.P. O'Brien offered the view that An Tóstal had taken its place as the major tourist event of the year, and he assured the delegates that overseas publicity for 1954 was well in hand. By the following month it had been decided that a historical and floral pageant, along with the military parade, should form the mainstay of a more extensive opening ceremony in Dublin, with Seán T. O'Kelly once again performing the honours.[45] However, the decrease in local organising committees from 172 in 1953 to 135 in 1954 was an indication of the decline in public interest, and although the Pageant of Saint Patrick at Tara was a triumph of voluntary effort and attracted a large audience, including over 3,000 people who travelled from Northern Ireland,[46] initial enthusiasm for the festival was not maintained over the following years. The 1955 Tóstal took place over the last three weeks in May, immediately after the Dublin Spring Show, as this was hoped that this might persuade visitors to the show to linger in the city, but the collapse of the Dublin Tóstal Committee immediately after the 1954 festival was a severe blow. By 1955 only fifty-five centres countrywide were involved, and it was apparent that such attractions as were proving successful were based in the cities, with little dissemination of tourists into smaller towns and villages. Nevertheless, John Costello, leader of the inter-party government, echoed the sentiments of de Valera in his speech at the opening of the 1955 Tóstal:

> If this festival has been designed with the primary purpose of attracting more tourists and extending our holiday season, it also seeks to impress itself in the widest sense on our whole way of life, to encourage us to realise that we have a heritage of tradition and culture, of language, music, dancing, song and games which can win the interest and, we hope, the admiration of every visitor to our shores.[47]

Regrettably, the power of the Catholic Church as exemplified by John Charles McQuaid, archbishop of Dublin, would prove the nemesis for the faltering festival in 1958. During the 1957 Tóstal, an international theatre festival was inaugurated in Dublin which proved a success with the public, but ended with the suppression of a production of *The Rose Tattoo* by the police. For 1958 the theatre festival director, Brendan Smith, commissioned Seán O'Casey to write a new play, *The Drums of Father Ned*, to be performed by Dublin's Globe Theatre Company, while the Edwards–MacLiammóir company planned an adaptation of *Ulysses*, by James Joyce. Controversy arose in January 1958 when it became known that McQuaid had refused permission for mass to be celebrated in the Pro-Cathedral to mark the opening of the festival, as in previous years, on learning of plans to present these plays. On 12 February O'Casey withdrew his play from the festival,[48] and the Dublin Tóstal Council then announced that the production of *Ulysses* would not proceed due to the contentiousness it had aroused.[49] Samuel Beckett, a close friend of Joyce, weighed in by withdrawing three new plays of his as a mark of protest,[50] and in the end a decision to cancel the 1958 theatre festival was taken at a Bord Fáilte board meeting on 10 April.[51] The *Irish Times*, in a leading article, was scathing in its condemnation:

> No evidence has been adduced that either of these productions contains a hint of obscenity or of blasphemy; yet pressure has been brought to bear against both of them from high places, and the [Tóstal] Council has kissed the rod ... Next year's Tóstal Council will be well advised to submit its programme to the Archbishop of Dublin in advance of publicity if it is to avoid a similar wastage of money and effort ... Will there, for that matter, be a Tóstal?[52]

The writer was not far out in his analysis of the situation, and the incident is yet another example of what John A. Murphy terms the 'backstairs diplomacy' of McQuaid, as exemplified in the Mother and Child controversy in 1951.[53] Although the 1958 Tóstal went ahead, Bord Fáilte concluded that the level of public support over its six years of existence was not sufficient to justify its continued financial scaffolding of the event.[54] Local contributions had declined progressively, the tourist board had spent £305,000 on An Tóstal since 1952, and they estimated that a mere 5,000 visitors had come to Ireland specifically for the festival in 1957, a year in which they had spent £32,000. At a meeting called by the ITB board on 24 July 1958 and attended by over 100 members of Tóstal councils, national and cultural organisations, it was overwhelmingly agreed that the timescale of the festival should be extended to cover the entire period from April to September.[55] The tourist board would promote and sponsor events as distinct from organising them, and the main programme would take place between June and September, with April and May being devoted to a campaign of spring-cleaning and preparation to improve the appearance of urban centres, the countryside and seaside resorts, and an extension of the Tidy Towns and Villages and Roadside Gardens competition. Once again, the *Irish Times* had its finger on the pulse:

> Tóstal is dead; long live Tóstal!! Thus oversimply and perhaps unkindly, one might summarise last Saturday's announcement by Bord Fáilte ... The concept of Tóstal was a noble one, but in its translation to reality it fell foul of adverse forces, some of them – such as our inability to fuse private gaiety and public pageant – inherent in the Irish character ... No one can quarrel with Bord Fáilte's desire to clean up our cities, towns and villages ... The danger is that by sticking a Tóstal label on this laudable work – and on any 'major tourist attraction' – the odour of failure may cling.[56]

Although the festival continued in many centres for some years, it was no longer a cohesive national effort enjoying committed government support, and it never achieved its primary goal of attracting hordes of Americans to Ireland in the off-peak season. However, it certainly succeeded in educating the Irish people as regards the importance of tourism in the national economy. It stimulated a tradition of community co-operation that bore fruit in the results of the Tidy Towns competition, transforming the appearance of Irish towns and villages. It extended the decoration of urban areas and floodlighting of public buildings. Angling competitions organised for the festival generated a demand for cheap accommodation in private homes, leading to the establishment of the Irish 'Bed and Breakfast', a reasonably priced facility providing a satisfactory alternative to hotel accommodation. These things are taken for granted today, but constituted a major step forward in tourism in the 1950s. In addition, many of the cultural festivals that sprang from An Tóstal have survived to this day, and none of these and the multitude of other festivals which now attract thousands every year to these shores could exist without the continued support of tourism bodies. According to Morash, it was also respon-sible for the phenomenal growth of amateur theatre in Ireland from that time onwards.[57] There was an opening up of artistic awareness, such as that which extended from the appreciation of the Gaelic tradition into the success of 'folk' singers in the 1960s, and a realisation that external influences in the shape of foreign tourists could assist the Irish people in both enjoying and exploiting the uniqueness of their own culture. For decades, visitors to Ireland, when asked for their favourite constituent of our tourism 'product', have replied simply 'the people', and An Tóstal generated the awareness of the value of that ingredient of the Irish package.

Another aspect of the integration of tourism and culture in 1950s Ireland was the realisation of the importance of preservation and protection of the natural and built environment. The year 1930 saw the passing of the National Monuments Act, which empowered the commissioners of public works to assume guardianship over monuments in private ownership.The Town and Regional Planning Act, 1934 was of special interest to the tourist industry, and the ITA undertook propaganda work in favour of the immediate general adoption of its provisions, particularly with regard to the preservation of important scenic and historical sites. In 1936 the government announced that its policy of substituting useful public works for the payment of the dole as a means of relieving unemployment was to be further extended, and the ITA prepared a comprehensive scheme of works for recommendation to the responsible minister.[58] The passage of the Acquisition of Derelict Sites Bill through the Dáil

10. Cover for *Ireland – an illustrated guide to the counties of Ireland*, published by Fógra Fáilte in 1953 and illustrating the multitude of activities available to visitors.

11. Irish farmers meet a creamery lorry – one of the first six postcards produced by John Hinde in 1957. *Courtesy of John Hinde Limited.*

12. A well-known image by John Hinde, of which he said that Bord Fáilte discouraged the use of donkeys in postcards because the government regarded them as symbols of a backward country and wanted portrayals of skyscrapers. *Courtesy of John Hinde Limited.*

13. Poster for the 1992 International James Joyce Symposium. Bord Fáilte was most instrumental in fostering the use of Irish literary figures such as Joyce in developing cultural tourism, especially as the number of Irish Nobel literary prize-winners was disproportionately large. *Courtesy of Robert Ballagh.*

14. Poster for the 'Today' radio programme in Australia featuring an Irish week, with co-operation from Cathay Pacific airlines, the Northern Ireland Tourist Board, the Traveland group and Tourism Ireland.

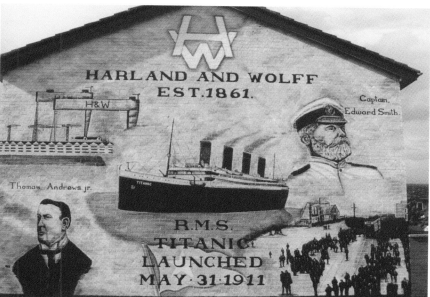

15. With 'black taxi' tours heralding a return to tourism in Belfast, loyalist and nationalist iconic images were popular attractions. These commemorate the building of the *Titanic* in Belfast in 1911 and Bobby Sands, the republican hunger-striker who died in 1981. *Courtesy of Irina Raffo.*

17. Bord Fáilte 1970s poster of a Paul Henry painting which was made available to overseas travel companies for promotion purposes. *Courtesy of National Museum of Ireland.*

16. Poster issued by Irish Airlines in 1959 featuring Shannon airport, with emphasis on the duty-free facilities available there. *Courtesy of National Museum of Ireland.*

18. Brochure illustrating charms of Northern Ireland's 'coast of beauty.'

19. Aer Lingus advertisement, 1960s

20. Illustration by Rowel Friers, a well-known Northern Ireland cartoonist, for a map of the province.

21. A brochure for Dublin.

22. John Hinde postcard for Dublin airport with glamorous Aer Lingus stewardess. *Courtesy of John Hinde Limited.*

in September 1940 was hailed as a progressive step in the elimination of 'Irish eyesores' so detrimental to the presentation of the country to foreign view. This legislation enabled local authorities to compulsorily purchase such sites and clear and dispose of them, but as with many matters provided for in legislation in Ireland, the following years would demonstrate a lack of will and commitment to avail of the provisions of either of these acts.[59]

However, moves were afoot to establish an organisation on the lines of the British National Trust, to safeguard objects and centres of aesthetic and historic interest. The Association for the Preservation of Places of Interest or Beauty in Ireland was set up during the summer of 1947, with a prestigious committee comprising Professor Felix Hackett, Dr R. Lloyd Praeger, Arthur Cox, Seán MacBride, Cearbhaill Ó Dálaigh and the Earl of Rosse.[60] To be known as An Taisce, meaning a safekeeping place, its aim was to acquire and maintain noteworthy buildings and lands for the nation.[61] The presence of such a body, with a number of prestigious personalities at the helm, was bound to have a beneficial effect in educating public opinion regarding the preservation of its natural and manmade environment. With public concern for conservation increasing, the government included a provision in regard to the development and acquisition of monuments in the Tourist Traffic Bill, 1952. The powers given to the tourist board under Section 5 of the 1952 Tourist Traffic Act were: 'To supply road signs to local authorities and also to protect and maintain and to aid in protecting and maintaining historic buildings, sites and shrines and places of scenic, historic, scientific or other interest to the public and to facilitate visitors thereto by the provision of notices and the provision and improvement of means of access.'[62] The ITB set up an Advisory Archaeological Council the following year to advise on activities related to national and historic monuments, and surveys were undertaken with a view to formulating improvement schemes for its consideration. However, the level of participation by the tourist board in the care of national monuments was threatened in 1954 when Gerard Sweetman, Minister for Finance in the second inter-party government, targeted tourism in his efforts to reduce expenditure in the estimates for 1955–56.[63] In a letter to Industry and Commerce he stated that certain schemes conducted by An Bord Fáilte encroached on the functions of other authorities and should be abandoned. He instanced the maintenance of historic monuments, the provision of means of access to these monuments or to beauty spots, and the supply of signposts. Industry and Commerce felt that the tourist board's activities did not overlap with those of the OPW or the local authorities, as those bodies could not be expected to take the initiative required from the point of view of tourism. With regard to signposts, the ITB supplied them but they were erected and maintained by the local authorities, as local government had objected in 1952 to the proposal to permit the tourist board to erect them.[64] It was agreed that the ITB should continue to fulfil its duties under these two headings, while Industry and Commerce promised to keep expenditure on tourism under review.[65] By 1956 there was an encouraging amount of work done under these provisions, with 4,845 signposts supplied in 1955, and 4,083 in the year ending March 1956. Sixty-three projects had been carried out on access works, carparks, shelters and toilet facilities, piers and landing stages, and other amenities at tourist resorts, fishing and sporting centres, and national monuments. Informative plaques had been erected at 170 historic sites, shrines and national monuments, while a photographic survey of national monuments at Newgrange, south Kilkenny and Ardmore had also been undertaken.[66] At last, the environment was a priority in tourism terms, but the depredations of the 1960s would take a terrible toll on Ireland's natural and constructed heritage.

Another matter that became the province of the ITB in this period was the production of Irish souvenirs of good calibre, and this resulted in the establishment of a thriving industry by the end of the 1950s. In his 1949 report on the arts in Ireland, the failure of the ITA to produce quality postcards was of concern to Thomas Bodkin, and he was equally critical of the absence of souvenirs of good design for visitors: 'They can still buy a mock bog-oak shillelagh, a jaunting-car or a "Paddy and his Pig".'[67] Bodkin pointed to the efforts of the Scottish Tourist Board, who were consulting the British Council for Industrial Design on developing a tourist souvenir industry. That body was preparing for the Festival of Britain in 1951 by discussing a range of quality souvenirs with British manufacturers. In addition, in August 1949 the ECA administrator, Hoffman, complained to Industry and Commerce that no Irish souvenirs were available at Shannon airport.[68] The arrangements for the sale of goods were discussed in September 1949 and a scheme was drawn up for the construction of a shop within the terminal building. As dollar receipts from the existing shop and the bar had amounted to $50,000 in the year 1947/48, the Working Party on Dollar Earnings considered the matter and suggested that officials from Finance and Industry and Commerce should inspect the airport together. The following year, the Cabinet Committee on Tourism proposed that the facilities at Dublin airport for the sale of works of art, books and souvenirs should be extended and improved.[69] However, Aer Rianta argued that the existing shop was intended only for the sale of newspapers, cigarettes, chocolates, and so forth, and that additional space as well as specialised staff would be required to expand their range of activities. Discussions took place between the ITB and the Industrial Development Authority (IDA) during 1950 with a view to the production of Irish souvenirs designed in harmony with the culture and history of the country.[70] At the IDA's suggestion, a Souvenir Committee was set up comprising Brendan O'Regan, representatives of the Departments of Lands, Education and Industry and Commerce, and a nominee from the tourist board.[71] Discussions were held with manufacturers and wholesalers and the committee submitted its final report in November 1953, recommending the setting-up of a permanent committee to be financed by the tourist board, who would provide secretarial assistance.[72] However, Lemass decided that the ITB should be asked to take responsibility for securing improvements in the type of souvenirs produced, by offering inducements such as permission to use a mark which would be indicative of an approved standard and, if necessary, the tourist board could set up an *ad hoc* committee of interested parties to assist it. The tourist board inserted advertisements in the press in February 1955, which resulted in more than eighty samples of souvenirs being received, along with many enquiries as to the type of article considered suitable.[73] Discussions were held with the Federation of Irish Manufacturers, and with the Design Research Unit of Ireland, and selected samples of current souvenirs were chosen for consideration. The result was the production of new types of souvenirs based on Irish motifs, such as a range of jewellery with earrings, brooches and cufflinks designed in Irish letters obtained from the Book of Kells. By the end of 1955, the tourist board had assembled a permanent collection of souvenirs in their offices in Dublin.[74] Acting as liaison between craftspeople, manufacturers and retailers, it continued to play a significant part in the development of the Irish souvenir industry. Valuable assistance was given by the Arts Council to improve quality and design, and increased sales resulted from the board's use of press publicity and displays at exhibitions, trade shows and tourist information centres. Along with a close relationship with fifty craftspeople and some manufacturers, the ITB also established contact during 1955 with vocational schools, the Irish Countrywomen's Association, Muintir na Tíre and Macra na Feirme with a view to stimulating interest in the home production of souvenirs, and that year the collection was shown at the Dublin Spring Show.[75] Exhibitions were held at Galway, Killarney, Shannon and Belfast, and sample collections were despatched for display in London, Sheffield, New York, Boston, Montreal and Helsinki. Close co-operation was maintained with the Arts Council, the National Museum, the Genealogical Office, the Folklore Commission and Córas Tráchtála.[76] Twelve new shops were opened for the sale of souvenirs during the following year, and the tourist board estimated that £1 million per year was spent on souvenirs, with 120 craftspeople engaged in production, thus providing employment for a large number of workers during the winter months.[77] By 1959 the number of craftspeople had grown to 350, with 1,350 visitors to the permanent exhibition. The only problem was that production was unable to keep pace with demand, as a survey of visitors showed that 43 per cent of those interviewed had bought souvenirs, at an average expenditure of £6.[78] A successful outcome to one of the tourist board's ventures was an achievement to savour as the 1960s approached. There was also progress on the postcard front, with British photographer John Hinde producing his first mass-produced works, six views of Ireland, in 1957. Hinde's bright foreground colours, often a result of 'gilding the lily', made his Irish postcards so popular and successful that they became 'synonymous with a rural view of the country as a paradise which in turn became a key part of its official marketing to the outside world'.[79] He eventually spread his wings abroad and today John Hinde Limited is a worldwide enterprise specialising in global souvenir gift and novelty solutions.

The second inter-party government, which came to power in May 1954, wasted no time in dealing with the administrative inefficiency and conflict arising from the existence of two statutory tourism bodies. Back in Industry and Commerce, William Norton reported that the relationship between the two bodies was 'distinctly unsatisfactory, if not openly hostile', and that Fógra Fáilte was failing to consult An Bord Fáilte on policy matters.[80] The 1955 Tourist Traffic Act provided for the dissolution of the former body and the transfer of its functions and funding to the latter.[81] Speaking on the second stage of the bill, Norton answered Lemass's query on the tourism policy of the inter-party administration by declaring:

> as long as I am Minister for Industry and Commerce, I will do my best to ensure that the policy of developing the tourist trade will be pushed as far as possible, and that every possible assistance will be given to any organisation or group which is concerned with promoting the immense possibilities which this country has from a tourist point of view.[82]

Some deputies pushed for the bestowing of statutory status on the ITA, but Lemass and Norton were in agreement on this question, insisting that it should retain its voluntary and independent status. Henceforth it would have three directors on the board of the new body, and the association would continue to operate tourist bureaux inside the country as it had done as an agent of Fógra Fáilte, relying on contributions from the local authorities, which at this stage were running at around £16,000 a year, to finance its activities. The point was made that from 1925 to 1951 the association had carried out all tourism promotion for the country at a cost of just £300,000, while the new state body would now receive £500,000 in one year, with half of that amount earmarked for publicity purposes alone.[83] The act became law on 21 March 1955 and Bord Fáilte Éireann became the sole statutory body dealing with tourism matters in the Republic of Ireland. In a sad coincidence, that year also saw the death of J.P. O'Brien, the man mainly responsible for the industry's profile at this time.

But cometh the hour, cometh the man. Perhaps the most significant event in the 1950s was the appointment of Timothy J. O'Driscoll as director-general of the tourist board in 1956. As former chief executive of Córas Tráchtála, the Irish export board, he had commercial experience in a foreign-marketing environment, and as former Irish ambassador to the Netherlands, he was accustomed to the diplomatic manoeuvring necessary to achieve success in difficult negotiations. Moreover, his earlier post as a public servant in Industry and Commerce meant that he was already on familiar terms with many of the leading lights in Irish tourism. O'Driscoll was to prove a charismatic and outward-looking chief executive who would steer the industry into a new dimension in the late 1950s and the 1960s, and who ensured that the ITB retained its role on the international stage, as he participated fully in global organisations in the tourism sphere. At the time that he took over, the question of tourism statistics remained a vexed question, due to the difficulty in computing the number of visitors entering a country as opposed to people travelling on business or returning from holidays abroad. In Ireland, it was only with the foundation of the Central Statistics Office in 1949 that some attempt could be made to assess the number of tourists entering the country. Prior to that, figures were based on numbers of passengers arriving by air or by sea, without any effort being made to discern the purpose of their journey. Figures published by the Central Statistics Office in 1956 reveal that the net income from tourism decreased each year in the first half of the 1950s, while spending by Irish holidaymakers abroad showed a marked increase.[84] However, it is worth also comparing the relative importance of tourism in the national economy with that of visible exports in 1955. In that year, the balance of payments showed that expenditure was £231.8 million, and receipts, including £31.8 million from tourism, totalled £195.4 million, leaving a deficit of £36.4 million. By 1958 the gap had closed to £29 million, as tourism receipts rose to £34.6, representing a figure of 5–6 per cent of Gross Domestic Product.[85]

Garret FitzGerald, writing in 1957 on Irish economic problems, felt that there were grounds for optimism as far as the tourist industry was concerned, provided leadership of a high quality was provided.[86] He listed the shortage and high cost of hotel accommodation, the short season and CIE's virtual monopoly of coach tours, along with a lack of adequate publicity in Britain, Ireland's largest market, as reasons for the adverse trend in tourist traffic, and concluded: ' We need a new spirit of ambition and urgency, a new horror of inefficiency and low productivity and a new, constructive and far-sighted attitude to employment problems.' Further legislation in 1957 and 1959 were attempts to put the industry on a better footing, but the fact remains that the First Programme for Economic Expansion of 1958 allocated tourism only £2.5 million out of a total provision of £220.5 million under all headings. In the event, the actual amount expended on the total programme amounted to £297 million, while the expenditure on tourism at £1.21 million was less than 50 per cent of the target.[87] Horgan speaks of Lemass's general difficulties in the period as being 'a shortage of capital funds, a lack of enthusiasm on the part of colleagues and the electoral unpredictability that marked the years between 1949 and 1957, combined with the obstacles placed in his path by the Department of Finance'.[88] The tourism industry was no exception to the rule, suffering these constraints to an advanced degree, and it is fair to say that tourism in Ireland in the 1950s was still on a learning curve. As Kennedy and Dowling put it: 'Frequently, one idea has to fail before a better one can replace it.'[89] They see the setting up of the two separate bodies in 1952 as the beginning of a conscious policy for tourism development, which failed to make a sizeable impact partly on account of inadequate funding, but also because it is often necessary to acquire experience in order to develop the most satisfactory schemes. Nevertheless, the late 1950s and early 1960s comprised the era when tourism made its largest relative contribution to the Irish economy, as Bord Fáilte Éireann under T.J. O'Driscoll achieved the kind of success dreamed of by Frederick Crossley at the turn of the century.

Swings
and roundabouts
1960–1980

Tourism develops the mind, promotes the awakening of a social consciousness, improves social relations, diminishes prejudices and elevates the soul.[1]

Citing the late Pope Pius XII on tourism, Bord Fáilte was highly optimistic about prospects as the 1960s began. This chapter will look at developments in the period up to 1980, mainly as seen from the perspective of the tourist board, accommodation providers and investors in the industry. In 1960 the outlook seemed positive, with revenue up by £3.2 million to £37.8 million, 780,000 British visitors and the number described as 'pure' tourists the highest ever at 294,000.[2] American earnings were estimated at £5 million spent by 70,000 visitors, an encouraging figure at a time when the new jet runway at Shannon was not yet complete and international services were over-flying Ireland. In the First Programme for Economic Expansion, tourism was one of the first areas selected for examination by the Economic Development branch established by the Department of Finance, which appointed a Tourism Study Group, comprising representatives of Finance, Industry and Commerce and Bord Fáilte to prepare reports on hotel accommodation, lengthening of the season, motor traffic, inclusive tours, package holidays and festivals. As a result the Tourist Traffic Act (1961) enabled the tourist board to spend up to £5 million on development works at home and publicity abroad in the following seven years. Jack Lynch, Minister for Industry and Commerce, introducing the proposed legislation, made the point that the tempo of development activities other than those of accommodation and major resorts should be increased. These included 'the training of hotel staff, the development of angling and other sporting attractions, the signposting of roads and the provision of easier access to beaches, rivers, lakes, scenic views and other places of special interest to tourists'.[3]

In 1962 tourism came under the remit of the Department of Transport and Power, with Erskine Childers as minister. Three years later the ITB was re-structured, with the creation of a technical department under Kevin Barry, comprising architects, engineers and an archaeologist, with responsibility for the development of major resorts, general planning and amenities, inland waterways, signposting, national monuments and the Tidy Towns competition.[4] An architectural consultancy service was also initiated, providing hotel and guest-house owners with advice on building and interior design, economic projects for new premises and extensions to existing hotels. At the same time, a public relations department under Aidan O'Hanlon was set up to deal with information and liaison, and a publicity department under Michael Gorman to handle advertising, printed publicity, enquiries, external public relations, films, overseas press and photography.

The following year saw the beginning of the second half of the Economic Programme decade and the ITB was encouraged by a sharp rise in the demand for marketing information and found a readiness to 'go out and sell', with groups from every sector of Irish tourism working on old and new markets. Thirty-two organisations in the tourism industry met at the annual co-ordinating meeting convened by the board to exchange information and evaluate progress in the industry. Realisation was dawning that inclusive holidays were no longer an optional refinement, but a necessity when doing business on the international market. It was evident that Ireland was attracting more visitors with a purpose, such as fishing, conferences, theatre and music, hostelling, studying, or visiting historic houses and gardens and ancient monuments. Hoteliers and special interest groups came together, many for the first time, and brought a new sense of organisation and purpose to this element of the tourism product: 'Business will continue to be lost until our portfolio includes holidays much more representative of what Ireland can offer.'[5] Thus began a five-year period in which annual earnings, at 1950 values, needed to be increased by an average of £5 million per annum in order to attain earnings of £90 million in 1970. The ITB felt that state investment in the industry needed to be scaled up and given encouragement that would bear comparison with help given to other important industries.[6] However, 1967 brought disappointing results, with revenue down £0.5 million to £77.7 million, the first drop in ten years. This meant a higher annual target of average increase of 9.5 per cent for the following four years, a difficult task as the base for calculation was rising each year.[7]

By 1967 tourism was the largest single item in world trade, endorsed by the United Nations and praised by the Vatican Council for its contribution 'to the refinement of man's character and his enrichment with understanding of others'.[8] The International Union of Official Tourist Organisations (IUOTO) declared 1967 to be 'International Tourist Year', and its motto, 'Tourism – passport to peace' was adopted by the United Nations Economic and Social Council. In Ireland, Bord Fáilte pointed out that the industry was responsible for raising national living standards and for increasingly benefiting the farming community, although they rarely saw the tourists who were their customers. With the multiplier effect, each £10 million of tourist revenue was likely to create over £18 million in additional income, £5 million in additional tax revenue through high consumption of heavily taxed articles like drink and petrol, and £3 million in savings, as tourists spent at a rate almost four times higher than the average expenditure rate of residents. This additional purchasing power was much more valuable than that of an additional residential population, as the money originated outside the country and represented an addition to the external purchasing power of the economy. Moreover, the import content was notably lower than that of domestic consumption. It was reliably calculated that around 15 per cent of all national employment, equivalent to 160,000 jobs, depended ultimately on tourism.[9] The tourist industry grew in constant money values at an average rate of 5.6 per cent from 1960 onwards, and by 1967 it was Ireland's largest single export, at £84.3 million, £31.3 million ahead of live animals. At that stage it played a more important part in the balance of payments than that in all other European countries except Spain and Austria.[10]

The devaluation of the pound in the autumn of 1967 had a twofold effect: better prices could be offered in non-devaluation areas, making it necessary to attract more visitors to enable the same amount of hard currency to be earned. Visitor numbers from Northern Ireland, for the two preceding years the Republic's most rewarding market, comprised the most significant reductions. While it was felt that the northern market was fairly well exploited, and that the economic recession was bound to have some effect, the situation was exacerbated by the British shipping strike, which

8.1
Brendan O'Regan,
Chairman of Bord
Fáilte, Taoiseach
Jack Lynch and
T.J. O'Driscoll,
Director-General of
Bord Fáilte, at a
promotion in the
late 1960s. *Courtesy
of Fáilte Ireland.*

affected 'through traffic' and especially motorists coming to the
South via cross-channel routes to Northern Ireland, at a loss of £2
million. Cross-channel sea traffic was also down, but passengers
arriving by air were well up. The strike revealed to the business
community how dependent the Irish economy was on visitors,
with traders in Dublin and other centres reporting a marked falling
off in business, not merely in souvenirs but also in clothing,
footwear, drink and a wide range of other goods. The serious economic situation in Britain, reflected in the continuing currency lim-
itations, made it difficult to know if any significant improvements

in visitor numbers could be expected the following year. However, the two-week visit to Ireland in 1969 by the former French president, Charles de Gaulle, was seen as a boost for potential French visitors. A target of £120 million was set for 1970, but revenues fell considerably short at £100 million in a year beset with difficulties at home and abroad. Under the Third Programme for Economic Expansion, a set revenue target for 1972 of £117 million at 1968 values was to be achieved by a growth rate of 6 per cent per annum in real money terms.[11]

However, the early 1970s proved a very difficult period for tourism in the Republic, as the effects of the troubles in Northern Ireland began to take effect, along with spiralling inflation that made the prices of accommodation, food and drink much less attractive to visitors. A period of decline saw a drop of almost 500,000 in visitor numbers in the years 1968–72, and this loss was not fully recovered until 1977, with growth being further consolidated in 1978.[12] The figures for visitors from Northern Ireland in 1970 showed revenue down 13 per cent to under £8 million and a decrease of 16 per cent for stays of more than twenty-four hours, while day trips were down to 12.75 million and corresponding revenue down 3 per cent at £10 million, although this may have been due in many cases to the political disturbances that left people disinclined to leave their homes.

In January 1971 a computerised reservation system was introduced and by 31 March 154 hotels and 18,500 bed nights worth at least £38,000 had been booked. This service was of particular value during the British postal strike lasting seven weeks in the early part of the year, as it was the only link between Irish hotels and guesthouses and prospective clients in Britain. In time it was hoped to include car rental, ferries, inland waterways cruising and inclusive holidays on the system. At the same time the government decided to increase Bord Fáilte's funds by £1.5 million, to be split between accommodation, resort development and marketing and promotion in an effort to halt the decline.[13] Meanwhile, students had come to the fore as world travellers, with over 19,000 coming to Ireland in 1970 for organised literature and language courses and spending £1,086,000. For the first time, a number of six-week advanced programmes were offered for university students. European students, especially the French, had heretofore been the most important group, but they were being steadily overtaken by the number of North Americans who came during the off-season. The Student Calendar for 1970 was revised and improved, with an information brochure for North America listing the more important summer schools and general educational programmes, along with information on work camp schemes, scouts, guides and youth hostelling. In 1971 over 30,000 students came to Ireland and spent £1.29 million, up 18.5 per cent on the previous year.[14]

Another area of growth during this time was that of conference travel, which in the mid-1960s was confined almost exclusively to Dublin. A new development was that of incentive holidays offered by major companies to employees and their wives as a bonus for good sales figures. In October and November 1966, the Norge organisation of Chicago sent 1,700 salesmen and their wives to Ireland and three British firms sent 500 staff, again with their wives, in the spring of 1967.[15] This was precisely the kind of business the tourist board sought, with its emphasis on off-peak travel and the distribution of these visitors in locations outside the capital. In 1967 sixty-two conferences brought 12,000 delegates and salesmen who spent £650,000, making an annual increase of 20 per cent in the previous couple of years. Unfortunately, in 1968 travel curbs by the US government interrupted the successful expansion of this initiative. Arrangements had been made for eight major firms to send staff on incentive holidays, some of whom arrived before the restrictions became an issue. The remainder cancelled in deference to government policy, and as a result almost 9,000 off-peak visitors were lost. Nevertheless, in 1968 there were eighty-five conferences, sales meetings and incentive holidays whose 17,000 participants spent £1.36 million. Interestingly, the troubles in Northern Ireland did not seem to affect conference business to the same extent as holiday visitors, and the numbers rose consistently throughout the 1970s. However, there were disadvantages to holding a conference in Ireland – the lack of late-night entertainment, the extensions of hotel peak rates, the increased cost of travel from Britain and the Continent, together with the fact that conference facilities were inadequate compared with what was offered elsewhere. The Convention Bureau of Ireland was set up in 1972 to assist potential visitors, and 1975 saw the arrival of 40,000 delegates and salesmen who contributed over £7.3 million to the tourism coffers.

An era ended in 1972 when T.J. O'Driscoll retired from the ITB and was succeeded by Éamon Ceannt, former deputy director-general. The following year, Brendan O'Regan also retired after sixteen years as chairman of the board, during which time he had become a seminal figure in Irish tourism and economic development. He was the driving force behind the establishment in 1959 of the Shannon Free Airport Development Company (SFADCO), the first regional economic development agency, which included tourist development in its brief.[16] One of its first initiatives was the restoration of the fifteenth-century Bunratty castle just five miles from Shannon airport, to which Bord Fáilte contributed £13,400, with the remainder shared between Lord Gort, the Office of Public Works and SFADCO. The inauguration of medieval tours from the airport by SFADCO was an increasingly powerful inducement for transatlantic transit passengers to stop off, and numbers rose from 5,000 in 1963 to 27,600 in 1970, while the Bunratty banquets attracted 20,000 visitors in 1969. In the meantime, the Bunratty Folk Park was set up in 1964, and Knappogue and Dunguaire castles opened for banquets in 1967. Castle Tours came into being in 1969, arranging package tours that were marketed in the USA. Along with the burgeoning development at the industrial zone at the airport, O'Regan was also responsible for the building of accommodation for workers there. His achievements in the period 1943–73 constituted a formidable accomplishment for any one man, and his retirement ended an epoch of great advancement in the tourist industry generally. The new chairman was P.V. Doyle, the builder turned hotelier, and the board of directors now included five hoteliers, who encouraged the formation of a task force in 1974 to demonstrate to the travel trade in Britain that Irish tourism was still operating normally.[17]

In 1975, Éamon Ceannt retired. His successor was Joe Malone, who had been the board's general manager for North America. Malone had an established record in tourism development, having been involved in the car hire business for seventeen years before joining Bord Fáilte. He set about re-organising the board and 1975 saw the preparation of a five-year tourism development plan. This comprehensive document outlined policies, objectives and standards for development of the entire tourist infrastructure in line with the expected future needs of tourism. Costs were brought down, with 15 per cent fewer staff, a 17 per cent reduction in travel and related expenses and the joint printing of promotional expenditure and sharing of offices in overseas markets with other Irish state bodies. In 1975 visitor revenue of £243.6 million from all sources, including carrier receipts, meant that total export and domestic tourism spending contributed 5.6 per cent to GNP. With the global economy still in recession and rising unemployment leading to the inevitable curtailment of normal growth in disposable income, world tourism was still recovering from a 3 per cent fall in tourism arrivals in 1974, the first decline since statistics were compiled.[18] In Ireland, tourism produced 9.2 per cent of all foreign earnings, about half of which were in sterling, and the balance mainly in dollars and hard European currencies, leaving net

8.2
From left: David
Kennedy, General
Manager of Aer
Lingus; *unknown*;
P.V. Doyle,
Chairman of Bord
Fáilte and Joe
Malone, Director-
General of Bord
Fáilte, at Dublin
Airport *en route* to
the United States for
a promotional
campaign in 1977.
*Courtesy of Fáilte
Ireland.*

retained foreign exchange earnings at 75 per cent.[19] Work on projects in the Five-Year Plan were carried out in 1976 at a cost of over
£2.5 million, under the headings of environment, facilities, accommodation and catering, transport and manpower. At that time, it
was estimated that 9 per cent of jobs in the Republic could be attributed directly or indirectly to tourism earnings.[20] Revenue was up to
a total of £181.4 million, but after deducting 18 per cent for inflation, the real increase was only 1 per cent. The British market was
down 4 per cent, an unsurprising result considering the state of the
economy there, with the falling value of sterling, continued unemployment and unabated inflation. An added deterrent to visitors
was the fear of an overspill of the Northern Ireland violence into
the Republic, but with a prediction of a recovery in world tourism,
the board hoped for a better outcome in 1977.[21]

And so it proved. The following year was a record year in every
way, with the highest-ever number of visitors at 1,963,000, up from
a previous best of 1,940,000 in 1969, and a total revenue record figure of £328 million, a rise of 32 per cent. A new tourism plan for the

years 1978–82 incorporated the major strategies of the previous development plan, and expansion programmes were revised to take account of the timings of planned projects and policy changes. The following two years saw the successful trend continue, with over two million visitors in 1978, and 2.36 million in 1979, bucking the trend in an OECD report that confirmed no growth in arrivals in other member states.[22] However, 1979 was also a year of problems, with initial uncertainty about Ireland's entry into the European Monetary System, a postal dispute lasting from February to June and petrol shortages beginning in April, along with widely publicised killings at Mullaghmore and Warrenpoint. A petrol voucher scheme for tourists was introduced with the support of the Departments of Tourism and Transport, Industry and Commerce and Energy, but the Irish situation received unusually large coverage overseas as it appeared to be the worst hit of tourist destinations in Europe. The uncertainty of supply in remote areas made tourists unwilling to travel and led to shorter stays, causing a 5 per cent drop in bed nights from overseas.[23] The visit of the Pope in September helped to counterbalance Ireland's negative image overseas, with a great deal of positive publicity and the 30,000 visitors who came especially for his trip helping to boost the figures. At the same time, an analysis of visitor profiles showed that the proportion of those coming to Ireland on business had increased, contributing to the growth of revenue and a relatively better performance in the main urban centres.

In the period 1949–58 there had been a steady decline in income from tourism in constant monetary values, but between then and 1964 revenue had increased by a yearly average of 4.3 per cent in real terms. With the aim of meeting two major needs – better marketing and better organisation of resources available locally – in 1964 a radical move was the formation of eight Regional Tourism Organisations (RTOs). In an attempt to decentralise Irish tourism, Bord Fáilte set about the formation of voluntary regional organisations to cover the country, with the co-operation of the Irish Tourist Association, the Irish Hotel and Restaurant Managers Association and the Irish Hotels Federation. The RTOs assumed the functions of the ITA and absorbed its staff. Its directors comprised local politicians, businessmen and tourism experts, and Bord Fáilte also anticipated the support and growing interest of the trade unions.[24] Funds for the new bodies were supplied mainly by local authorities, the business community and the tourist board, and a close working relationship was envisaged between the RTOs and the board. Local authorities were to be enabled to play a more

8.3
Robert Hall,
General Manager of
the Northern
Ireland Tourist
Board; John Carroll
of the Irish
Transport and
General Workers'
Union, Acting
Chairman of Bord
Fáilte; Lord O'Neill,
Chairman of the
Northern Ireland
Tourist Board; and
Joe Malone,
Director-General
Bord Fáilte, after
Bord Fáilte's May
1979 board meeting
in Belfast. *Courtesy
of the Northern
Ireland Tourist Board.*

active part in tourist development and would nominate RTO directors. Planning for the regions included an emphasis on a fuller use of accommodation; improved visitor information services; the provision of recreational facilities and entertainment and the encouragement of local voluntary efforts in the provision of tourism facilities. Eight managers were chosen in 1965 from more than 1,000 applicants and despatched for training at the Irish Management Institute.[25] Local authorities increased their contributions to the new organisations by one third, and by 1966 the target set for supplementary accommodation, namely bed and breakfast establishments, was achieved due to the personalised local approach, which also helped in locating accommodation and classrooms for increasing student traffic.[26] In conjunction with Comhaltas Ceoltóirí Éireann, initial plans were made for extended visitor entertainment in hotels. The RTOs assisted local enterprises and advised Bord Fáilte on commercial propositions needing examination at local level. They took over the administration of the Joyce tower at Sandycove, W.B. Yeats's former home at Thoor Ballylee, Gort, and the information centre at Newgrange, thus enhancing the investment by Bord Fáilte and other bodies interested in the restoration of historic and cultural places. In 1969, 453,000 bed nights were booked at 100 telex-linked information offices, and the companies produced 3.5 million holiday information folders, which were distributed abroad by Bord Fáilte and at home in the tourist information offices. Information supplied by the RTOs to the tourist board on tourism resources in the eight regions made a considerable contribution to the planning aspect of physical development, and the bodies also continued to provide commercial intelligence on effective marketing methods.[27]

In 1971 ninety-two local authorities contributed £94,000 to the regional bodies, up from £24,000 in 1965, and support from the business community was up to almost £100,000. Tourist information offices handled 1.6 million enquiries and booked 380,000 bed nights for 220,000 people. The RTOs also handled travel writers, film and television units, and travel agents, while at the same time encouraging more Irish people to spend holidays at home.[28] However, in 1972 local authority and commercial contributions stalled at their 1970 levels, while the tourist board had to put in £305,000.[29] The following year the RTOs collaborated with the ITB on the administration of a special fund allocated by the Department of Transport and Power for general resort development. In addition, over thirty regional staff joined a Bord Fáilte promotion force in Britain and were also deployed in sales work in France, Germany and North America.[30] However, the organisations' income was stagnant at this stage, while the tourist board's contribution had risen to £465,000, and their financial situation was only secured by a special allocation of £120,000 by the board in relief overdrafts over the previous two years.[31] By 1975, despite contributions of £138,000 by local authorities, Bord Fáilte's expenditure was £780,000, representing over 80 per cent of their funds, which was a great deal higher than that envisaged when these bodies were established.[32] Nevertheless, the board continued to support the RTOs financially, and by 1981 the cost had risen to almost £1.9 million.

Along with progress in cross-border co-operation with Northern Ireland, the tourist board felt that it would benefit Britain and Ireland, north and south, if the two islands could be offered as a single tourist area to potential North American and continental visitors. However, efforts to achieve this in the late 1950s were effectively stymied by the northern board. In 1960, J.B. MacCarthy, secretary of the Department of Industry and Commerce, wrote to Con Cremin in the Department of Foreign Affairs explaining the course of events. During a meeting in London in November 1957, the then president of the Board of Trade suggested to Seán Lemass that there was scope for co-operation between the two countries in the field of tourism. This was pursued by Bord Fáilte and the British Travel and Holidays Association (BTHA), with some enthusiasm on the part of the latter, and after talks with T.J. O'Driscoll their director-general suggested plans for joint promotional activities between the two bodies. Lemass sanctioned Bord Fáilte's participation provided that his clearance was obtained in the event of any political complications. Plans were made for a distribution of literature on request about the respective areas, with the BTHA willing to provide representation for the ITB at trade fairs and exhibitions where it had none. In addition, the association would undertake certain distribution activities on behalf of the board in countries where the board had no office, provided the expenses involved, such as postage, were reimbursed. When parties of travel agents, journalists or other sponsored visits were organised by either body, consideration would be given to including parts of the UK or the Republic on such tours. In future publicity material, particularly those including maps, consideration would be given by both organisations to the addition of information on transport connections between Great Britain and Ireland and other information of mutual interest; statistics, research and other technical information would be freely exchanged, with the exception of any confidential documentation, which would not in any case be made available to members of the BTHA or to constituents of Bord Fáilte. Needless to say, this seemed like a most advantageous offer to the tourist board, in a situation where they were getting much more than they were giving.

However, much to their surprise, the BTHA declined to follow up the plans and adopted a reserved attitude towards the question of co-operation. According to information given confidentially to O'Driscoll, the committee and board of the BTHA had refused to endorse the propositions because the NITB, a constituent of the BTHA, objected strongly to the proposals, mainly on the grounds that their tourist publicity material would be overshadowed by the larger quantities and better variety of publications which Bord Fáilte could make available and which would be distributed side by side with NITB literature in the overseas offices of the BTHA. Subsequently, Bord Fáilte found out that the NITB also found its tourist literature politically 'tendentious'. In an effort to compromise, Bord Fáilte offered to limit the range of publications to BTHA offices abroad, to select for NITB perusal specimens of literature which might not be considered tendentious, and to examine the possibility of participating in joint publicity to cover the whole country, or, alternatively, joint publicity embracing both islands. There was no response to these suggestions and negotiations with the BTHA ended. While MacCarthy was in London some time later, he mentioned the matter informally to a Board of Trade official, who later wrote to say that co-operation on the lines suggested was not 'practical politics'.[33] A letter from O'Driscoll to MacCarthy explained Bord Fáilte's position on the matter:

> Since one of our major concerns is the promotion of Irish tourism in overseas markets, we are primarily interested in an extension of practical co-operation with BTHA, rather than with the Six Counties Tourist Board ... both BTHA and ourselves are agreed on the proposition that the holiday attractions of Britain and Ireland could be more effectively publicised abroad if these islands were presented as a single tourist area. Co-operation with the Six-County people is not

really of much practical touristic importance, though obviously attractive for other reasons.[34]

In the event, it was 1966 before a meeting took place in Dublin with representatives of the Northern Ireland Tourist Board and Len Lickorish and Lord Geddes of the British Travel and Holidays Association. Agreement was reached on the production of a joint folder for Ireland and Britain for distribution in North America, and it was hoped that a common hotel grading system for the whole island of Ireland could be achieved with the co-operation of the NITB.[35] Bord Fáilte also hoped that in time a uniform system could be introduced to include Britain, which would be of considerable benefit to combined marketing endeavours in North America. In 1969, for the first time, familiarisation tours of Ireland and Britain by overseas agents were organised jointly with the NITB and the new British Tourist Authority, which had replaced the BTHA. Bord Fáilte also participated in BTA workshops in Copenhagen, Paris, Madrid, the Far East and Australia.[36] With common research activities and a standardisation of information, this tripartite co-operation gave the board the opportunity to explore new business, particularly in areas where it was not represented.

The tourist board also continued its international involvement during the 1960s. The International Union of Official Tourist Organisations (IUOTO), representing national tourism authorities in ninety-six countries, was established in 1947 with Bord Fáilte as a founder member. The organisation worked with the Organisation

8.4
Robert Frizell, General Manager of the Northern Ireland Tourist Board; Leonard Lickorish, General Manager, and Lord Geddes, Chairman, of the British Travel Association; Brendan O'Regan, Chairman of Bord Fáilte; W.L. Stephens, Chairman of the Northern Ireland Tourist Board; and T.J. O'Driscoll, Director-General of Bord Fáilte, at tripartite talks held in Dublin in 1966 to discuss co-operation between the three bodies.

for Economic Co-operation and Development (OECD) at government level, and advances made in facilitating world travel were
largely due to its efforts. It also had consultative status at the
United Nations, and in view of his work as president of the organisation and of the international standing of the Irish Tourist Board,
T.J. O'Driscoll was asked by the secretary-general of the UN in 1967
to act as their high-level consultant on tourism. This post involved
a review of the functions of international groups in tourism and
advice on the organisation of tourism, particularly for the benefit of
developing countries. Bord Fáilte was selected for a second term to
provide the chairman and secretarial service for the European
Travel Commission, an alliance of the national tourism bodies of
twenty-one European countries.[37] In 1969 Ireland was chosen as the
venue for the twenty-first general assembly of IUOTO, which was
held in Dublin and attended by representatives of seventy-five
countries and thirty-three other organisations connected with
tourism. O'Driscoll was elected chairman of the ETC for a third
successive term, and during that year the tourist board was also
closely involved in the organisation in Amsterdam of the Third
Transatlantic Travel Congress, sponsored by the ETC and the
national tourism organisations of Canada, Mexico and the USA.[38]

The provision of adequate accommodation for the growing
numbers of visitors during the 1960s was a constant headache for
the tourist board, but in 1960 it secured tax concessions and
approval to extend the scope of loans and grants. For income tax
purposes, annual depreciation was allowed of 10 per cent of capital
expenditure incurred from 1 January 1960 for extensions and
improvements, and for the construction of new premises, including
motels. Grants of up to 20 per cent of the total cost became available
for works in existing hotels, in addition to the existing 20 per cent
grant for new bedrooms. But the great leap forward in the early
1960s was the arrival of large, modern hotels built by the Irish and
Inter-Continental group in Dublin, Cork and Limerick. These were
followed by the building of medium-sized hotels offering accommodation at reasonable prices by P.V. Doyle. The success of these
hotels persuaded Irish entrepreneurs to invest in the business, as
tourist numbers began to rise dramatically during the 1960s. The
growth of coach-tour business meant that extra accommodation
was necessary, especially in the west, and in 1967 Bord Fáilte was
empowered to offer additional incentives in that region. The board
encouraged prospective developers to think in terms of motor inns
and medium-priced hotels suited to the mobile visitor, with less
emphasis on public areas but provision of adequate, inexpensive

meal facilities. A major study in accommodation needs in terms of quantity, quality and distribution up to 1985 was commissioned in 1970, and the building of 'authentic' Irish cottages in a traditional local style for rent by SFADCO in small villages such as Ballyvaughan and Corofin in County Clare was a welcome innovation. In 1975 work began on a new hotel classification system in consultation with the IHF, the NITB and the Northern Ireland Hotel and Catering Association, and the Hotel Marketing Advisory Unit was established in co-operation with the IHF and the RTOs. A new grant scheme for additional hotel accommodation was approved in 1978, with an emphasis on expanding and improving existing premises, and the high volume of applications was a healthy indication of the confidence of the industry in future prospects.

The shortage of trained staff continued to be a chronic problem and in 1961 the ITB set up a working group to examine all aspects of staff recruitment and training, while still funding scholarships to the tune of £16,000 at various venues around the country. As a result, the Council for Education, Recruitment and Training (CERT) came into being in 1963, funded by Bord Fáilte to the tune of £15,000, and by 1966 there were 600 students in training at nine training centres, with the board planning to double that number by 1970.[39] It was also decided that in-service programmes should be organised for people already in the industry. With 800 students trained by 1968, including 124 in management, national recruitment campaigns were undertaken in vocational and secondary schools over the following years. However, finances were inadequate and the board looked to central and local authorities for assistance in this respect. During 1968 T.J. O'Driscoll became the chairman of CERT and at the annual Tourism Co-ordination Meeting in 1969 there was unanimity that more professionalism was needed in an international field of intense competition. With France, Germany, Britain and the USA according recognition to tourism in third-level courses, the Irish performance would continue to fall short until there was substantial investment in advanced education.[40] To add to the problem, recruitment to an industry with a reputation for low pay and poor conditions was difficult. In June 1969 the recruitment campaign attracted 1,000 school-leavers, but over two-thirds of them did not follow through to the training stage.[41] The following year, a new school opened at Killybegs, and in 1971 a programme of rationalisation saw CERT divide the country into seven regions, each with its own registered training advisor. Day-release and sandwich courses were set up in conjunction with local vocational schools and regional technical colleges in order to supplement existing residential hotel schools.[42] Then in 1974 the role of CERT was expanded to take responsibility for all tourism training and related manpower research and planning under the auspices of the Department of Labour. A survey was completed early in 1977 with a view to giving indications of requirements throughout the industry and a more detailed picture in relation to specific sectors.[43] From 1978 on, with the support of European Economic Community funds, courses were rationalised and services increased, and in 1982 a National Craft Curricula and Certification Board was set up.[44]

As regards major resorts, the White Paper on Economic Expansion published in 1959 provided for £1 million to be set aside for a ten-year programme of development. This was catered for in the 1959 Tourist Traffic Act and consisted of grants to be administered by local authorities in conjunction with local committees. This provision found general acceptance in the Dáil, although Donough O'Malley queried the term 'major' when applied to Irish resorts: 'Who is the competent authority to interpret the meaning of the word "major" in this Bill? Surely the word could be omitted and just "tourist resort" left in? Are places such as Kilkee, Lahinch, Lisdoonvarna and Dingle, allowed to qualify under this Bill, or would Limerick City be considered "a major tourist resort"?'[45] Liam Cosgrave pointed out that local committees wishing to improve their amenities often lacked the necessary funds, and that some local authorities were reluctant to get involved for fear of being held responsible for any accident or injury that might occur.[46] The board proceeded with preliminary works in 1960, spending £10,000 in Dun Laoghaire, Arklow, Greystones and Salthill in Galway. However, progress was slow, with delays in purchasing sites for development and some local authorities adopting a 'go slow' policy so that they could spread their share of the cost over longer periods.[47] With the fund exhausted by 1966, legislation was enacted to provide an additional £2.25 million to be split between twelve resorts and five resort areas already in the programme, and preliminary works on a number of additional resorts, almost all of which were on the coast.[48] By 1975 the major resort scheme begun in 1958 was completed, with £4 million spent by the board in five resort areas and fourteen resort centres. The Tourism Development Plan 1976–1980 entailed the examination of over 14,000 projects, which were whittled down to 1,500 in the final plan with a projected expenditure of almost £50 million.[49]

Another concern for the ITB was the expansion of the North American market, and intensive efforts to this end were made during the 1960s, as the growth in jet transport and the absence of new major events in Europe resulted in significant US traffic being diverted to the Caribbean and the Pacific. In 1961, 85,000 transatlantic visitors to Ireland spent £6.1 million, but traffic to Europe as a whole declined.[50] By the mid-1960s numbers had risen to 137,000, who spent £8.1 million. A lack of knowledge about Ireland on the part of US travel agents and the tendency at American government level to discourage pleasure travel abroad was thought to have had an effect on numbers. An extra 75,000 airline seats to Ireland were on offer in 1967 by Aer Lingus, Pan American Airways, Trans World Airways and Air Canada, including a Chicago–Ireland direct link, thus opening up the mid-west, second only to the east coast region in the volume of tourist traffic to Europe. In 1968 transatlantic air traffic was up 17 per cent, and the number of cruise ships calling at Irish ports was also on the increase. However, proposed travel curbs in the USA left the market in an uncertain state, and Bord Fáilte opposed the Washington proposals by contributing material for submission to the Ways and Means Committee of the House of Representatives by the European Travel Commission and the Ireland–US Council for Commerce and Industry, a group of American business executives that rendered valuable practical assistance to Ireland in this difficult situation. A campaign to encourage special interest and package holidays spread over the autumn, winter and spring months in 1970 produced encouraging results. A particular success was the 'Fall through Spring' programme, under which forty-three special tours generated 8,000 visitors. By the end of the year transatlantic traffic was up 25.7 per cent from 183,000 to 230,000, while revenue increased by 31.6 per cent, from £15.5 million to £20.4 million. This was quite an achievement and brought the North American market to its target ahead of time in a year marked by a number of adverse factors, including difficulties in the US economy. Under-capacity on North American routes was a recurring problem in the peak season, with scheduled traffic up 16 per cent in 1971, and non-scheduled down 30 per cent due to the rigorous application of charter regulations. A decision by Aer Lingus to increase charter flights in 1971 was good news, as was the liberal policy statement by the Minister for Transport and Power on the granting of authorisation for transatlantic charter flights. A proposed new fare structure submitted to the International Air Transport Association's conference in September 1970 could have led to serious reductions in US traffic to Ireland. Bord Fáilte briefed Aer Lingus prior to the conference and the proposals were defeated due to the lively opposition led by

Irish delegates, thus ensuring that Ireland maintained its competitiveness. However, the worldwide recession in following years led to a serious decline in North American traffic, and it was 1977 before a meaningful improvement was seen. After two good years, tension in the international sphere in 1980 characterised by the taking of American hostages by Iran, the Russian invasion of Afghanistan and the consequent American boycott of the Olympic Games in Moscow, added to an election year in the USA, combined to depress North American travel to Europe.

Publicity and promotion abroad played an increasingly large part in the 1960s and 1970s, especially as events in Northern Ireland began to radically affect tourism in the Republic. In 1962, Bord Fáilte spent £247,000 on publicity abroad and sought an additional state allocation for the expansion of such activities. The board also participated in a Publicity Co-ordination Committee with Aer Lingus, Córas Tráchtála, the Department of Foreign Affairs, SFADCO, CIE and the Industrial Development Authority, which met every two months to help ensure the effective presentation of Ireland abroad. It was felt that tourist publicity did much more than project Ireland as a desirable place for holidays; in speaking of Irish history, culture, industrial achievement and standards of living, it dispelled many of the antiquated notions about the country that still existed abroad. In April 1963 one successful outcome was the publication by *Holiday* magazine of an issue entirely given over to Ireland, with articles by V.S. Pritchett, Frank O'Connor, Brian Friel, Seán Ó Faoláin and Desmond Guinness. The board's policy was also to encourage top-level commentators in every medium to make their own assessments and correct the many misconceptions about Ireland. Where before there was indifference or even hostility, familiarisation visits by representatives of some of the world's most influential magazines, newspapers, radio, film and television networks assisted Irish political, social and economic aspirations abroad. Publicity had to be intensified to meet unforeseen situations such as that created by the devaluation of sterling in 1968, while also explaining to British visitors the essential precautions taken by Ireland against foot and mouth disease in the same year. The board also carried out what amounted to an educational campaign in the USA in order to counter the threat of travel restrictions there. Its claim to expertise in general promotional effectiveness was vindicated when Michael Whelan, marketing manager, delivered a paper on the subject to the European Society for Opinion Surveys and Market Research at its seminar on Travel and Tourism in Switzerland in 1969. His paper was well received and was offered as a case study for discussion at selected graduate schools of business administration in the US and elsewhere.

At this time the board's publicity emphasis was on extending the holiday season, with concentrated promotional activities abroad that it hoped would lead to the industry being active for ten months of the year, with the balance of time being spent on refurbishment and preparation for the year ahead. However, the negative worldwide publicity that attended the Northern Ireland troubles in the 1970s shattered the peaceful and friendly image of the island, and much of the publicity and promotion undertaken during this time consisted of attempting to reassure potential visitors that the Republic was a separate and unaffected entity, although events such as the 1974 Dublin and Monaghan bombings, the assassination of the British ambassador in 1976, and that of Lord Mountbatten in 1979 clearly contradicted this assertion and made promotional efforts abroad even more crucial.

Many improvements in transport facilities for visitors took place during the 1960s and 1970s, with the most effective being the provision of cross-channel and continental car ferry services. A depressing development was the demise of the transatlantic liner service to Cobh, where an improvement scheme was completed in 1960 to which the tourist board contributed £32,000, only to see operations cease there in 1963. Cross-border motoring traffic increased spectacularly, with 4.5 million car entries in 1963, largely due to the easing of customs regulations. With 1964 dubbed 'the year of the motorist' by tourist interests in the Republic, the number of cars brought by sea and air increased by 7,000, a 28 per cent rise to 30,000, while cross-border motoring traffic rose by 1.5 million to 6 million. In 1965 a further improvement was the removal of the triptyque and its substitution by a simple temporary importation permit, which also allowed visitors from Britain to cross the border northwards in hired cars. The introduction of the British Rail Holyhead–Dun Laoghaire car ferry in July 1965 with a capacity for 155 cars and 1,000 passengers, extra space for cars on the Fishguard–Rosslare route and the Aer Lingus air ferry all contributed to hopes for an immediate increase of 50 per cent in cross-channel motoring traffic. By 1968 the shipping companies had spent £15 million on car ferries and were contemplating another £6 million. The fruits of their investment were seen in 1970 when 114,389 accompanied cars arrived in the Republic, up 24 per cent, while another 73,903 entered Northern Ireland, of which an estimated 60 per cent travelled south. The main contributory factors were the new Cork–Swansea B+I route; the new B+I ferry from Dublin to Liverpool; increased capacity by British Rail to Dun Laoghaire and Rosslare; and the doubling of the capacity of the Normandy Ferries service between Le Havre and Rosslare, which had begun in 1968. An innovative development, at the instigation of Bord Fáilte, was the introduction of express coach services from Paris to Dublin, Glasgow to Dublin, and Glasgow to Derry, to benefit the generation and facility of pedestrian family traffic and eliminate any feeling of discrimination against non-car-owning passengers. The increase in passenger numbers called for better facilities at arrival points, and these were provided with a permanent car ferry terminal in Dun Laoghaire in 1969, along with a new B+I terminal in Cork and improvements by CIE at Rosslare harbour to be completed in 1973 at a cost of £200,000. That year also saw the inauguration of the Irish Continental Line direct service to Le Havre to replace the Normandy Ferries operation that had ceased abruptly in 1971.

Festivals became a major component in the drive to lengthen the season as the 1960s unfolded. Despite the effective demise of An Tóstal, with only sixteen events bringing 6,000 visitors who spent £80,000 in 1960, the ITB decided to guarantee certain major events for the following years. The criteria for financial support included the number of foreign visitors attracted, especially in the off-season; publicity value abroad; the extent of local support; and the internal value of gaining support for tourism. Festivals supported in 1961 were: Grand Opera and Theatre in Dublin; the Irish Hospitals £5,000 Golf Tournament at Woodbrook; the Yeats Summer School, Sligo; choral and folk dance in Cork; Light Opera in Waterford; and the Festival of Kerry. Six years later grants of £31,000 to nine major events attracted 12,000 visitors who spent £250,000, and, as importantly, strengthened Ireland's cultural image abroad. Backing was guaranteed for selected off-season festivals up to 1970, but the board lamented the lack of high-level administration, while encouraging organising committees to form limited companies. Local commercial sponsorship was disappointing, with a tendency to fall back on the board and to a lesser extent on the same handful of national firms, even though many businesses around the country could thank local festivals for a sizeable increase in turnover.[51] By 1970 ten major events were being supported financially by Bord Fáilte, while an average of ten others were being assisted by each Regional Tourism Organisation: 'There are now over 300 festival-type events in the Twenty-six Counties, some of cultural importance, many others whose entertainment and glamour quality gives them visitor appeal.' Some major events, such as the Dublin Theatre Festival, the Cork Choral Festival and the Waterford

Festival of Light Opera, had achieved international status, and in addition to attracting considerable numbers, helped to secure positive publicity for Ireland abroad at a time when escalating violence in the North was grabbing headlines all over the world. The St Patrick's Day festival, inaugurated in 1967, was extended to a week in 1971 and attracted 2,200 visitors from North America, Germany, Britain and Northern Ireland, generating 16,750 bed nights. It was considerably helped by moving into March a number of events previously held during the high and late seasons, such as the Dublin Festival of Arts and Theatre Festival, the Wexford Festival of Living Music, Siamsa, and the Limerick Pageant Week.[52]

During the 1960s and 1970s Bord Fáilte continued its campaign to encourage the best standards of design while preserving natural amenities. Although the Derelict Sites Act of 1960 allowed for the removal of abandoned sites and a scheme of amenity grants was put in place enabling eyesores to be cleared and tasteful planning carried out, the board called for further legislation to protect towns and the countryside from tasteless exploitation and urged local authorities to participate more fully in such activities. It was felt that until tourism was totally accepted as a local as well as a national responsibility, it would never achieve the performance of which it was capable, and that spending on amenities and local promotion should be recognised as investments that would enhance the appeal of a district to visitors and benefit local ratepayers. While a country such as Ireland, which had come late to industrialisation, gained greatly by having preserved its natural beauty and unspoilt countryside, more resources were needed for the care and presentation of ancient and historic sites. Since 1953 the board had spent over £60,000 on ancillary works at national monuments, and planned another £50,000 in expenditure over the following five years on comprehensive works at Newgrange and improvements at Mellifont, Cashel, Ardee castle, Four Knocks and Clonmacnoise. In 1961 CIE brought 38,500 visitors to Glendalough, while 9,500 people took tours of the Boyne Valley, and it was probable that these figures were doubled by private transport and charter bus. The National Museum of Ireland had 170,000 visitors, while Bunratty castle attracted 30,000, proving that Ireland's historical and cultural heritage was high on the list of many tourists.

The 1963 Local Government (Planning and Development) Act gave the ITB an advisory role on applications for planning permission, and by 1964 it had given recommendations on thirty submissions, including the proposed siting of hotel, chalet and housing projects, the erection of overhead cables in scenic areas, the demolition of an old bridge and commercial developments in a number of resorts. For those interested in local improvement schemes it published a free booklet entitled *Eye to Progress*, which was in such demand that a revised edition had to be issued. The Planning Act was designed to protect natural resources from erosion by population, industrial and other pressures. Section 6.2 (a) empowered local authorities to 'make examinations of tourist potential, interest and need', and the board anxiously awaited its implementation. Its first full year of operation was 1966 and each of the eighty-seven local authorities was required to produce a development plan, including an amenity section, by 1967. In this they were backed by the Minister for Local Government; An Foras Forbartha, the National Institute for Physical Planning and Construction Research, established in 1964; and various consultant bodies including Bord Fáilte, the Arts Council and An Taisce. By 1966 the board had been consulted on 250 cases by various planning authorities and had participated in regular consultations with specialist firms engaged by the Department of Local Government to prepare prototype plans for such selected regions as Dublin, Limerick and Donegal.

The preservation of countryside, coastline, areas of botanic and geological interest and the protection of wildlife were of continuous concern to Bord Fáilte, which gave priority to matters arising from the Planning Act at this time, even at the expense of progress in tourism development, as despoliation of any area would be irretrievable. In 1969 the board and An Foras Forbartha jointly initiated a survey to investigate the problem of building on the coastline to help formulate and guide local authority planning and future strategies for conservation and development in coastal areas. By 1970 the number of planning applications processed by the Technical Department had risen to 2,560, which placed a considerable toll on the workload of that section. The board reviewed its amenity policy, with its concern for social and environmental problems, and welcomed the growing interest in conservation issues, while participating in the establishment of Derrynane National Park and the planning of Killarney National Park. The following year it was decided to reduce the board's involvement in planning matters, and action was taken on only some of the 1,500 referred projects. A liaison plan was inaugurated with local authorities, with the stress on initiating and furthering of specialised studies on planning and amenity. The Tourism Development Plan for 1976–80 laid strong emphasis on conserving scenic resources and called for the tackling of the deteriorating environment with pollution,

despoliation of the countryside, litter and inappropriate development. In 1977 the Planning and Development Act dealt with water
pollution and the conservation and protection of wildlife. Two
years later, Bord Fáilte jointly funded a national anti-litter campaign with industrial interests, launched at the behest of the
Department of Tourism and Transport at a cost of £200,000, and successfully motivated over 2,000 anti-litter projects by residents' associations, voluntary groups and local committees.

However, the most effective initiative for enhancing rural
Ireland from the late 1950s onwards was the Tidy Towns competition, which was organised and financed by the tourist board. A
National Roadside Gardens competition, designed to brighten up
approaches to towns and villages, was run by the Irish
Countrywomen's Association in co-operation with Bord Fáilte as
part of An Tóstal. The board also organised a National Spring Clean
campaign each year as part of the festival, and this developed into
the Tidy Towns and Villages Competition in 1958, with the aim of
finding the best-kept town in the country. With voluntary councils
already organised for An Tóstal, it was an easy evolution to Tidy
Towns involvement as the festival foundered in the late 1950s. In
1958 the ITB set up an independent panel of assessors comprising
architects, town planners and landscape architects under the aegis
of the Technical Department, which also offered advice and support
to local committees. Fifty-two centres entered and the national winner, Glenties in County Donegal, was awarded a perpetual plaque
and a cash prize, while there were also awards for towns and villages in the different categories of size, based on population, and
county. The board encouraged development of natural amenities
such as lakes, rivers and green spaces, and called for the preservation of distinctive items such as traditional shop-fronts and street
furniture. It also waged war on derelict buildings, advising that if
they could not be demolished they should be cleaned up and
painted in attractive colours. Other organisations interested in
rural society and heritage, such as Muintir na Tíre and An Taisce,
became involved, and press and television reporting of the annual
results gave the competition further standing. By 1960 there were
over 200 entries, along with 3,000 roadside gardens, and an encouraging feature of the competitions was the growing participation of
local authorities and vocational groups, and the willingness of
commercial interests to award prizes. In 1966 there was a record
entry of 377 centres, and the ITB emphasised that marking would
favour communities giving sympathetic treatment to village greens
and town parks, showing feeling for trees and shrubs as well as

8.5
P.V. Doyle,
Chairman of Bord
Fáilte; James Tully,
Minister for Local
Government and
Father J. Kelly,
Chairman of Trim
Tidy Towns
Committee at an
awards ceremony in
1974 in Trim.
*Courtesy of Fáilte
Ireland.*

flowers, and using colour in a restrained, harmonious way. The competition grew from an entry of 557 in 1970 to 729 in 1977, at which stage the competition was extended to major population centres in Dublin, Dun Laoghaire, Limerick, Waterford, Cork and Galway with the introduction of the National Tidy Districts Award Scheme. By then expenditure on this and other community projects, together with the National Gardens competition, was running at £60,000.[53] In 1978 the board celebrated the competition's coming of age with a film entitled 'Our Tidy Towns – Twenty-One Years of Community Effort'. The film focuses on the 1978 prize-giving ceremony in Glaslough in County Monaghan, but covers twenty-three towns and villages, examining the layout and architectural details of a number of urban design types. Activities associated with Tidy Towns improvement schemes are shown, including tree-planting, shop-front design and park development. Padraig Faulkner, Minister for Transport and Power, P.V. Doyle, chairman of Bord Fáilte, and Joe Malone, director-general of the board, are featured, with the minister making a strong plea for a concerted national campaign to tackle Ireland's growing litter problem.[54]

The development of inland waterways for fishing and cruising holidays was an important priority for Bord Fáilte during the 1960s. A five-year development programme for fishing was inaugurated in 1958 and the tourist board made a significant commitment to it in financial terms, with expenditure of £190,000 on facilities and £54,000 on promotion abroad by 1960.[55] In 1962 the plan achieved its target of £1.2 million at a cost to the tourist board of £236,000.[56] The money was well spent. In 1963 angling earned £1.35 million and by 1965 a record 90,000 fishermen, up from 39,000 in 1960, spent £3.15 million. The importance of this industry to the midland regions cannot be overstated, as it brought economic and social benefits to areas with limited opportunities for industrial or any other tourism development. On the other hand, these numbers also created an urgent need for yet more accommodation, boats, access roads, carparks and fishing stands, which the board looked to the RTOs to assist in providing. By 1967 fishing numbers were up 4 per cent to 106,000 and spending was up correspondingly to £3.74 million. At the same time, preparations were in hand for a second five-year plan for the development of both sea and coarse fishing, with the aim of generating a £5 million contribution to the Second Programme for Economic Development.[57] By 1975, despite problems elsewhere in the industry, angling remained the most resilient activity. However, pollution of fishery resources was growing, and it was hoped that the 1977 Planning and Development Act would be implemented in a manner that would protect inland fisheries. It contained new obligations for planning permission for piggeries, one of the worse offenders as regards contamination, along with creamery effluent, discharge of untreated town sewage, and growth peat deposits on rivers and lakes, the last being particularly bad on the Shannon from Shannonbridge to Lough Derg.[58]

While fishing development helped to lengthen the tourist season, the board also looked to cruising holidays on inland waterways to become a major attraction. In 1961, at the time of the first Irish Boat Show in Dublin there were just twelve boats for hire, but the following year there were fifty craft on offer, aided by loans to the tune of £40,000 from Bord Fáilte, who aimed to have 100 boats by the end of 1962. The Shannon waterway was designated a major resort in 1963, and in 1964, with sixty-four boats in operation mainly financed by the ITB, it was decided to spend £100,000 over five years developing the waterway and another £40,000 on marketing.[59] Earnings from hire cruisers in 1963 were £50,000 and this jumped to £100,000 in 1964, a good return on the £25,000 spent by the board. By then there were 100 boats for hire, and at this stage 75 per cent of hirers

8.6
Joe Malone,
Director-General of
Bord Fáilte and
Robert Hall, General
Manager of the
Northern Ireland
Tourist Board, with
members of the
California Highway
Patrol in Los Angeles
during the Irish
Open golf
championship at the
Association of British
Travel Agents
convention in 1979.
*Courtesy of the
Northern Ireland
Tourist Board.*

were from Britain, but as the business developed increasing numbers of continental visitors took to the water, mainly from France, Germany and Holland. The growth in popularity of boating holidays, worth £180,000 in 1965, led to a need for improved facilities along the waterways. In 1966, having expended £100,000 on development, the board calculated that £5 million was needed to service 1,000 craft with shore installations and adequate protection services, and that this would require private investment. The new marina at Carrick-on-Shannon was completed in 1967 and cost £120,000, of which Bord Fáilte paid £97,000 and Leitrim County Council the balance. It stimulated the growth of hire craft, with 171 on the river in 1971, representing an investment of £400,000, including £158,000 from the tourist board. Among the operators was Emerald Star Line, a new cruising venture by the Guinness company. In that year, 10,000 boating visitors spent £250,000, and with so much traffic on the river, an increase in the number of accidents underlined the need for a co-ordinated safety service. The Office of Public Works approved the final draft of new navigational by-laws, although some legal objections delayed their implementation. A Waterways Inspectorate was appointed with a priority task of setting up a warning and rescue service.

To sum up, the 1970s brought mixed fortunes to Irish tourism after the growth of the 1960s, as civil unrest in Northern Ireland led to a period of decline. The loss was not fully recovered until 1977 and growth was further consolidated in 1978, but the following two years signalled another period of world recession, with belt-tightening by tourists leading to shorter stays in less expensive accommodation and generally more cost-conscious visitors. Although an early promotional campaign of special offers and reduced fares in 1980 was instrumental in stimulating some additional traffic, Bord Fáilte could only predict that more oil price rises and even higher inflation would erode real disposable spending in many tourism producing countries: 'Growth in spending on discretionary items like tourism is likely to be curtailed in the short term. Price resistance is growing, which is usual in a recessionary period, and future progress in Irish tourism may well depend on achieving a viable balance between price and value for money.'[60] As expected, 1980 proved a disappointing year as yet another worldwide recession hurt international tourism. Other factors included a strike by Aer Lingus mechanics in June and July, a blockade of French ports by fishermen and a petrol tanker drivers' strike. While total revenue amounted to an impressive £529 million, this represented a 3 per cent decrease in real terms.[61] As this trend persisted into the 1980s, the continuing negative image of Northern Ireland became a major stumbling block in promotion for the Republic, especially in Britain, where at one stage in 1981 enquiries at the board's London office were down to almost zero as a result of saturation coverage in the media.[62] However, one positive result of the 1960–80 period was a new awareness of the economic importance of tourism among a significant proportion of the Irish population, as a survey carried out on behalf of the tourist board indicated that a majority regarded tourism as a vital national industry, crucial for its contribution to foreign earnings and jobs. Furthermore, it remained Ireland's third largest export, with out-of-state earnings accounting for around 7 per cent of the country's exports of goods and services, and 76,000 jobs depending on the industry.

Postscript

> We will re-examine from scratch our marketing stance, in the light of today's tourists. We will determine the most effective marketing positioning for Ireland in the world of tourism, then focus our resources on building a secure future within that chosen niche. Policy-makers need to learn the lesson of recent years. Our over-dependence on the US market has increased the vulnerability of the industry in the aftermath of … terrorist attacks and the slump in the value of the dollar … Americans will probably be reluctant to visit Europe for some time … If the decline of the Irish tourism industry is to be halted, we will have to address the problem posed by the sharp fall in competitiveness over the past number of years.[1]

The reader could be forgiven for assuming that the above statement was made in 2008. Not so – in fact, it comes from a policy document issued by Fianna Fáil in 1987, at a time when tourism in Ireland was once again in the doldrums as a result of international events. However, in the aftermath of recent terrorist attacks at high-profile tourist destinations, it serves well to illustrate a constant underlying theme in this book. The industry is fragile, fickle and always at the mercy of events outside the ambit and control of any nation's tourism interests. So it has always been in Ireland, as international and national conflicts, together with economic constraints, have combined to render difficult its consistent development.

Tourism in Ireland up to the Great War was promoted by a coalition of those engaged in the industry, such as hoteliers, transport companies, peers of the realm whose properties were opened to the public to subsidise their falling incomes, and some individual entrepreneurs like Frederick Crossley. As such, it was an unusual phenomenon in the late Victorian age, as it brought together people from all classes who were united in a common aim, and might be construed as one of the earliest arenas of egalitarianism in action in Ireland. The depredation visited on the country's infrastructure by the War of Independence and by the Civil War was such as to render ludicrous the idea of attracting visitors in search of pleasure, comfort and relaxation. This was not a country for the delectation of discerning tourists, and the priorities of the Free State Cosgrave government lay far away from seaside resorts and hotel reconstruction. The years from 1922 to 1960 were an era of struggle in Ireland; not the struggle for political independence or religious toleration or land reform that had occupied patriotic Irishmen of all persuasions and none during the preceding centuries, but the growing pains of an infant state attempting to carve out its niche in the world. The instigation of self-government in 1922 came accompanied by massive responsibilities, and the various administrations that took on the task of forming the New Ireland were hampered by internal and external developments that affected the conduct of government and their attitude to the multitude of problems that arose during the first half of the twentieth century.

At the same time, there was a glimmering recognition of the potential of the country as a tourist destination. The inheritance of the 1909 Health Resorts and Watering-Places Act was a reminder that such an industry had existed before the European war, and the resurrection of the Irish Tourist Association in 1925 was a small step in the right direction. The irony was that the people who were now involved in publicising the charms of Ireland for mainly British consumption were the very same people who had fought so fiercely to rid the country of that influence. The rabid republicans who had opposed the Anglo-Irish Treaty in 1922, and who went to war against their former comrades in an effort to overturn its provisions, were to prove the backbone of tourism promotion aimed principally at perfidious Albion. What is even more striking is the fact that the Cosgrave administration was prepared to support this organisation by word and by deed, by taking steps to halt the harassment of its staff by the police on account of their political affiliation. The integrity of that government stemmed from its leader, and his appearances at the annual meetings of the association were a further proof of his determination to put behind him the vicious divisions of the internecine period.

The contributions of local authorities to the advertising of their districts as tourist destinations, initiated in 1909, was to prove a lasting tradition which had the effect of forcing budding politicians to engage with the industry. However, with donations neither fixed nor compulsory, the result was that the Irish Tourist Association was not assured of a certain income but was dependent on the goodwill of councillors, which was a variable quantity from time to time. As a result, the association had difficulty in planning a publicity programme and the publication of promotional material, and in any case, the funds from local authorities did not amount to a meaningful sum for the purpose for which they were needed. The 1931 Tourist Traffic Act did ensure that the ITA was the official beneficiary of all such contributions, but pressure continued from its administrators for the setting-up of a statutory body to develop all facets of the industry, including accommodation, publicity, infrastructure, amenities and facilities for tourists.

The driving force in the promotion of Irish tourism was John P. O'Brien, and it was due to his unceasing efforts that Seán Lemass and John Leydon became convinced of the industry's potential as a panacea for the economic woes of the state. As a former comrade in the Civil War, and later as fundraiser for Fianna Fáil, O'Brien capitalised on his closeness to Lemass by putting tourism on the political agenda when that party assumed office in 1932. Despite the deprivations of the Economic War and its profoundly negative effects on the Free State's principal industry, agriculture, O'Brien held fast to his vision of state intervention as the matrix in which the industry could flourish. In a country where entrepreneurs were thin on the ground, and in an economic climate that led Lemass to see the establishment of semi-state bodies as the only means of establishing new industries, O'Brien's energy and determination were attractive qualities. He was successful in persuading Lemass and Leydon of the wisdom of his cause, and he was mainly responsible for the provisions of the 1939 Tourist Traffic Act.

While this legislation incorporated many of the accepted constituents of tourist development elsewhere, such as the registration and grading of hotels, it also delivered some rather startling features, which seemed to denote a totalitarian approach to the organisation of Irish tourism. The provision that allowed for the establishment of special areas, in which all aspects of commerce connected to tourism in any way in that area could become subject to registration and licensing by the tourist board, was one such, and was deemed intolerable by the residents of one town so designated. The involvement of the tourist board in the purchasing, building and running of hotels was another, as was their financial involvement in the development of holiday resorts. These provisions seem of a piece with the attitude of O'Brien to the development of recreational facilities by the state, as he strongly advocated the approach of enforced organisation of leisure time for workers who received paid holidays as a part of social legislation by the Fianna Fáil government.

The intervention of the Second World War halted the application of the 1939 legislation, and it may well be that the climate of public opinion in Ireland had changed during that conflict to such an extent that O'Brien's ideas were out of date by 1946. On the other hand, the organisation of holiday savings clubs during the war was a successful initiative on the part of the Irish Tourist Association, and a welcome adjunct to the holidays-with-pay legislation. Unfortunately, the post-war boom occasioned by the influx of British tourists led to complacency on the part of the hotel industry as regards their accommodation facilities, and this was accompanied by a shortage of construction materials that would have rendered meaningful improvement impossible in any event. The various schemes provided for in the 1939 legislation gradually foundered in the post-war period. Registration and grading ground to a halt in 1951, the Fáilte Teoranta hotel scheme was abandoned in 1949, the institution of special areas ended with only one town surveyed, the loans scheme for hoteliers never got off the ground and the large-scale resort development planned by O'Brien and Lemass to counter unemployment after the war was stymied by a lack of finance and building materials. The cancellation of the transatlantic air service by the inter-party government in 1948 was a powerful psychological blow to tourism interests, and it was only the entrance of American players onto the stage as a result of Marshall Aid loans to Ireland that concentrated the mind of that administration on the dollar potential of tourism.

Its defeat in the 1951 general election resulted in the Tourism Traffic Bill of that year being superseded by another from Seán Lemass, which went against all received wisdom in the tourism sphere at the time in creating yet another tourism body – Fógra Fáilte – in addition to the Irish Tourist Association and An Bord Fáilte, the successor to An Bord Cuartaíochta. Set up expressly in order to provide a position for J.P. O'Brien, this organisation hived off the publicity function from both the established bodies, but it was a short-lived experiment. William Norton, back in power in May 1954, dissolved it in 1955 under the provisions of the Tourist Traffic Act. Its functions and finance were transferred to Bord Fáilte Éireann, the new body created by the legislation, which became responsible for all aspects of Irish tourism until the late 1990s. The prime mover of the state promotion of Irish tourism during its infancy was Seán Lemass, and although many of his hopes for the industry were to come to nought during that period, he never gave up his efforts to develop the industry. Speaking to the Institute of Public Administration in 1959, he categorised tourism as one of the country's most important industries and stated that Bord Fáilte Éireann had a big role to play in the development of an industry, which was a substantial factor in the country's balance of payments.[2] Nor was he afraid to think big. When Kevin O'Doherty resigned from the civil service to join the tourist board in 1946, Lemass wished him well and signed a photo as a souvenir. They exchanged a few words about tourism development and O'Doherty mentioned the possibility of reviving the Tailteann Games, which had not been held since 1932. Lemass's response was: 'Try and get the Olympic Games for Ireland, I'll back that.'[3]

As the rising tide of economic prosperity in the 1960s lifted all boats, tourism was not excluded and enjoyed a dramatic success, rising in value between 1961 and 1968 at an average annual rate more than two and half times the rate for the period 1949–61.[4] In fact, tourism represented over one-third of invisible exports between 1949 and 1968, when receipts amounted to £75.7 million.[5] However, the outbreak of the troubles in Northern Ireland in the early 1970s devastated the tourist industry, with steady growth in real terms suffering a 30 per cent reduction between 1969 and 1972.[6] The number of visitors declined from 1.95 million to 1.47 million in the same period, and the 1969 peak was not reached again until 1977.[7] The realisation of the vulnerability of the British market, which combined with that of Northern Ireland accounted for almost 70 per cent of visitors in the 1970s, forced Bord Fáilte to concentrate their efforts on attracting more tourists from continental Europe, and the results were encouraging, as they accounted for a 14 per cent share by 1979.[8]

However, the overall pattern was one of continued fluctuation up to 1986, partly due to the international recession, and a White Paper published in 1985 attempted to clarify government thinking on tourism and specify the broad objectives of policy. These were the economic and social benefits accruing from the industry, consisting of the potential for job creation, the quality of life and development of the community, the enhancement and preservation of the nation's cultural heritage, the conservation of the physical resources of the country and the contribution to rural development.[9] By 1990 tourism receipts had passed the one billion pounds mark, and by 1994 had increased to IR£1,455.2 million, as a result of sustained growth in visitor numbers.[10] Between 1988 and 1994, earnings from travel and tourism converted the balance of payments deficit into a surplus in three of those years, and were responsible for increasing that surplus in another three. The application of European Union regional funding under two Operational Programmes for Tourism in 1989–93 and 1994–99 ensured an investment of over IR£500 million in tourism facilities, and IR£350 million was allocated to specific measures for tourism marketing, product development and training in the National Development Plan 2000–2006.[11] Tourism was established as a key contributor to the Irish economy in the 1990s, thanks to regained competitiveness, new product development and infrastructure, a welcome 'fashionability' and the beneficial impact of the peace process in Northern Ireland, as well as a heightened interest in Irish culture.[12]

Then, in 2000, a new chapter in the history of tourism development in Ireland was opened as Northern Ireland and the Republic came together under the terms of the Belfast Agreement of 1998. A new North/South company, Tourism Ireland Limited, to be jointly funded by the two governments, was set up with responsibility for strategic destination marketing in all markets outside the island of Ireland.[13] Tourism Ireland's role is to grow overseas tourism revenue and visitor numbers to the island of Ireland, and to help Northern Ireland to realise its tourism potential. It devises and delivers marketing programmes in over twenty markets across the world and works in close co-operation with industry partners on the island of Ireland as well as with the travel trade, online operators, media, air and sea carriers overseas to encourage consumers to 'Discover the island of Ireland'. In November 2001 the Irish government gave approval for the creation of a new body, Fáilte Ireland, to promote the development of the industry, encompassing the range of functions of Bord Fáilte and CERT, the national training body for the industry. This body was established under the National Tourism Development Authority Act, 2003, to guide and promote tourism as a leading indigenous component of the Irish economy. It provides strategic and practical support to develop and sustain Ireland as a high-quality and competitive tourist destination. Its key role is to help the industry to meet the challenges facing the entire global tourism market and to sustain, or increase, the level of activity in the sector. The emphasis is on strategic partnership, with all the interests in Irish tourism at national, local and regional levels working together towards a common goal. There are three principal areas of operation: helping to develop product offerings for both the domestic and overseas markets and lead the marketing effort to promote Irish holidays to the domestic consumer; supporting enterprise development in Irish tourism, promoting best practice in operations, quality and standards and facilitating investment in tourism infrastructure; and building human resource capability in the industry, investing heavily in training provision and standards across the publicly supported educational system, and through executive and management development programmes for the tourism industry.[14] Fáilte Ireland operates an extensive marketing programme including consumer and trade shows, regional marketing co-ordination and home holidays promotion. A 'Discover Ireland' home holidays campaign was launched in April 2007 and focuses on 'things to do' in Ireland, and in particular on regional and rural activity. In addition, Fáilte Ireland operates seventy-five tourist information offices nationwide.

On a regional level, July 2006 saw a radical change, when five of the seven Regional Tourism Authorities were subsumed into Fáilte Ireland, resulting in a new Regional Development Directorate covering their regional functions and activities. Five new Regional Tourism Development Boards are working on three-year Strategic Tourism Development Plans for significant undertakings under the Fáilte Ireland Tourism Product Development Strategy. It is intended that they should also devise targets for growth and performance in their regions. Their responsibilities will include organisation development and staff management, production and market development and enterprise development.

The combination of the foot and mouth scare and terrorist attacks in the United States in 2001 had a detrimental effect on the industry during the following years. The number of jobs in the Irish economy supported by tourism dropped by 7,000 by the end of 2001,[15] while overseas visitor numbers decreased by 7 per cent. A Bord Fáilte survey conducted in August 2002 showed a downturn across all the principal industry sectors, with most enterprises reporting a marked decline in their American business.[16] At a time when fears were already being expressed about the non-competitiveness of the Irish product, made even more visible by the adoption of the euro as the common European currency, and of a deterioration in the public attitude towards the industry and visitors,[17] yet again international events demonstrated the fragility of the industry. Threats were posed by the greater range of attractively presented tourism products from the emerging market economies of central and eastern Europe.[18] It was also feared that a trend towards less 'Irishness' could have a negative impact on the quality of the Irish product, which has people contact and conviviality as a core benefit, if in future years it became more difficult to attract Irish people to work in front-line customer contact roles within the industry.

POSTSCRIPT

Apart altogether from Irish tourism's economic role over the last forty years, it cannot be denied that it has become widely accepted as an integral part of Irish society, and the question has been posed: 'Is tourism the patron saint of Ireland?' Certainly, many positive elements in Irish life today are the result of the public realisation of the crucial importance of the industry in the Irish economy, and many changes in the country in the last fifty years have resulted from its impact. While its effect on the Gross Domestic Product has not increased dramatically since the 1950s, its influence on rural development has been critical, as it has become the saviour of many small communities around Ireland, which have nothing to sell but their physical environment, their hospitality and their past. As a major factor in the distribution of regional economic growth, tourism has generated financial support for the provision of recreational facilities for sport and leisure and has been responsible for the preponderance of hotels and restaurants and the mushrooming of Irish culture in the form of music, literature and the dramatic arts on a local basis. The growth of cultural tourism in recent years has been spectacular, as visitors flock to museums, interpretive centres, art galleries, historical homes and gardens and language schools. In this connection, literary tourism, in a country which has the largest relative number of Nobel prize-winners in that genre, has proved to be of inestimable value, and the proliferation of summer schools, winter schools and weekend seminars devoted to Irish authors continues to expand. As Irish culture achieves world wide recognition in the fields of music, literature, art and design, it should be borne in mind that tourists do not come only for high art – Riverdance and U2, Father Ted and Westlife are as likely to persuade foreigners to visit the country as the Book of Kells or Newgrange. Television series and film-making in Ireland have also proved another boon for the tourist industry, as they marry images of landscapes of outstanding natural beauty with contemporary drama, and the success of a series like *Ballykissangel* can bring enormous economic benefits for its location. The proliferation of festivals in Ireland over the last twenty years has also been prodigious. In 2008 goireland.com lists 676 festivals and fairs on its website, with Fáilte Ireland offering roughly the same number. They range from the usual and well-established artistic, literary and musical offerings to activities such as walking, sand sculpting, storytelling, fireworks, film, maritime, comedy and agriculture. Some of the more esoteric are the matchmaking festival in Lisdoonvarna, the largest 'singles' event in Europe, running for five weeks in the autumn; the Ballyjamesduff Pork Festival, where the visitor can enjoy pig racing and roasting, along with the usual 'craic' of music and mayhem; and the 'Culchie of the Year' festival in Clonbur, Co. Galway, which is confined to men from outside the Pale and seen as the male equivalent of the Rose of Tralee. Under the Festivals and Cultural Events Initiative administered by Fáilte Ireland, 270 events were awarded funding of €4.2 million in 2007.[19]

At the same time, the intrusion of tourists into one of the most authentic countrysides in Europe, given 'added value' by reason of its cultural heritage, has brought about a dichotomy. As European Structural Funds became available under the Operational Programme for Tourism in the late 1990s, many new projects were supported without a corresponding conservation of existing heritage items. This has led to a conflict in heritage-related tourism, where one side supports a project for economic and social reasons, and the other side opposes it for cultural or ecological reasons.[20] Ironically, Fáilte Ireland has a key role in establishing policies and co-ordinating the diverse strands of Irish culture, as the government recognises that culture and heritage products have a crucial part to play in extending the tourism season. The question of the cultural impact of tourism continues to be debated, and the jury is still out on whether it has a detrimental effect or not. Cultural tourism is one of the most significant growth areas in the Irish product, and some commentators see it, in turn, as the constructor of Irish culture today: 'The tourist could be seen as the patron of culture … one who gives financial or other support to a person, activity or cause. Within this role, the tourist is the patron of traditional rural lifestyles and ethnic minority cultures that are now packaged in glossy brochures, activity holidays and festivals.'[21] It is possible, nonetheless, that the development and commodification of our cultural assets for foreign consumption may bring about undesirable and degrading change which will destroy the authenticity of that culture, and that the images of Ireland which prove effective in attracting tourists may influence the delicate sense of identity which is still being constructed after centuries of foreign rule.

While it is easy to imagine the effect of an alien culture on an isolated rural community, it is more difficult to accept that the metropolis would be so susceptible to outside influence as to undergo a cultural sea change in order to accommodate itself to the demands of the tourist, but this is the case on the occasion of the annual Saint Patrick's Day parade in Dublin. Anthropologists have developed the concept of 'cultural fixation' to explain how, under certain social and economic circumstances, selected cultural icons are conserved, with their meaning reduced to a stereotypical badge of identity.[22] The Dublin parade is a perfect illustration of this phenomenon, having metamorphosed into an event more American than Irish, with throngs of Irish-Americans participating in it, as opposed to being mere observers. What is even more bizarre is the corresponding rise in the number of Irish majorette bands, modelled on the American tradition, who stomp their way around Dublin on the day in costumes that owe everything to North America and nothing at all to Ireland. Yet this parade is billed as one of the great cultural events of the Irish calendar, despite the fact that it is superimposing an alien culture onto an Irish icon just to please the tourists. The supreme irony is that the parade attracts more native Dubliners in its present form than it ever did when it consisted mainly of quasi-religious floats representing the 'isle of saints and scholars'. As Irish tourists travel to North America in ever-greater numbers and are exposed to the culture there, they are prepared for its importation into Ireland, and this may be a greater factor in putting Irish culture at risk than that posed by the incursion of tourists. In the same way, the commodification of Ireland today may entail the manipulation of history and the fabrication of new myths, but it has also been responsible for the restoration and preservation of many of our national monuments and for the emergence of a renewed interest in Irish history by the natives of the country. Irish culture is now physically exported as a result of tourism, as the manufacturing and despatching of 'Irish' pubs around the globe has become commonplace. With over forty Irish pubs in Paris alone at the last count, for example, it stands to reason that they assist in selling the country as a tourist destination, while often also providing employment for young Irish people abroad.

Personalities from all walks of life have regarded Irish tourism in different ways over the years. Bishop Cornelius Lucey of Cork, whose confirmation sermons touched on various contemporary issues in Irish life, had a somewhat ambivalent attitude to the industry. Speaking at Goleen in 1952, he deplored the lack of initiative in promoting the tourist industry in that area,[23] and ten years later he praised the people of Inchigeelagh for providing a holiday centre there.[24] However, by 1973 he was not so positive; speaking in Blackrock, he criticised 'those who cry "pollution" or "tourist attraction ruined" whenever there is talk of industrial development along the coast … Blackrock existed to be lived in by our own people … rather than preserved as an old world area full of empty spaces, an atmosphere for the delectation of fly-by-summer tourists from abroad.'[25] Éamon de Valera, speaking at the Fianna Fáil árd-fheis in

1957 on the subject of partition, declared that the proper way to solve it was to endeavour to have as close relations as possible with the people of Northern Ireland: 'In the case of tourism, was it not obvious that they should combine with the people of the Six Counties to induce visitors to come not to the Twenty-six or the Six Counties but to Ireland?'[26] Writing in 1966, T.P. Coogan regarded tourism as one of Ireland's greatest hopes for the future, and numbered Bord Fáilte among those state-sponsored companies that had been fortunate in recruiting a particularly good type of executive.[27] There is no doubt that Timothy J. O'Driscoll, who was appointed to the tourist board in 1956, was one such, and he was responsible for a dramatic transformation in the public attitude to tourism and to its promotion and development on a professional basis. Seán Ó Faoláin, looking back in 1969 on the progress made over the previous fifty years in rural Ireland, considered that one of the most welcome modern developments was 'the appearance of the farm guesthouse, fostered by the tourist board, which insists on baths, hot and cold water, comfortable beds, electricity, cleanliness and good plain cooking. Such an amenity was unthinkable in my youth.'[28]

In the international sphere, a dignified presentation of the country's history and traditions through tourism can undo many harmful misconceptions of Ireland and the Irish existing abroad. At the same time, having visitors here from other countries, we can ourselves be enriched in our social and economic lives. Tourism in the economy injects the same purchasing power as if we had an additional residential population and is an excellent way of selling Irish goods and services to non-residents, as they come to us to make their purchases. What they pay is mostly retained within the country, because goods and services are usually home-produced. Tourism reverses the normal trend of economic activity to seek centres of population, and in Ireland this trend has particularly affected the west, making tourism one of the most effective redistributive factors in international economy relationships. Bord Fáilte's annual report for 1970 pointed out that it recognised full well that the rate of growth of Irish tourism, while outstanding in a national context, was less than average in the international table. It emphasised the difference in promoting what was, in tourism jargon – if not in our own thinking – a secondary tourism destination. The prescription was enterprise and co-operation, backed by financial investment, by individuals and also the public and private sector.[29] In this way, in the years since then, tourism has assisted every region in Ireland, with its role in regional development significantly helping to provide many infrastructural facilities such as adequate roads, improved water supplies and general living conditions that benefit local communities and make areas more attractive for subsequent industrial development.

A case in point is the Tidy Towns competition, which was initiated to improve the appearance of Irish towns and villages, and has gone from strength to strength in the fifty years since its launch. By the use of bright colours, floral arrangements and floodlighting of attractive buildings, it was hoped to make provincial Ireland more appealing to visitors. Along with this has come the amelioration of the environment for residents, pride in their place and pride in their past, as the competitive spirit has moved the community. Better still, it has united people of all ages, creeds and classes in a concerted effort to make the most of their own habitat. Bord Fáilte continued to organise the competition until 1995, when it was taken over by the Department of the Environment. Its main sponsor since 1992 has been the Super-Valu chain of supermarkets, and this financial support is secure until 2013. Aughrim in County Wicklow was the 2007 overall winner, with 299 points out of a possible 400, and received a prize of €15,000 and a trophy. County and regional awards are also given, as well as one for the best new entry. Special prizes are awarded in categories such as shop-fronts, recycling banks, landscaping, schools, biodiversity projects and anti-gum litter efforts. In 2008 the competition will celebrate fifty years of getting Ireland tidy, and with an increasing population and massive changes in infrastructure and industrial growth around what were sleepy towns and villages twenty years ago, there is work still to be done.

In Northern Ireland, the restoration of normal life to the province, along with improved access and investment, has transformed the tourism situation there. From a figure of 1.1 million visitors in 1967, numbers dropped to below 500,000 in 1972, but in three years of dramatic growth topped 900,000 in 1984, before declining again by 5 per cent in 1985.[30] Early in 1986 the Northern Ireland government issued a Tourism Policy Guidelines Statement defining its development objectives for the following three years and set down proposals for achieving them.[31] Continuing civil unrest led to more fluctuations over the following decade, but by 1999 revenue was up to £322 million, and the board looked forward to the establishment of an all-Ireland marketing body that would bring larger budgets and a wider network of overseas offices.[32] In 2002 visitor numbers were up to 1.74 million, but expenditure fell by 5 per cent in real terms, partly due to shorter stays by visitors.[33] Preliminary results for 2007 suggest an increase of over 4 per cent in total visits to Northern Ireland, with good growth in particular from mainland Europe, North America and the Republic of Ireland. Most encouraging has been the significant return to growth in holiday visitors from Great Britain, of the order of 26 per cent. There has also been double-digit growth in holidaymakers from mainland Europe and North America. This will build on the momentum of the last six years which has seen Northern Ireland earn more than £1.8 billion from eleven million overnight visitors.

In November 2007, Tourism Ireland and the Northern Ireland Tourist Board launched marketing plans and a growth strategy for 2008 and beyond, aiming to grow holidaymaker traffic to Northern Ireland at a faster rate than that to the rest of the island. By 2010 it is anticipated that over two million overseas visitors a year to Northern Ireland will generate £458 million in revenue, and that over the next three years Northern Ireland will secure up to £1.28 billion in earnings from overseas tourism, surpassing both world and European levels of performance. The draft Programme for Government recognises tourism's future role in the Northern Ireland economy and has set ambitious targets for tourism that require substantial growth from all markets and on visitor spend. The NITB also sees further work to be done on overcoming engrained perceptions about Northern Ireland among potential visitors arriving from and via the Republic of Ireland.[34]

In the Republic, a Tourism Policy Review Group was appointed by the government in December 2002 and asked to identify key elements of strategy for the sustainable development of the industry. Its report, *New Horizons for Irish Tourism: An Agenda for Action*, was finalised in September 2003 and made a number of disquieting points, including the fact that competitiveness had been lost in previous years, while a certain complacency had set in among many parts of the industry.[35] It said that urgent and comprehensive changes in the policies and actions of the government and the tourist industry itself were necessary in order to maintain the success of the industry in the recent past. The key targets in the report were to double overseas tourism revenue to €6 billion in the period 2003–12, and to increase visitor numbers from just under six million in 2002 to ten million in 2012. The National Development Plan 2007–2013 endorsed the group's findings and contains the largest ever public programme for tourism expansion, with exchequer investment of €800 million out of a total of €184 billion.[36] This comprises €317 million on product development and infrastructure, €148 million for upgrading upgrading the infrastructure of firms and for staff training and development, and €355 million for promoting the island of Ireland at international markets.[37] In addition, it is anticipated that tourism will benefit greatly from investment in other areas such as transport and the environment.

To sum up, it is almost a hundred years since the first political recognition of the potential of tourism for the island of Ireland. We have come a long way in that time in terms of government recognition, entrepreneurial commitment and public acceptance of the potential and importance of the tourism industry to the economic, social and cultural life of its citizens. As we move into the third millennium, and with tourism currently the fastest-growing industry on the planet, it is fascinating to conjecture whether Ireland can achieve even greater success by achieving the targets set for the island in the century to come.

Notes

INTRODUCTION

1. G.B. Shaw, *John Bull's Other Island* (London: A. Constable, 1907), p.155.
2. J. Urry, *The Tourist Gaze* (London: Sage Publications, 1990), p.1.
3. M. Nic Eoin, 'The native gaze: literary perceptions of tourists in the West Kerry Gaeltacht', paper delivered to Joint Faculty of Humanities, DCU/St Patrick's College, 20 February 1998.
4. Ibid.
5. T. O'Crohan, *The Islandman* (Oxford: Oxford University Press, 1951), p.241.
6. L. O'Flaherty, *A Tourist's Guide to Ireland* (London: Mandrake, 1929), p.24.
7. Ibid., p.33.
8. Ibid., p.36.
9. P. O'Donnell, 'Tourist guide to Irish politics', *The Bell*, 14, 5 (1947), pp.1–3.
10. G. Hooper, *The Tourist's Gaze: Travellers to Ireland, 1800–2000* (Cork: Cork University Press, 2001), p.xiv.
11. A.J. Durie, *Scotland for the Holidays: A History of Tourism in Scotland 1780–1939* (East Linton: Tuckwell Press, 2003), pp.6–7.
12. I. Jackson, *An Introduction to Tourism* (Melbourne: Hospitality Press, 1998), p.3.
13. Bord Fáilte, *Report and Financial Statement 2001* (Dublin: Bord Fáilte, 2001), p.3.
14. Central Statistics Office, *Tourism and Travel 2007* (Dublin: Central Statistics Office, 2008), p.11.
15. Ibid.
16. Fáilte Ireland, *Annual Report 2006* (Dublin: Fáilte Ireland, 2007), p.20.
17. Fáilte Ireland, 'Tourism Facts' 2007 (Dublin: Fáilte Ireland, 2008), p.1.
18. Northern Ireland Tourist Board, *Tourism Performance 2007* (Belfast: www.nitb.com/research, 7 August 2008.
19. P. Brendon, *Thomas Cook: 150 Years of Popular Tourism* (London: Secker & Warburg, 1991), p.6.
20. S. Rigge, 'On tour around the Empire', in Harold C. Field (ed.), *The British Empire*, 41 (Norwich: Time-Life Books, 1972), p.1,172.
21. Ibid.
22. C.S. Andrews, *Man of No Property* (Cork: Mercier Press, 1982), p.68.

CHAPTER 1: TURN OF THE CENTURY TOURISM IN IRELAND

1. S.C. Hall, *A Week in Killarney* (London: Jeremiah How, 1843), p.216.
2. R. Delany, *The Grand Canal of Ireland* (Dublin: Lilliput Press, 1995), p.21.
3. Ibid., p.128.
4. Bord Fáilte, *The Fáilte Business: Tourism's Role in Economic Growth* (Dublin: Bord Fáilte, 1997), p.24.
5. Ibid.
6. F. Corr, *Hotels in Ireland* (Dublin: Jemma Publications, 1994), p.20.
7. G.S.J. Williams, *A Sea-Grey House: The Story of Renvyle House* (Galway: Renvyle House Hotel, 1995), p.65.

NOTES

8. J.P. Harrington (ed.), *The English Traveller in Ireland* (Dublin: Wolfhound Press, 1991), p.187.
9. H. Martineau, *Letters from Ireland* (Dublin: Irish Academic Press, 2001), p.273.
10. Bord Fáilte, *Fáilte Business*, p.25.
11. I. Moylan, 'The development of modern Bray 1750–1900', in J. O'Sullivan, T. Dunne and S. Cannon (eds), *The Book of Bray* (Dublin: Blackrock Teachers' Centre, 1989), p.50.
12. Ibid., p.51.
13. P. Brendon, *Thomas Cook: 150 Years of Popular Tourism* (London: Secker & Warburg, 1991), p.8.
14. Ibid., p.64.
15. Ibid., p.168.
16. Ibid., p.248.
17. A. Young, *A Tour in Ireland* (London: G. Bell & Sons, 1892), pp.363–4.
18. Ibid.
19. K.M. Davies, 'For health and pleasure in the British fashion: Bray, Co. Wicklow as a tourist resort, 1750–1914', in B. O'Connor and M. Cronin (eds), *Tourism in Ireland: A Critical Analysis* (Cork: Cork University Press, 1993), p.31.
20. S. Nenadic, 'Land, the landed and relationships with England: literature and perception 1760–1830', in S.J. Connolly, R.A. Houston and R.J. Morris (eds), *Conflict, Identity and Economic Development* (Preston: Carnegie Publications, 1995), p.159.
21, Oral history interview with Allie Pigot, 16 July 2002.
22. J. Walsh, 'The Development of Public Policy for the Irish Tourist Industry', MA thesis, NUI Galway (1998), p.55.
23. *Irish Tourist*, 2, 3 (1895), p.1.
24. *Irish Tourist*, 1, 1 (1894), p.1.
25. Ibid., p.11.
26. Corr, *Hotels in Ireland*, p.59.
27. *Irish Tourist*, 1, 2 (1984), p.63.
28. Ibid., p.33.
29. *Irish Tourist*, 1, 3 (1894), p.77.
30. *Irish Times*, 18 April 1895, p.4.
31. Ibid.
32. G. Hall 'The tourist question', *New Ireland Review*, 3 (1895) p.152.
33. *Irish Times*, 13 May 1895, p.12.
34. *Irish Tourist*, 2, 3 (1895), p.1.
35. Ibid.
36. *Irish Tourist*, 2, 7 (1895), p.1.
37. *Times*, 8 October 1895, p.3.
38. F.W. Crossley to *The Times*, 10 October 1895.
39. *Irish Tourist*, 2, 3 (1895), p.13.
40. Ibid., p.42.
41. *Irish Tourist*, 3, 5 (1896), p.85.
42. *Irish Tourist*, 3, 3 (1896), p.56.
43. *Travel Express*, 10 June 1974, p.15.
44. Corr, *Hotels in Ireland*, p.59.
45. *Travel Express*, 10 June 1974, p.15.
46. Shannon Development Company Limited, dissolved companies files (NA 2023).
47. *Irish Tourist*, 4, 1 (1896), p.5.
48. Shannon Development Company Limited, dissolved companies files (NA 2023).
49. F.W. Crossley Publishing Company Limited, dissolved companies files (NA 2008).
50. *Irish Tourist*, 3, 3 (1896), p.53.
51. *Irish Tourist*, 3, 5 (1896), p.92.
52. H. Forde, *Around the Coast of Northern Ireland* (Belfast: R. Carswell, 1938), p.90.
53. Ibid., p.92.
54. *Irish Tourist*, 4, 1 (1897), p.4.
55. *Irish Times*, 13 June 1901.
56. Ibid.
57. R.A.S. Macalister, 'The debit account of the tourist movement', *New Ireland Review*, 8 (1897) pp. 87–92.
58. *Irish Tourist*, 4, 7 (1897) p.122.
59. *Irish Tourist*, 1, 4 (1894), p.98.
60. J.H. Murphy, *Abject Loyalty: Nationalism and Monarchy in Ireland during the Reign of Queen Victoria* (Cork: Cork University Press, 2001), p.187.

61. Ibid., p.132.
62. Ibid., p.129.
63. R.V. Comerford, *The Fenians in Context: Irish Politics and Society 1848–82* (Dublin: Wolfhound Press, 1998), p.18.
64. Murphy, *Abject Loyalty*, p.151.
65. Ibid., p.163.
66. Ibid., p.189.
67. *Irish Tourist*, 4, 1 (1897), p.23.
68. Corr, *Hotels in Ireland*, p.59.
69. Allie Pigot interview.
70. *Irish Tourist*, 4, 6 (1897), p.109.
71. Murphy, *Abject Loyalty*, p.275.
72. Ibid., p.279.
73. Ibid., p.288.
74. Ibid., p.283.
75. *Irish Tourist* 9, 4 (1902), p.1.
76. F.W. Crossley, *A Concise Guide to Ireland: A Descriptive and Illustrative Guide* (Dublin: F.W. Crossley Publishing Co., 1903), p.96.
77. M. O'Neill, *From Parnell to de Valera: A Biography of Jennie Wyse Power* (Dublin: Blackwater Press, 1991), p.57.
78. *Irish Tourist*, 10, 4 (1903), p.1.
79. Ibid., p.2.
80. F.W. Crossley to *The Times*, 4 June 1904.
81. *Irish Tourist*, 11, 3 (1904), p.4.
82. *Irish Tourist*, 11, 5 (1904), p.1.
83. Ibid.
84. *Irish Tourist*, 12, 1 (1905), p.1.
85. *Irish Tourist*, 13, 1 (1906), p.1.
86. Ibid.
87. *Statist*, 10 February 1906, p.18.
88. M. Daly, 'The return to the roads', in K.B. Nowlan (ed.), *Travel and Transport in Ireland* (Dublin: Gill & Macmillan, 1974), p.134.
89. *Irish Tourist*, 14, 1 (1907), p.1.
90. *Annual Report of the Local Government Board for Year Ending 31 March 1910* (Dublin: Local Government Board, 1910), p.i.
91. *Annual Report of the Local Government Board for Year Ending 31 March 1912* (Dublin: Local Government Board, 1912), p.xi.
92. *Annual Report of the Local Government Board for Year 1914–1915* (Dublin: Local Government Board, 1915), p.viii.
93. *Irish Tourist*, 13, 1 (1906), p.3.
94. *Irish Tourist*, 14, 1 (1907), p.3.
95. *Irish Tourist*, 14, 3 (1907), p.1.
96. *Parliamentary Debates 1906*, vol. 10, col. 187 (London: Hansard, 1906).
97. *Annual Report of the Local Government Board for Year Ending 31 March 1910* (Dublin: Local Government Board, 1910), p.i.
98. Interview with Allie Pigot.

CHAPTER 2: THE IRISH TOURIST ASSOCIATION 1925–1939

1. *Irish Travel* (June 1926), p.210.
2. J. Meehan, *The Economic and Social State of the Nation* (Dublin: Economic and Social Research Institute, 1982), p.12.
3. M.E. Daly, *Industrial Development and Irish National Identity 1922–1939* (Syracuse, NY: Gill & Macmillan, 1992), p.18.
4. Director of Publicity memorandum, 'Irish tourist development', 18 January 1924 (NA S5472A).
5. Irish Tourist Association, dissolved companies files (NA 7282).
6. Director of Publicity memorandum.
7. *Irish Travel* (September 1925), p.1.
8. Local Government (1925) Act, Section 67, 2, p.89.
9. Irish Tourist Association, dissolved companies files (NA 7282).
10. *Irish Travel* (September 1925), p.9.
11. C.S. Andrews, *A Man of No Property* (Cork: Mercier Press, 1982) p.71.

NOTES

12. Martin O'Dwyer, *Tipperary's Sons and Daughters 1916–1923* (Tipperary: Folk Village, 2001), p.10.
13. Andrews, *Man of No Property*, p.68.
14. Ibid., p.67.
15. Ibid.
16. *Irish Travel* (September 1925), p.3.
17. Ibid., p.8.
18. Glenister to Department of External Affairs, 4 May 1925 (NA GR 459-2).
19. *Irish Travel* (November 1925), p.1.
20. T.P. Coogan, *The IRA* (London: Pall Mall Press, 1970), p.69.
21. G. Keown, 'Taking the world stage: creating an Irish foreign policy in the 1920s', in M. Kennedy and J.M. Skelly (eds), *Irish Foreign Policy 1919–1966* (Dublin: Four Courts Press, 2000).
22. S. Cronin, *Frank Ryan: The Search for the Republic* (Dublin: Repsol Publications, 1980), p.24.
23. Ibid.
24. Andrews, *Man of No Property*, p.68.
25. *Irish Travel* (October 1925), p.33.
26. *Irish Travel* (July 1926) p.244.
27. Department of External Affairs (NA Gr 459).
28. B. Hobson (ed.), *The Official Dublin Civic Week 1927 Handbook* (Dublin: Dublin Corporation, 1927), p.4.
29. *Irish Travel* (October 1925), p.33.
30. *Irish Travel* (November 1925), p.57.
31. C. Curran, 'Tourist development at home and abroad', *Studies*, 15, 58 (1928), p.4.
32. *Irish Travel* (February 1926), p.121.
33. Minutes of General Council of Irish County Councils, 26 October 1927 (NA 999/408).
34. Ibid., 26 April 1928.
35. Seán Ó Muircheadha, secretary, Department of External Affairs, enclosing memorandum of conference held in Washington, 28 June 1927 (NA S5472A).
36. Keown, *Irish Foreign Policy*, p.37.
37. Department of Finance note April 1928 (NA F 6/1/27).
38. Irish Tourist Association annual general meeting, 24 April 1928 (NA S5819A).
39. Ibid.
40. *Irish Travel*, 3, 1 (1928), p.5.
41. Ibid., p.3.
42. *Irish Travel*, 3, 4 (1928), p.64.
43. *Irish Travel*, 3, 6 (1929), p.72.
44. *Irish Travel*, 3, 3 (1928), p.78.
45. *Irish Travel*, 3, 8 (1929) p.1.
46. *Better Business* (October 1929), p.5.
47. Department of Industry and Commerce, 'Memorandum on the subject of amending tourist legislation', 1 May 1930 (NA S5482).
48. *Better Business* (May, 1930), p.16.
49. *Dáil Debates 1926–39*, vol. 37, col. 1932, 20 March 1931.
50. *Dáil Debates 1926–39*, vol. 38 col. 33, 22 April 1931.
51. T. de Vere White, 'Social life in Ireland 1927–1937', in F. MacManus (ed.), *The Years of the Great Test* (Cork: Mercier Press, 1967) p.27.
52. *Irish Travel*, 8, 1 (1932), p.16.
53. *Irish Travel*, 8, 3 (1932), p.66.
54. *Irish Travel*, 9, 2 (1933), p.23.
55. Daly, *Industrial Development*, p.64.
56. R. Dunphy, *The Making of Fianna Fáil Power in Ireland* (Oxford: Clarendon Press, 1995), p.45.
57. *Irish Travel*, 8, 4 ((1932), p.14.
58. D. Roche, 'John Leydon', *Administration*, 27, 7 (1979), p.234.
59. R. Fanning, *The Irish Department of Finance* (Dublin: Institute of Public Administration, 1978), p.214.
60. Andrews, *Man of No Property*, p.76.
61. J. Horgan, *Seán Lemass: Enigmatic Patriot* (Dublin: Gill & Macmillan, 1997), p.67.
62. *Irish Travel*, 8, 5 (1933), p.99.
63. *Irish Travel*, 8, 6 (1933), p.131.
64. P. Maume, *D.P. Moran* (Dundalk: Dundealgan Press, 1995), p.50.
65. *Irish Travel*, 9, 7 (1934), p.113.
66. Ibid.

67. *Irish Travel*, 10, 2 (1934), p.25.
68. *Irish Travel*, 10, 8 (1935), p.147.
69. *Irish Times*, 'The motorist in Ireland' supplement, 8 April 1936, p.5.
70. *Irish Travel*, 11, 11 (1936), p.227.
71. *Irish Travel*, 12, 2 (1936), p.26.
72. Ibid.
73. *Irish Travel*, 12, 3 (1936), p.45.
74. *Irish Independent*, 30 October 1936, p.4.
75. *Irish Travel*, 12, 7 (1937), p.166.
76. *Irish Travel*, 13, 1 (1937), p.17.
77. *Irish Travel*, 13, 2 (1937), p.41.
78. Department of the Taoiseach, 'Memorandum from Professor Felix Hackett', n.d. (NA S9215A).
79. Department of the Taoiseach, J.P. Walshe to M. Moynihan, memorandum to Taoiseach 'Cultural propaganda in the US', 2 November 1938 (NA S9215A).
80. Department of the Taoiseach, Roisín Walsh to Éamon de Valera, 17 February 1939 (NA S9215A).
81. Ibid.

CHAPTER 3: THE IRISH TOURIST BOARD: MARKING TIME 1939–1945

1. *Dáil Debates*, lxxxv, col. 1173, 27 April 1939.
2. F.S.L. Lyons, *Ireland Since the Famine* (London: Collins Fontana, 1973), p.558.
3. *Tourist Traffic Act, 1939* (Dublin: Stationery Office, 1939).
4. *Dáil Debates*, lxxxv, col. 2675, 17 May 1939.
5. Ibid., col. 1198, 27 April 1939.
6. *Seanad Debates*, xxii, col. 2422, 28 June 1936.
7. T.W. Moody and F.X. Martin, *The Course of Irish History* (Cork: Mercier Press, 1984), p.443.
8. *Dáil Debates*, lxxvi, cols 1305–6, 20 June 1939.
9. *Seanad Debates*, xxiii, cols 382–3, 12 July 1939.
10. *Dáil Debates*, lxxvi, cols 1305–6, 20 June 1939.
11. Secretary, Department of Justice to M. Moynihan, Department of the Taoiseach, 17 July 1939 (NA S11346).
12. *Irish Times*, 26 June 1939, p.7.
13. *Seanad Debates*, xxiii, col. 965, 26 July 1939.
14. Ibid., col. 960.
15. J.B. Bell, *The Secret Army* (London: Sphere Books, 1970), p.193.
16. Department of the Taoiseach note, 25 July 1939 (NA S11356A).
17. Seaghan Ó Briain interview.
18. Thomas O'Gorman interview.
19. Ibid.
20. Ó Briain interview.
21. *Irish Travel*, 15, 2 (1939), p.18.
22. F. Corr, *Hotels in Ireland* (Dublin: Jemma Publications, 1997), p.83.
23. Ibid., p.84.
24. *Irish Travel*, 15, 2 (1939), p.37.
25. *Irish Travel*, 15, 3 (1939), p.53.
26. *Irish Travel*, 15, 4 (1940), p.67.
27. *Irish Travel*, 15, 7 (1940), p.192.
28. *Irish Travel*, 15, 9 (1940), p.177.
29. *Irish Travel*, 16, 2 (1940), p.27.
30. Ibid.
31. *Leader*, lxxxi, 14 (1940), p.917.
32. *Irish Travel*, 16, 2 (1940), p.50.
33. *Irish Travel*, 17, 3 (1941), pp. 44–5.
34. Ibid., p.296.
35. *Irish Travel*, 16, 7 (1941), p.138.
36. *Irish Travel*, 17, 7 (1942), p.119.
37. *Irish Travel*, 15, 5 (1940), p.105.
38. *Irish Travel*, 17, 12 (1942), p.235.
39. *An Bord Cuartaíochta Annual Report for Year Ending 31 March 1943*, p.11.
40. Department of the Taoiseach, Seán Lemass to Éamon de Valera, 1 December 1942 (NA S12886).

41. Department of the Taoiseach, minutes of meeting of Cabinet Committee on Economic Planning, 7 January 1943 (NA S13087A).
42. Department of the Taoiseach, John Leydon to Secretary, 3 March 1943 (NA 13087A).
43. Department of the Taoiseach, minutes of meeting of Cabinet Committee on Economic Planning, 7 April 1943 (NA S13087A).
44. Department of the Taoiseach, Private Secretary to Minister for Industry and Commerce to P.Ó Cinnéide, 1 October 1943 (NA S13087A).
45. Department of the Taoiseach, memorandum from the Irish Tourist Board, 'Towards an Irish recreation policy', n.d. (NA S10387A).
46. Department of the Taoiseach, minutes of meeting of Cabinet Committee on Economic Planning on 'Recreational facilities', 2 February 1944 (NA 13087A).
47. J.J. Lee, *Ireland 1912–1985: Politics and Society* (Cambridge: Cambridge University Press, 1989), p.238.
48. Department of the Taoiseach, observations of the Minister for Local Government and Public Health to the Secretary of the Cabinet Committee on Economic Planning on a memorandum from the Irish Tourist Board entitled 'Towards an Irish recreational policy', 29 April 1944 (NA S13087A).
49. Department of the Taoiseach, note, 2 May 1944 (NA 13087A).
50. Department of Local Government and Public Health, memorandum on recreational facilities to Secretary, Department of the Taoiseach, 17 June 1944.
51. Ibid.
52. *Irish Travel*, 17, 12 (1942), p.239.
53. Kerry County Council minutes, 18 February 1943.
54. *Irish Travel*, 18, 2 (1942), p.17.
55. *An Bord Cuartaíochta Annual Report for Year Ending 31 March 1943*, p.23.
56. *An Bord Cuartaíochta Annual Report for Year Ending 31 March 1944*, p.11.
57. *Irish Travel*, 18, 8 (1943), p.121.
58. *Irish Travel*, 18, 12 (1944), p.333.
59. *An Bord Cuartaíochta Annual Report for Year Ending 31 March 1944*, p.15.
60. *Irish Travel*, 19, 12 (1944), p.457.
61. *Report of the Commission on Vocational Education* (Dublin: Stationery Office, 1944), p.418.
62. *Irish Independent*, 4 October 1944, p.5.
63. *Irish Travel*, 20, 2 (1944), p.22.
64. *Caterer and Hotel-keeper* (April 1945), p. 45.
65. *Irish Travel*, 20, 11 (1945), p.205.
66. Department of the Taoiseach, M. McDunphy to M. Moynihan, Secretary to the Government, 2 October 1945 (NA S10936A).
67. *Irish Travel*, 21, 2 (1945), p.21.
68. *Irish Travel*, 21, 3 (1945), p.45.
69. Ibid.

CHAPTER 4: IRISH CIVIL AVIATION AND THE STATE

1. Irish Tourist Association annual general meeting, 24 April 1928 (NA S5819A).
2. R. Fanning, *The Irish Department of Finance, 1922–58* (Dublin: Institute of Public Administration, 1978), p.34.
3. *Irish Times*, 23 November 1935, p.4.
4. J.J. Horgan, 'Irish ports and common sense', *Studies*, 20, 79 (1931), p.361.
5. B. Share, *The Flight of the Iolar* (Dublin: Gill & Macmillan, 1986), p.5.
6. Horgan, *Lemass*, p.88.
7. D. Roche, 'John Leydon', *Administration*, 27, 7 (1979), p.236.
8. Industry and Commerce memorandum, 'Commercial aviation in Saorstát Éireann', 9 January 1934 (NA S2410).
9. Share, *Iolar*, p.10.
10. Industry and Commerce memorandum, 'Proposals for the development of commercial air transport facilities in the Saorstát and between the Saorstát and other countries', 7 December 1934 (NA S2410).
11. *Irish Times*, 9 November 1934, p.3.
12. Industry and Commerce memorandum for Executive Council, 'Air services between the Saorstát and Great Britain', 12 April 1935 (NA S2410).
13. Ibid.
14. Cabinet minutes, 20 August 1935 (NA 7/252).
15. *Irish Times*, 11 May 1936, p.4.

16. M. Ó Riain, *Aer Lingus 1936–1986: A Business Monograph* (Dublin: Aer Lingus, 1986), p.9.
17. Share, *Iolar*, p.26.
18. Ibid., p.30.
19. Ibid.
20. *Dáil Debates*, lxiii, col. 2434, 30 July 1936.
21. Ó Riain, *Aer Lingus*, p.11.
22. H. Oram, *Dublin Airport: The History* (Dublin: Aer Rianta, 1990), p.27.
23. *Irish Times*, 10 April 1936, p.4.
24. Ó Riain, *Aer Lingus*, p.10.
25. Share, *Iolar*, p.43.
26. Industry and Commerce, T. Bertram to J.W. Dulanty, 11 December 1933 (NA S2410).
27. Industry and Commerce memorandum, 'Proposals for the development of air transport facilities', 7 December 1934.
28. Industry and Commerce memorandum, 'Transatlantic airport – arrangements for construction', 16 July 1936 (NA S8814A).
29. Interview with Kevin O'Doherty.
30. Industry and Commerce, 'Transport air services discussions – instructions to Saorstát representatives in discussions at Ottawa and Washington', 7 November 1935 (NA S8238).
31. Industry and Commerce, 'Minutes of final meeting held at Ottawa on December 2, 1935 – transatlantic air services' (NA S8238).
32. Industry and Commerce memorandum, 'Transatlantic air services – incidence of cost', 14 August 1936 (NA 7/347).
33. Cabinet minutes, 17 July 1936 (NA 7/341).
34. Ibid., 'Transatlantic air services – construction of airport', 14 August 1936 (NA 7/437).
35. Industry and Commerce, memorandum for Executive Council Meeting, 1 December 1936 (NA S8814A).
36. Seán MacEntee to Éamon de Valera, 18 January 1937 (NA 8814A).
37. B. Share, *Shannon Departures: A Study in Regional Initiatives* (Dublin: Gill & Macmillan, 1992), p.29.
38. Ibid., p.37.
39. Industry and Commerce memorandum, 'Revised estimate of capital cost of land aerodrome at Shannon airport', 24 November 1937 (NA S8814A).
40. Department of Finance, S. MacEntee to H. Flinn, 19 January 1939 (NA S8814A).
41. Industry and Commerce, S. Lemass to S. MacEntee, 6 January 1939 (NA S8814A).
42. Share, *Shannon*, p.52.
43. Interview with Dr G. FitzGerald.
44. Horgan, *Lemass*, p.156.
45. Share, *Shannon*, p.33.
46. Industry and Commerce memorandum, 'The development of civil aviation', 27 November 1946 (NA S13090 B/C1).
47. Industry and Commerce, 'Report on civil aviation for 1949, 4 March 1950 (NA S13090 B/C1).
48. Share, *Shannon*, p.51.
49. Industry and Commerce Conference no. 371, 22 October 1954 (NA 2000/13/10).
50. Industry and Commerce memorandum, 'Civil Aviation', 11 October 1945 (NA S13090A).
51. Ó Riain, *Aer Lingus*, p.13.
52. Share, *Iolar*, p.54.
53. Oram, *Dublin Airport*, p.86.
54. *Irish Press*, 19 January 1948, p.3.
55. *Irish Times*, 28 February 1948, p.7.
56. Department of the Taoiseach, telegram to John Costello, 2 March 1948 (NA S14209).
57. Industry and Commerce memorandum, 'Report on civil aviation for 1948', 28 April 1949 (NA S13090).
58. Ibid.
59. Industry and Commerce memorandum, 'Air companies staffing position – superannuation', 25 May 1948 (NA S13090 C/1).
60. Industry and Commerce, J. Leydon to M. Moynihan, 12 July 1948 (NA S13090 C/1).
61. Department of Finance memorandum, 'Superannuation scheme for air companies' staffs', 27 June 1949 (NA S13090 C/1).
62. Industry and Commerce memorandum, 'Report on civil aviation for 1949', 4 March 1950 (NA S13090 C/1).
63. *An Bord Fáilte Annual Report for Year Ending 31 March 1954*, p.6.
64. Department of Finance memorandum, 'Aer Rianta Teo, Aer Lingus Teo and Aerlínte Teo. Accounts for the year ended 31 March 1953', 21 July 1953 (NA S13090 B/C2).

65. Share, *Iolar*, p.79

66. Ibid., p.80.

67. Industry and Commerce memorandum, 'Bilateral agreement on air transport with the United States of America', 25 January 1945 (NA S13090A).

68. Industry and Commerce memorandum, 'Report on civil aviation for 1947', 23 April 1948 (NA S13090A).

69. Industry and Commerce memorandum, 'Report on civil aviation for 1948', 28 April 1949 (NA S13090A).

70. Industry and Commerce, 'Statement by United States delegation on first day of discussions', 14 September 1949 (NA S10325C).

71. Industry and Commerce memorandum, 'Request by the United States Government for revision of the Air Agreement of 3 February 1945', Appendix C, 17 September 1949 (NA S13090A).

72. Industry and Commerce Conference no. 313, 7 September 1953 (NA 2000/13/8).

73. Aer Lingus, *Annual Report for Year Ended 31 March 1974*, p.10.

74. Aer Lingus, *Annual Report for Year Ended 31 March 1978*, p.3.

75. Aer Lingus, *Annual Report for Year Ended 31 March 1972*, p.2.

76. Aer Lingus, *Annual Report for Year Ended 31 March 1974*, p.19.

77. Aer Lingus, *Annual Report for Year Ended 31 March 1979*, p.13.

CHAPTER 5: FALSE BEGINNINGS 1946–1951

1. Tourist Development Programme 1946 (Dublin: Stationery Office, 1946), p.6.

2. *Irish Times*, 13 April 1946, p.5.

3. *Dáil Debates*, col. 2038, 30 April 1946.

4. Ibid., col. 2052.

5. Ibid., col. 2132.

6. Interview with Kevin O'Doherty.

7. *Irish Independent*, 1 May 1946, p.9.

8. Interview with Seán Ó Briain.

9. *An Bord Cuartaíochta Annual Report for Year Ending 31 March 1945*, p.4.

10. *An Bord Cuartaíochta Annual Report for Year Ending 31 March 1946*, p.5.

11. *Irish Travel*, 21, 12 (1946), p.245.

12. *An Bord Cuartaíochta Annual Report for Year Ending 31 March 1947*, p.4.

13. *An Bord Cuartaíochta Annual Report for Year Ending 31 March 1948*, p.4.

14. *Irish Travel*, 23, 8 (1946), p.145.

15. *An Bord Cuartaíochta Annual Report for Year Ending 31 March 1950*, p.7.

16. *An Bord Cuartaíochta Annual Report for Year Ending 31 March 1949*, p.4.

17. *An Bord Cuartíochta Annual Report for Year Ending 31 March 1952*, p.5.

18. Fáilte Teoranta, dissolved companies files (NA 11492).

19. Ó Briain interview.

20. O'Doherty interview.

21. Ó Briain interview.

22. O'Doherty interview.

23. *An Bord Cuartaíochta Annual Report for Year Ending 31 March 1949*, p.9.

24. J. Walsh, 'The development of public policy for the Irish tourist industry', MA thesis, NUI Galway, 1998.

25. Industry and Commerce memorandum, 'Fáilte Teoranta', 21 November 1949 (NA S13087).

26. Dáil Éireann parliamentary question no. 58, 9 March 1947.

27. Fáilte Teoranta, dissolved companies files (NA 11492).

28. O'Doherty interview.

29. Industry and Commerce memorandum, 'Tourist Traffic Development', 27 November 1945 (NA S13087A).

30. *An Bord Cuartaíochta Annual Report for Year Ending 31 March 1947*, p.8.

31. *Irish Travel*, 24, 9 (1949), p.178.

32. *An Bord Fáilte Annual Report for Year Ending 31 March 1952*, p.11.

33. Tourist Traffic Act, 1939 (Dublin: Stationery Office, 1939).

34. *An Bord Cuartaíochta Annual Report for Year Ending 31 March 1943*, p.11.

35. *An Bord Cuartaíochta Annual Report for Year Ending 31 March 1945*, p.12.

36. *An Bord Cuartaíochta Annual Report for Year Ending 31 March 1948*, p.6.

37. Ó Briain interview.

38. Industry and Commerce Conference no. 234, 17 December 1951 (NA 2000/13/5).

39. O'Doherty interview.
40. Horgan, *Lemass*, p.325.
41. Department of Finance note, 'Irish Tourist Board', n.d. (NA S13087B).
42. Lee, *Ireland*, p.308.
43. Dáil Éireann parliamentary question no. 48, 13 July 1948.
44. O'Doherty interview.
45. Department of the Taoiseach, John A. Costello to all government ministers, 12 June 1948 (NA S14270).
46. Department of Finance, extract from budget speech by Patrick McGilligan, n.d. (NA S13087B).
47. *Irish Travel*, 24, 2 (1948), p.29.
48. *Irish Independent*, 29 October 1948, p.7.
49. T.D. Davis, *Dublin's American Policy: Irish-American Diplomatic Relations 1945–1982* (Washington: Catholic University of America Press, 1998), p.108.
50. Department of Finance memorandum, 'Inter-departmental Working Party on dollar earnings – first Interim Report', 19 November 1949 (NA S13087B).
51. Industry and Commerce memorandum, 'Joint technical assistance for the tourist industry for countries participating in the European Recovery Programme', 8 December 1949 (NA S13087B).
52. O'Doherty interview.
53. Industry and Commerce memorandum, 'Joint technical assistance', 8 December 1949.
54. *Irish Travel*, 25, 2 (1949), p.29.
55. Ibid., p.35.
56. *Irish Travel* (January 1927), p.97.
57. Ibid.
58. Corr, *Hotels in Ireland*, p.75.
59. Ibid., p.85.
60. *Irish Travel*, 15, 9 (1940), p.177.
61. *Irish Travel*, 16, 10 (1942), p.246.
62. *Irish Times*, 3 October 1944, p.5.
63. *Irish Travel*, 21, 9 (1946), p.186.
64. *An Bord Cuartaíochta Annual Report for Year Ending 31 March 1948*, p.19.
65. *An Bord Cuartaíochta Annual Report for Year Ending 31 March 1949*, p.14.
66. *An Bord Cuartaíochta Annual Report for Year Ending 31 March 1951*, p.15.
67. Industry and Commerce Conference no. 183, 2 June 1950 (NA 2000/13/5).
68. Share, *Shannon Departures*, p.48.
69. Industry and Commerce Conference no. 212, 9 July 1951 (NA 2000/13/5).
70. *An Bord Fáilte Annual Report for Year Ending 31 March 1953*, p.20.
71. Corr, *Hotels in Ireland*, p.75.
72. Ibid., p.76.
73. *Irish Independent*, 9 October 1950, p.3.
74. Department of Finance memorandum, 'The tourist industry', 16 February 1950 (NA S13087B)
75. Department of the Taoiseach, unsigned minute, 24 May 1950 (NA S13087B).
76. *Irish Travel*, 25, 11 (1950), p.207.
77. *Irish Travel*, 25, 5 (1950), p.88.
78. Department of the Taoiseach memorandum, 'Report of the committee on tourism', 13 June 1950 (NA S13087B).
79. Department of the Taoiseach, R. Beamish to J.A. Costello, 7 July 1950 (NA S13087B).
80. O'Doherty interview.
81. Department of the Taoiseach, P. Reynolds to É. de Valera, 17 January 1952 (NA S11356C).
82. O'Doherty interview.
83. *Irish Travel*, 27, 12 (1950), p.227.
84. O'Doherty interview.
85. *Irish Independent*, 18 October 1950, p.8.
86. *Irish Travel*, 26, 2 (1950), p.30.
87. *Irish Press*, 12 October 1950, p.11.
88. *Irish Travel*, 26, 2 (1950), p.30

CHAPTER 6: NORTH OF THE BORDER 1922–1980

1. Ulster Tourist Development Association, *Sixty Years On* (Ballymoney: Ulster Tourist Development Association, 1984), p.7.

NOTES

2. Ibid.
3. Ulster Tourist Development Association, *Ulster for your Holidays* (Belfast: Ulster Tourist Development Association, 1928), p.2.
4. Interview with Desmond McGimpsey, 24 August 2005.
5. Keown, 'Taking the world stage', p.38.
6. UTDA, *Sixty Years On*, p.11.
7. *Irish Travel*, 15, 7 (1940), p.142.
8. UTDA, *Sixty Years On*, p.11.
9. Interview with Ken Powles.
10. UTDA, *Sixty Years On*, p.14.
11. Northern Ireland Tourist Board, *Annual Report for the Period 4 February 1948 to 31 March 1949*, p.1.
12. Ibid., p.4.
13. Ibid., p.5.
14. Ibid., p.10.
15. Ibid., p.12.
16. Northern Ireland Tourist Board, *Annual Report for the Year Ended 31 March 1954*, p.12.
17. Powles interview.
18. Northern Ireland Tourist Board, *Annual Report for the Year Ended 31 March 1954*, p.3.
19. Interview with Robert Blair, 24 August 2005.
20. Northern Ireland Tourist Board, *Annual Report for the Year Ended 31 March 1955*, p.8.
21. Ulster Tourist Development Association and Northern Ireland Tourist Board, *Northern Ireland Gives a Great Welcome* (Belfast, 1954), p.4.
22. Ibid., p.18.
23. Interview with Thomas O'Gorman.
24. Northern Ireland Tourist Board, *Annual Report for the Year Ended 31 March 1957*, p.3.
25. Northern Ireland Tourist Board, *Annual Report for the Year Ended 31 March 1956*, p.6.
26. Northern Ireland Tourist Board, *Annual Report for the Year Ended 31 March 1958*, p.3.
27. Ibid., p.14.
28. Blair interview.
29. Interview with Major Jock Affleck, 25 August 2005.
30. Northern Ireland Tourist Board, *Annual Report for the Year Ended 30 September 1963*, p.7.
31. Northern Ireland Tourist Board, *Annual Report for the Year Ended 30 September 1964*, p.5.
32. Northern Ireland Tourist Board, *Annual Report for the Year Ended 30 September 1966*, p.14.
33. McGimpsey interview.
34. Northern Ireland Tourist Board, *Annual Report for the Year Ended 30 September 1964*, p.5.
35. McGimpsey interview.
36. Lord O'Neill of the Maine, *The Autobiography of Terence O'Neill* (London: Rupert Hart-Davis, 1972), p.64.
37. McGimpsey interview.
38. M.J. Kennedy, *Division and Consensus: The Politics of Cross-Border Relations in Ireland 1925–1969* (Dublin: Institute of Public Administration, 2000), p.176.
39. Ibid., p.206.
40. Northern Ireland Tourist Board, *Annual Report for the Year Ended 30 September 1962*, p.12.
41. Horgan, *Lemass*, p.279.
42. Northern Ireland Tourist Board, *Annual Report for the Year Ended 30 September 1965*, p.16.
43. McGimpsey interview.
44. Kennedy, *Division and Consensus*, p.249.
45. Ibid., p.297.
46. Northern Ireland Tourist Board, *Annual Report for the Year Ended 31 December 1969*, p.6.
47. McGimpsey interview.
48. Blair interview.
49. Northern Ireland Tourist Board, *Annual Report for the Year Ended 31 December 1970*, p.25.
50. Northern Ireland Tourist Board, *Annual Report for the Year Ended 31 December 1971*, p.7.
51. Ibid., p.10.
52. Northern Ireland Tourist Board, *Annual Report for the Year Ended 31 December 1973*, p.11.
53. Northern Ireland Tourist Board, *Annual Report for the Year Ended 31 December 1974*, p.10.
54. Northern Ireland Tourist Board, *Annual Report for the Year Ended 31 December 1975*, p.13.
55. Ibid., p.6.
56. Northern Ireland Tourist Board, *Annual Report for the Year Ended 31 December 1977*, p.14.
57. Blair interview.
58. Northern Ireland Tourist Board, *Annual Report for the Year Ended 31 December 1980*, p.6.
59. Northern Ireland Tourist Board, *Annual Report for the Year Ended 31 December 1981*, p.3.

60. Ibid.
61. Northern Ireland Tourist Board, *Annual Report for the Year Ended 31 December 1975*, p.6.
62. Northern Ireland Tourist Board, *Annual Report for the Year Ended 31 December 1978*, p.19.
63. Blair interview.
64. Northern Ireland Tourist Board, *Annual Report for the Year Ended 31 December 1980*, p.2.
65. Northern Ireland Tourist Board, *Annual Report for the Year Ended 31 December 1981*, p.3.
66. Ibid., p.10.

CHAPTER 7: TAKING TOURISM SERIOUSLY 1951–1960

1. *Irish Travel*, 24, 4 (1949), p.65.
2. *Irish Travel*, 24, 6 (1949), p.92
3. *Irish Travel*, 24, 7 (1949), p.105.
4. An Bord Cuartaíochta, *Annual Report for Year Ending 31 March 1947*, p.4.
5. An Bord Cuartaíochta, *Annual Report for Year Ending 31 March 1948*, p.5.
6. An Bord Cuartaíochta, *Annual Report for Year Ending 31 March 1949*, p.7.
7. T. Bodkin, *Report on the Arts in Ireland* (Dublin: Stationery Office, 1949), p.11.
8. Industry and Commerce Conference no. 177, 20 February 1950 (NA 2000/13/2).
9. Industry and Commerce Conference no. 222, 24 September 1951 (NA 2000/13/5).
10. J.C. Coleman, 'Publicity and tourism – a general report on publicity methods applicable to the tourist industry', April 1949.
11. Interview with Kevin O'Doherty.
12. An Bord Fáilte, *Annual Report for Year Ending 31 March 1952*, p.13.
13. Industry and Commerce memorandum, 'Report submitted by the Irish delegation on the study of American hotel methods', May 1950 (NA 13087B).
14. Department of Industry and Commerce, *Synthesis of Reports on Tourism 1950–51* (Dublin: Stationery Office, 1951).
15. Department of the Taoiseach, 'Preliminary Report of the Irish Hotels' Commission for American Tourism', 30 September 1950 (NA S13087B).
16. Industry and Commerce memorandum, 'Reports submitted by Irish delegation', May 1950.
17. Department of External Affairs memorandum, 'Dollar earnings', 4 May 1950 (NA S13087B).
18. Department of the Taoiseach note, 'Tourist Industry', 30 May 1950 (NA 13087B).
19. *Irish Independent*, 27 October 1950, p.7.
20. Department of the Taoiseach note, 17 July 1951 (NA S11356C).
21. *Tourist Traffic Act, 1952* (Dublin: Stationery Office, 1952).
22. *Dáil Debates*, xxxix, col. 1118, 27 February 1952.
23. *Dáil Debates*, xxxix, col. 1384, 28 February 1952.
24. Department of the Taoiseach, J. Leydon to M. Moynihan, 29 April 1953 (NA S13087D).
25. Industry and Commerce Conference no. 232, 3 December 1951 (NA 2000/13/5).
26. *Irish Press*, 8 March 1952, p.7.
27. *Irish Press*, 7 April 1952, p.3.
28. *Irish Times*, 13 March 1952, p.5.
29. Department of the Taoiseach, D. Shanagher to M. Moynihan, 24 June 1952 (NA 13087D).
30. *Irish Press*, 30 October 1952, p.5.
31. Department of Local Government memorandum, 'Decoration of urban districts and towns', 24 December 1952 (NA S13087D).
32. Department of Finance, confidential circular 2/53 to all departments, 'An Tóstal seals', 11 January 1953 (NA S113087D).
33. *Irish Independent*, 12 January 1953, p.6.
34. Department of the Taoiseach, W. Fletcher to É. de Valera, 30 January 1953 (NA S13087D).
35. E.F. Booth and C. Weir to É. de Valera, 30 January 1953 (NA S13087D).
36. *Daily Mirror*, 7 April 1953, p.7.
37. *Daily Mirror*, 9 April 1953, p.6.
38. *Irish Times*, 18 April 1953, p.3.
39. Dáil Éireann, parliamentary question, 23 April 1953.
40. *Irish Times*, 22 April 1953, p.8.
41. *Irish Press*, 27 March 1953, p.2.
42. *Evening Herald*, 28 April 1953, p.4.
43. An Bord Fáilte, *Annual Report for Year Ending 31 March 1953*, p.12.
44. *Irish Tourist Bulletin*, October 1953, p.3.
45. Department of the Taoiseach, M.K. O'Doherty to M. McDunphy, 6 November 1953 (NA S13087D).

46. Department of the Taoiseach, 'Note from An Bord Fáilte', 25 April 1954 (NA S13087D).
47. *Irish Independent*, 9 May 1955, p.5.
48. *Irish Times*, 12 February 1958, p.8.
49. *Irish Press*, 31 February 1958, p.5.
50. *Irish Times*, 17 February 1958, p.3.
51. *Sunday Press*, 27 April 1958, p.7.
52. *Irish Times*, 15 February 1958, p.10.
53. J.A. Murphy, *Ireland in the Twentieth Century* (Dublin: Gill & Macmillan, 1975), p.133.
54. Department of the Taoiseach, 'Report of Bord Fáilte Board Meeting', 29 May 1958 (NA S13087D).
55. *Evening Herald*, 24 July 1958, p.8.
56. *Irish Times*, 27 July 1958, p.4.
57. C. Morash, *A History of Irish Theatre 1601–2000* (Cambridge: Cambridge University Press, 2002), p.257.
58. *Irish Travel*, 11, 5 (1936), p.83.
59. *Irish Travel*, 15, 12 (1940), p.298.
60. *Irish Travel*, 22, 10 (1947), p.187.
61. *Irish Travel*, 23, 11 (1948), p.217.
62. *Tourist Traffic Act, 1952* (Dublin: Stationery Office, 1952).
63. Industry and Commerce Conference no. 378, 13 December 1954 (NA 2000/13/10).
64. Industry and Commerce Conference no. 238, 21 January 1952 (NA 2000/13/6).
65. Industry and Commerce Conference no. 378.
66. Bord Fáilte Éireann, *Annual Report for Year Ending 31 March 1956*, p.13.
67. Bodkin, *Report on the Arts*, p.13.
68. Industry and Commerce Conference no. 161, 6 September 1949 (NA 2000/13/2).
69. Industry and Commerce Conference no. 192, 6 November 1950 (NA 2000/13/2).
70. An Bord Cuartaíochta, *Annual Report for Year Ending 31 March 1951*, p.11.
71. Industry and Commerce Conference no. 223, 2 October 1951 (NA 2000/13/5).
72. Industry and Commerce Conference no. 322, 30 November 1953 (NA 2000/13/8).
73. An Bord Fáilte, *Annual Report for Year Ending 31 March 1955*, p.13.
74. Industry and Commerce Conference no. 420, 29 October 1955 (NA 2000/13/14).
75. Bord Fáilte Éireann, *Annual Report for Year Ending 31 March 1956*, p.11.
76. Bord Fáilte Éireann, *Annual Report for Year Ending 31 March 1957*, p.8.
77. Bord Fáilte Éireann, *Annual Report for Year Ending 31 March 1958*, p.8.
78. Bord Fáilte Éireann, *Annual Report for Year Ending 31 March 1960*, p.12.
79. Irish Museum of Modern Art, *Hindesight* (Dublin: Irish Museum of Modern Art, 1993), p.12.
80. *Dáil Debates*, cxxxxix, col. 130, 9 February 1955.
81. Ibid., col. 133.
82. Ibid., col. 135.
83. Ibid., col. 444.
84. Bord Fáilte Éireann, *Annual Report for Year Ending 31 March 1956*, p.13.
85. Bord Fáilte Éireann, *Annual Report for Year Ending 31 March 1958*, p.7.
86. G. FitzGerald, 'Irish economic problems', *Studies*, 46, 3 (1957), p.294.
87. J. Deegan and D.A. Dineen, *Tourism Policy and Performance: The Irish Experience* (London: International Thomson Business Press, 1997), p.26.
88. Horgan, *Lemass*, p.108.
89. K.A. Kennedy and B.R. Dowling, *Economic Growth in Ireland: The Experience Since 1947* (Dublin: Gill & Macmillan, 1975), p.143.

CHAPTER 8: SWINGS AND ROUNDABOUTS 1960–1980

1. Bórd Failte, *Annual Report for Year Ending 31 March 1960*, p.47.
2. Ibid., p.9.
3. *Dáil Debates*, col. 1776, 25 July 1961.
4. Bord Fáilte, *Annual Report for Year Ending 31 March 1965*, p.2.
5. Bord Fáilte, *Annual Report for Year Ending 31 March 1966*, p.9.
6. Ibid., p.12.
7. Bord Fáilte, *Annual Report for Year Ending 31 March 1967*, p.6.
8. Bord Fáilte, *Annual Report for Year Ending 31 March 1966*, p.44.
9. Bord Fáilte, *Annual Report for Year Ending 31 March 1967*, p.14.
10. Bord Fáilte, *Annual Report for Year Ending 31 March 1968*, p.31.
11. Bord Fáilte, *Annual Report for Year Ending 31 March 1969*, p.11.

12. Bord Fáilte, *Annual Report for Year Ending 31 December 1979*, p.2.
13. *Dáil Debates*, col. 1589, 28 October 1971.
14. Bord Fáilte, *Annual Report for Year Ending 30 September 1971*, p.22.
15. Bord Fáilte, *Annual Report for Year Ending 31 March 1967*, p.39.
16. Share, *Shannon Departures*, p.59.
17. Corr, *Hotels in Ireland*, p.67.
18. Bord Fáilte, *Annual Report for Year Ending 31 December 1975*, p.2.
19. Bord Fáilte, *Annual Report for Year Ending 31 March 1976*, p.3.
20. Bord Fáilte, *Annual Report for Year Ending 31 December 1979*, p.7.
21. Bord Fáilte, *Annual Report for Year Ending 31 December 1976*, p.1.
22. Bord Fáilte, *Annual Report for Year Ending 31 December 1979*, p.2.
23. Ibid., p.9.
24. Bord Fáilte, *Annual Report for Year Ending 31 March 1964*, p.21.
25. Bord Fáilte, *Annual Report for Year Ending 31 March 1965*, p.22.
26. Bord Fáilte, *Annual Report for Year Ending 31 March 1966*, p.25.
27. Bord Fáilte, *Annual Report for Year Ending 31 March 1970*, p.18.
28. Bord Fáilte, *Annual Report for Year Ending 31 March 1971*, p.15.
29. Bord Fáilte, *Annual Report for Year Ending 31 March 1971*, p.19.
30. Bord Fáilte, *Annual Report for Year Ending 30 September 1973*, p.15.
31. Ibid., p.17.
32. Bord Fáilte, *Annual Report for Year Ending 30 September 1975*, p.15.
33. Department of the Taoiseach, J.B. MacCarthy, to C.C. Cremin, 7 September 1960 (NA S13087E).
34. Ibid., T.J. O'Driscoll to J.B. MacCarthy, 30 August 1960.
35. Ibid., p.10.
36. Bord Fáilte, *Annual Report for Year Ending 31 March 1969*, p.23.
37. Bord Fáilte, *Annual Report for Year Ending 31 March 1967*, p.12.
38. Bord Fáilte, *Annual Report for Year Ending 31 March 1969*, p.13.
39. Bord Fáilte, *Annual Report for Year Ending 31 March 1966*, p.27.
40. Bord Fáilte, *Annual Report for Year Ending 31 March 1969*, p.28.
41. Corr, *Hotels in Ireland*, p.77.
42. Bord Fáilte, *Annual Report for Year Ending 31 March 1970*, p.16.
43. Bord Fáilte, *Annual Report for Year Ending 30 September 1976*, p.14.
44. Corr, *Hotels in Ireland*, p.78.
45. *Dáil Debates*, col. 943, 9 July 1959.
46. Ibid., col. 924.
47. Bord Fáilte, *Annual Report for Year Ending 31 March 1964*, p.23.
48. Bord Fáilte, *Annual Report for Year Ending 31 March 1966*, p.7.
49. Bord Fáilte, *Annual Report for Year Ending 30 September 1975*, p.11.
50. Bord Fáilte, *Annual Report for Year Ending 31 March 1961*, p.14.
51. Bord Fáilte, *Annual Report for Year Ending 31 March 1967*, p.29.
52. Bord Fáilte, *Annual Report for Year Ending 31 December 1971*, p.18.
53. Bord Fáilte, *Annual Report for Year Ending 31 December 1977*, p.13.
54. http://www.tcd.ie/irishfilm/showfilm.php?fid=37671
55. Bord Fáilte, *Annual Report for Year Ending 30 September 1960*, p.29.
56. Bord Fáilte, *Annual Report for Year Ending 30 September 1962*, p.10.
57. Bord Fáilte, *Annual Report for Year Ending 30 September 1967*, p.29.
58. Bord Fáilte, *Annual Report for Year Ending 31 December 1975*, p.11.
59. Bord Fáilte, *Annual Report for Year Ending 30 September 1963*, p.6.
60. Bord Fáilte, *Annual Report for Year Ending 31 December 1979*, p.27.
61. Bord Fáilte, *Annual Report for Year Ending 31 December 1980*, p.2.
62. Bord Fáilte, *Annual Report for Year Ending 31 December 1981*, p.10.

POSTSCRIPT

1. Fianna Fáil, *Putting Growth Back into Tourism* (Dublin: Fianna Fáil, 1987), p.7.
2. Ibid., p.11.
3. S. Lemass, 'The role of the State-sponsored bodies in the economy', *Administration*, 7, 4 (1959), p.282.
4. O'Doherty interview.
5. Kennedy and Dowling, *Economic Growth in Ireland*, p.133.
6. Ibid., p.126.
7. J. Deegan and D. Dineen, 'Irish tourism policy: targets, outcomes and environmental

NOTES

considerations', in B. O'Connor and M. Cronin (eds), *Tourism in Ireland: A Critical Analysis* (Cork: Cork University Press, 1993), p.121.

8. J.P. Haughton and D.A. Gillmor, *The Geography of Ireland* (Dublin: Department of Foreign Affairs, 1979), p.49.

9. Ibid.

10. Deegan and Dineen, *Tourism Policy and Performance*, p.90.

11. See Deegan and Dineen, 'Irish tourism policy', p.117.

12. Bord Fáilte, *Tourism Development Strategy 2000–2006* (Dublin: Bord Fáilte, 2000), p.2.

13. Bord Fáilte, *A Business Plan for Irish Tourism Marketing 1998–2003* (Dublin: Bord Fáilte, 1998), p.19.

14. Bord Fáilte, *Report and Financial Statements 2000* (Dublin: Bord Fáilte, 2001), p.4.

15. http://www.failteireland.ie

16. Bord Fáilte, *Annual Review 2001 and Outlook 2002* (Dublin: Bord Fáilte, 2002), p.8.

17. Bord Fáilte, *Link*, October 2002 (Dublin: Bord Fáilte, 2002), p.6.

18. Irish Tourist Industry Federation, *Strategy for Growth Beyond 2000* (Dublin, 1988), p.42.

19. Bord Fáilte, *Business Plan for Irish Tourism Marketing*, p.21.

20. Fáilte Ireland, *Tourism Matters* (Dublin: Fáilte Ireland, 2007), p.2.

21. P. Duffy, 'Conflicts in heritage and tourism', in U. Kockel (ed.), *Culture, Tourism and Development: The Case of Ireland* (Liverpool: Liverpool University Press, 1994), p.77.

22. M. Kneafsey, 'The cultural tourist', in Kockel, *Culture, Tourism and Development*, p.105.

23. C. Ryan, *Recreational Tourism: A Social Science Perspective* (London: Routledge, 1991), p.183.

24. *Cork Examiner*, 11 April 1956, p.7.

25. *Cork Examiner*, 4 June 1962, p.3.

26. *Irish Times*, 8 May 1973, p.4.

27. M. Moynihan (ed.), *Speeches and Statements by Éamon de Valera 1917–1973* (New York: St Martin's Press, 1980), p.584.

28. T.P. Coogan, *Ireland Since the Rising* (London: Pall Mall Press, 1966), p.157.

29. S. Ó Faoláin, *The Irish* (Harmondsworth: Penguin, 1969), p.83.

30. Bord Fáilte, *Annual Report for Year Ending 31 December 1970*, p.34.

31. Northern Ireland Tourist Board, *Annual Report for Year Ended 31 March 1986*, p.4.

32. Ibid., p.5.

33. NITB, *Annual Report 2002–2003*, p.10.

34. http://www.nitb.com/article.aspx?ArticleID=1692 29 November 2007.

35. Tourism Policy Review Group, *New Horizons for Irish Tourism: An Agenda for Action* (Dublin, 2003), p.11.

36. *National Development Plan 2007–2013: 'Transforming Ireland – A Better Quality of Life for All'* (Dublin: Stationery Office, 2007), p.171.

37. Fáilte Ireland, *Annual Report for Year Ended 31 December 2006* (Dublin, 2007), p.2.

References

PRIMARY SOURCES

Dublin: National Archives of Ireland
Chief Secretary's office – registered papers
Department of External Affairs files
Department of Finance files
Department of Industry and Commerce conferences
Department of Industry and Commerce files
Department of the Taoiseach files
Dissolved companies files
Minutes of General Council of Irish County Councils
Minutes of Wicklow County Council

Tralee, Co. Kerry: Kerry County Council
Minutes of Kerry County Council

Tralee, Co. Kerry: Kerry County Library
Irish Tourist Association topographical survey of Co. Kerry

Killarney, Co. Kerry: Killarney Urban District Council
Minutes of Killarney Urban District Council

Bray, Co. Wicklow: Wicklow County Council
Minutes of Bray Urban District Council
Minutes of Bray Harbour Committee

Bray, Co. Wicklow: Wicklow County Library
Irish Tourist Association topographical survey of Co. Wicklow

Ennis, Co. Clare: Clare County Library
Irish Tourist Association topographical survey of Co. Clare

REFERENCES

Official and semi-state publications

Aer Rianta/Aer Lingus, annual reports and accounts (Dublin, 1936–80).

An Bord Cuartaíochta, annual reports and accounts (Dublin, 1940–51).

An Bord Fáilte, annual reports and accounts (Dublin, 1952–55).

Bodkin, Thomas, *Report on the Arts in Ireland* (Dublin: Stationery Office, 1949).

Bord Fáilte Éireann, annual reports and accounts (Dublin, 1956–60).

Bord Fáilte, *A Business Plan for Irish Tourism Marketing 1998–2003* (Dublin, 1998).

Bord Fáilte, *Annual Review 2001 and Outlook 2002* (Dublin, 2000).

Bord Fáilte, *Report and Financial Statement 2001* (Dublin, 2001).

Bord Fáilte, *The Fáilte Business: Tourism's Role in Economic Growth* (Dublin, 1997).

Bord Fáilte, *The Welcome Business* (Dublin, 1987).

Bord Fáilte, *Tourism Development Strategy 2000–2006* (Dublin, 2000).

Bord Fáilte, *Tourism Facts* (Dublin, 1995–2001).

Central Statistics Office, *That Was Then, This Is Now – Change in Ireland 1949–1999* (Dublin, 2000).

Central Statistics Office, *Tourism and Travel 2006* (Dublin, 2007).

Dáil Éireann parliamentary debates (Dublin, 1925–55).

Department of External Affairs, *Ireland – An Introduction* (Dublin: Stationery Office, 1950).Fáilte Ireland annual reports.

Department of Finance, *National Development Plan 2007–2013* (Dublin: Stationery Office, 2007).

Department of Industry and Commerce, *Synthesis of reports on tourism 1950-51* (Dublin: Stationery Office, 1951).

Department of Industry and Commerce, *Tourism Development Programme 1946* (Dublin: Stationery Office, 1946).

Fáilte Ireland, *Tourism Matters* (Dublin, 2007).

Fógra Fáilte, annual reports and accounts (Dublin, 1953–55).

Hansard, *House of Commons Debates* (London, 1909).

Local Government Board annual reports (Dublin, 1909–18).

Northern Ireland Tourist Board, annual reports (1948–56).

Northern Ireland Tourist Board, *Knowing the Visitor – Tourism Facts 2006* (Belfast, 2006).

Report of the Commission on Vocational Organisation (Dublin: Stationery Office, 1944).

Seanad Éireann Parliamentary Debates (1925–55).

Tourism Policy Review Group, *New Horizons for Irish Tourism: An Agenda for Action* (Dublin, 2003).

SECONDARY SOURCES

Andrews, C.S. *Man of No Property* (Cork: Mercier Press, 1982).

Bell, J.B. *The Secret Army* (London: Sphere Books, 1970).

Bodkin, T. *Report on the Arts in Ireland* (Dublin: Stationery Office, 1949).

Brendon, P. *Thomas Cook: 150 Years of Popular Tourism* (London: Secker & Warburg, 1991).

Comerford, R.V. *The Fenians in Context: Irish Politics and Society 1848–82* (Dublin: Wolfhound Press, 1998).

Coogan, T.P. *Ireland Since the Rising* (London: Pall Mall Press, 1966).

—— *The IRA* (London: Pall Mall Press, 1970).

Corr, F. *Hotels in Ireland* (Dublin: Jemma Publications, 1997).

Cronin, S. *Frank Ryan: The Search for the Republic* (Dublin: Repsol Publications, 1980).

Crossley, F.W. *A Concise Guide to Ireland* (Dublin: Crossley Publishing Company, 1903).

Curran, C. 'Tourist development at home and abroad', *Studies*, 15, 58 (1928).

Daly, M.E. *Industrial Development and Irish National Identity 1922–1939* (Syracus, NY: Gill & Macmillan, 1992).

Daly, M. 'The return to the roads', in K.B. Nowlan (ed.), *Travel and Transport in Ireland* (Dublin: Gill & Macmillan, 1974).

Davies, K.M. 'For health and pleasure in the British fashion: Bray, Co. Wicklow as a tourist resort 1750–1914', in B. O'Connor and M. Cronin (eds), *Tourism in Ireland: A Critical Analysis* (Cork: Cork University Press, 1993).

Davis, T.D. *Dublin's American Policy: Irish–American Diplomatic Relations 1945–1982* (Washington: Catholic University of America Press, 1998).

Deegan, J. and Dineen, D.A. *Tourism Policy and Performance: The Irish Experience* (London: International Thomson Business Press, 1997).

—— 'Irish Tourism policy: targets, outcomes and environmental considerations', in B O'Connor and M. Cronin (eds), *Tourism in Ireland: A Critical Analysis* (Cork: Cork University Press, 1993).

Delany, R. *The Grand Canal of Ireland* (Dublin: Lilliput Press, 1995).

De Vere White, T. 'Social life in Ireland 1927–1937', in F. MacManus (ed.), *The Years of the Great Test 1926–39* (Cork: Mercier Press, 1967).

Duffy, P. 'Conflicts in heritage and tourism', in U. Kockel (ed.), *Culture, Tourism and Development: The Case of Ireland* (Liverpool: Institute of Irish Studies, 1994).

Dunphy, R. *The Making of Fianna Fáil Power in Ireland* (Oxford: Clarendon Press, 1995).

REFERENCES

Durie, A.J. *Scotland for the Holidays: A History of Tourism in Scotland 1780–1939* (East Linton: Tuckwell Press, 2003).

Fanning, F. *The Irish Department of Finance 1922–58* (Dublin: Institute of Public Administration, 1978).

Fianna Fáil, *Putting Growth Back into Tourism* (Dublin: Fianna Fáil, 1987).

FitzGerald, G. 'Irish economic problems', *Studies*, 46, 3 (1957).

Forde, H. *Around the Coast of Northern Ireland* (Belfast: R. Carswell, 1938).

Hall, G. 'The tourist question', *New Ireland Review*, 3 (1895).

Hall, S.C. *A Week in Killarney* (London: Jeremiah How, 1843).

Harrington, J.P. (ed.), *The English Traveller in Ireland* (Dublin: Wolfhound Press, 1991).

Hobson, B. *The Official Dublin Civic Week 1927 Handbook* (Dublin: Dublin Corporation, 1927).

Hooper, G. *The Tourist's Gaze: Travellers to Ireland 1800–2000* (Cork: Cork University Press, 2001).

Horgan, J. *Seán Lemass: Enigmatic Patriot* (Dublin: Gill & Macmillan, 1998).

Horgan, J.J. 'Irish ports and common sense', *Studies*, 20, 79 (1931).

Houghton, J.P. and Gillmor, D.A. *The Geography of Ireland* (Dublin: Department of Foreign Affairs, 1979).

Irish Tourist Industry Federation, *Strategy for Growth Beyond 2000* (Dublin: Irish Tourist Industry Federation, 1988).

Jackson, I. *An Introduction to Tourism* (Melbourne: Hospitality Press, 1998).

Kennedy, K.A. and Dowling, B.R. *Economic Growth in Ireland: The Experience Since 1947* (Dublin: Gill & Macmillan, 1975).

Kennedy, M.J. *Division and Consensus: The Politics of Cross-Border Relations in Ireland 1925–1969* (Dublin: Institute of Public Administration, 2000).

Keown, G. 'Taking the world stage: creating an Irish foreign policy in the 1920s', in M. Kennedy and J.M. Skelly (eds), *Irish Foreign Policy 1919–1966* (Dublin: Four Courts Press, 2000).

Kneafsey, M. 'The cultural tourist', in U. Kockel (ed.), *Culture, Tourism and Development: The Case of Ireland* (Liverpool: Institute of Irish Studies, 1994).

Lee, J.J. *Ireland 1912–1985: Politics and Society* (Cambridge: Cambridge University Press, 1989).

Lemass, S. 'The role of the State-sponsored bodies in the economy', *Administration*, 7, 4 (1959).

Lyons, F.S.L. *Ireland Since the Famine* (London: Collins Fontana, 1973).

Macalister, R.A.S. 'The debit account of the tourist movement', *New Ireland Review*, 8 (1897).

Martineau, H. *Letters from Ireland* (Dublin: Irish Academic Press, 2001).

Maume, P. *D.P. Moran* (Dundalk: Dun Dealgan Press, 1995).

Meehan, J. *The Economic and Social State of the Nation* (Dublin: Economic and Social Research Institute, 1982).

Moody, T.W. and Martin, F.X. *The Course of Irish History* (Cork: Mercier Press, 1984).

Morash, C. *A History of Irish Theatre 1601–2000* (Cambridge: Cambridge University Press, 2002).

Moylan, I. 'The development of modern Bray 1750–1900', in J. O'Sullivan, T. Dunne and S. Cannon (eds), *The Book of Bray* (Dublin: Blackrock Teachers' Centre, 1989).

Moynihan, M. (ed.), *Speeches and Statements by Éamon de Valera 1917–1973* (New York: St Martin's Press, 1980).

Murphy, J.A. *Ireland in the Twentieth Century* (Dublin: Gill & Macmillan 1975).

Murphy, J.H. *Abject Loyalty: Nationalism and Monarchy in Ireland during the Reign of Queen Victoria* (Cork: Cork University Press, 2001).

Nenadic, S. 'Land, the landed and relationships with England: literature and perception 1760–1830', in S.J. Connolly, R.A. Houston and R.J. Morris (eds), *Conflict, Identity and Economic Development* (Preston: Carnegie Publications, 1995).

Northern Ireland Tourist Board and Ulster Tourist Development Association, *Northern Ireland Gives a Great Welcome* (Belfast: 1954).

O'Crohan, T. *The Islandman* (Oxford: Oxford University Press, 1951).

O'Dwyer, M. *Tipperary's Sons and Daughters 1916–1923* (Tipperary: Folk Village, 2001).

Ó Faoláin, S. *The Irish* (Harmondsworth: Penguin, 1969).

O'Flaherty, L. *A Tourist's Guide to Ireland* (London: Mandrake, 1929).

O'Neill of the Maine, Lord, *The Autobiography of Terence O'Neill* (London: Rupert Hart-Davis, 1972).

O'Neill, M. *From Parnell to de Valera: A Biography of Jennie Wyse Power* (Dublin: Blackwater Press, 1991).

Oram, H. *Dublin Airport: The History* (Dublin: Aer Rianta, 1990).

Ó Riain, M. *Aer Lingus 1936–1986: A Business Monograph* (Dublin: Aer Lingus, 1986).

Rigge, S. 'On tour around the Empire', in Harold C. Field (ed.), *The British Empire*, 41 (Norwich: Time-Life Books, 1972), p.1,172.

Roche, D. 'John Leydon', *Administration*, 27, 7 (1979).

Ryan, C. *Recreational Tourism: A Social Science Perspective* (London:

REFERENCES

Routledge, 1991).

Share, B. *The Flight of the Iolar* (Dublin: Gill & Macmillan, 1986).

—— *Shannon Departures: A Study in Regional Initiatives* (Dublin: Gill & Macmillan, 1992).

Shaw, G.B. *John Bull's Other Island* (London: A. Constable, 1907).

Ulster Tourist Development Association, *Sixty Years On* (Ballymoney: Ulster Tourist Development Association, 1984).

—— *Ulster for Your Holidays* (Belfast: Ulster Tourist Development Association, 1928).

Urry, J. *The Tourist Gaze* (London: Sage Publications, 1990).

Walsh, J. 'The Development of Public Policy for the Irish Tourist Industry', MA thesis, NUI Galway, 1998.

Williams, G.S.J. *A Sea-Grey House: The History of Renvyle House* (Galway: Renvyle House Hotel, 1995).

Young, A. *A Tour in Ireland 1776–1777* (London: G. Bell & Sons, 1892).

PERIODICALS AND NEWSPAPERS

Administration (Dublin)
Belfast Newsletter (Belfast)
Bell (Dublin)
Better Business (Dublin)
British Empire (London)
Caterer and Hotel Keeper (London)
Cork Examiner (Cork)
Evening Herald (Dublin)
Evening Press (Dublin)
Irish Hotelier (Tralee)
Irish Hotel Review (Dublin)
Irish Independent (Dublin)
Irish Press (Dublin)
Irish Times (Dublin)
Irish Tourist (Dublin)
Irish Tourist Bulletin (Dublin)
Irish Travel (Dublin)
Leader (Dublin)
Link (Dublin)
New Ireland Review (Dublin)
Statist (Dublin)
Studies (Dublin)
Sunday Press (Dublin)

The Times (London)
Travel Express (Dublin)

INTERVIEWS

Major Jock Affleck: 26 August 2005
Robert Blair: 24 August 2005
Dr Garret FitzGerald: 2 November 1999
Michael Gorman: 16 July 2002
Kathleen Kinsella: 12 January 2000
Desmond McGimpsey: 24 August 2005
Seaghan Ó Briain: 8 November 2001, 3 March 2002
Thomas O'Gorman: 9/10/11 March 2000
Kevin O'Doherty: 3 March 2002, 16 July 2002,
    19 July 2002, 31 July 2002
Allie Pigot: 17 July 2002
Ken Powles: 14 July 2005

Index

INDEX

de Gaulle, Charles, 187
de Valera, Eamon, 42, 65–6, 67, 72, 80, 130, 173
  air transport and, 93, 94, *95*, 96, 97, 99, 100, 107, 119
  economic war against Britain (1930s), 55, 56, 65, 91, 212
  An Tóstal and, 170, 172–3
  on tourism, 56–7, 219–20
  WW2 and, 68, 76, 137–8
Defence department, 89, 91, 95, 97, 107, 170
Delargy, Séamus, 59–60
Dempsey, J.F., 99, 100, 107
Denmark, 165
Derelict Sites Act (1960), 203
Derrig, Tom, 58, 92, 125
Derrynane National Park, 204
Design Research Unit of Ireland, 179
Development of Tourism Traffic Act (Northern Ireland, 1948), 138, 140
development schemes, 75–8, 82, 111–14, 119, 212
Development Syndicate (Ireland) Ltd, 23, 27
Devlin, Paddy, 154
Dillon, James, 91–2, 130
'Discover Ireland' campaign (2007), 216
Donegal, 134, 142
Dornan, Patrick F., 164, 165–6
Dowling, B.R., 182
Doyle, P.V., 189, *190*, 196, *206*, 207
Drennan, Dr William, 9
The Drums of Father Ned (Seán O'Casey), 174–5
Dublin, P21, 14, 18, 19, 40, 43, 44, 46, 50, 93, 125
  airport *see* Collinstown airport
  Industrial Exhibition (1853), 17, 27
  Saint Patrick's Day parade, 218–19
  Spring Show, 21, 33, 70, 163, 174, 180
  Theatre Festival, 203
  An Tóstal and, 169, 170, 171–2, 173, 174
Dublin Corporation, 30, 92, 93
Dulanty, J.W., 52, 85, 93
Dun Laoghaire (Kingstown), 15, 23, 35, 85, 159, 165, 198
  ferry services, 201, 202
Dunguaire castle, 189
Durie, Alastair, 4

E

Eason, Kathleen, 115, 117, *166*
Easter Rising (1916), 10, 37–8
eastern and central Europe, 216
economy, Irish, 2–4, 5, 10–11, 113, 122–3, 176–7, 223
  1960s/70s period, 110, 185–7, 189–90, 209, 214, 220–1
  Cabinet Committee on Economic Planning, 76, 78, 80–1
  Dollar Exports Advisory Committee', 167
  economic war against Britain (1930s), 55, 56, 65, 91, 212
  international events and, 110, 216
  Marshall Plan and, 123–4, 159, 161, 163–4, 213
  National Development Plans, 215, 222
  programmes for economic expansion, 108, 182, 183, 184–5, 187, 207
  protectionism, 53, 56
  recession (started late 1920s), 51, 55, 88

White Paper on Economic Expansion (1959), 198
  Working Party on Dollar Earnings (est. 1948), 123, 178
  see also revenue from tourism
economy, world, 50–1, 55, 88, 110, 146, 185–7, 209, 214, 216
Edgeworth, Maria, 19
education and training, 42, 117, 124–7, 144, 165, 184, 192, 197–8
'Emerald Isle' term, 9, 18
Emerald Star Line, 208
Emergency Powers Act (1940), 68
Emerson, Michael, 150
emigration, 56–7, 82, 128–9
England, 42, 60, 67–8, 134, 142, 202
Erne-Shannon canal link proposals, 152
Ervine, St John, 136
Eucharistic Congress (1932), 55, 58
European Civil Aviation Conference, 105
European Co-operation Agency (ECA), 122, 123–4, 127, 132, 163–4, 167, 178
European Monetary System, 191
European Recovery 1948-1951 and the Tourist Industry (E. Wimble, 1948), 165
European Recovery Programme (Marshall Plan), 123–4, 159, 161, 163–4, 213
European Travel Commission (ETC), 131, 196, 199
European Union (formerly EEC), 198, 215, 218
Evans, Professor E. Estyn, 139, 140
External Affairs department, 95, 106, 107, 166–7
Eye to Progress (ITB booklet), 204

F

Fáilte Ireland (est. 2003), 6, 7, 8, 127, 215–18
Fáilte Teoranta, 117–18, 213
'Fall through Spring' programme (1970), 199
Fanning, Ronan, 55, 89
Farmers' Union, 152
farming, P11, 58, 63–4
Faulkner, Brian, 151, *152*
Faulkner, Padraig, 206–7
Federated Employers Limited, 73
Federation of Irish Manufacturers, 73, 179
Fermanagh lake-lands, 134
Festival of Britain (1951), 142, 178
festivals, 168–76, 202–3, 205, 217–18
Fianna Fáil, 39, 42, 53, 101, 119, 132, 159, 212, 213, 219–20
  aviation and, 89, 90, 92
'fifth freedom rights' (aviation), 99
films and television, 40, 52–3, 141, 144, 149, 217
Finance, Department of, 11, 38, 48, 50, 53, 59, 100, 177, 182, 183
  aviation and, 88–9, 95, 98, 101, 103, 106, 107
Fine Gael, 65, 100, 113
Finland, 60
First World War, 10, 23, 24, 34, 36, 37, 135
fishing, P4, 140, 155, 176, 184, 207
FitzGerald, Desmond, 66, 93
FitzGerald, Garret, 182
Fitzmaurice, Major James C., 87–8, *88*
Fitzpatrick, Seán, 42
Flaherty, Robert, 52–3

247

INDEX